FIREWALKING
ON
JUPITER

A Therapist's Guide to
Fearless Self-Discovery

MICHAEL KINZER, JD, MA, LMFT

For Krissy,

To all those firewalkers who never made it to the end of their path,
you never knew how beautiful you were.

TABLE OF CONTENTS

ACKNOWLEDGMENTS

To every client with whom I have had the opportunity to work: for everything you have taught me about you, your struggles, your accomplishments, and for letting me share in all of it for a time in your life. The rewards I have received for having this opportunity continue to surprise and amaze me. Every idea in this book owes its origination to at least one client, and usually very many clients. You all have my most sincere gratitude for giving me so much.

To my therapy colleagues: for your willingness to share your ideas and feelings about how to do therapy in a way that is helpful to all of our clients.

To everyone in my personal life: for supporting me without being able to ever know the full details of my professional life.

To my mother: for graciously agreeing to proofread this book and your untiring enthusiasm reading my writings as they've become available over the years.

INITIAL THOUGHTS

An old friend, no longer with us in this life, once called me "firewalker." He told me he called me firewalker because I had a way of living my life as I saw fit, with confidence, not needing to justify who I was or the decisions I made—that this ability was the result of a difficult but necessary process of facing my many personal demons and re-experiencing traumatic events in my childhood. You will find references in this book to the idea that it is possible to live a life in which you have no fear of any part of yourself or your past because you have accepted yourself fully, including the parts of yourself you may not particularly like. My experience as a therapy client in adulthood, and then later as a therapist helping others, tells me the process is not easy, but it is possible. Although I do not describe in detail the environment of abuse and chaos I survived as a child in this book, I have written about it elsewhere, given talks about it, and may publish someday the memoir I have written about it, called Twelfth Child. My need to fully explore very painful memories and relationships has galvanized my commitment to helping others realize they can do the same—they can become their own firewalkers.

Just in case you were wondering, I do realize that it would be pretty difficult to go "Firewalking on Jupiter," where the average temperature is -234 degrees (*www.space.com*). The name of the book reflects the sentiments just explained and also references the name of my therapy practice, Jupiter Center. Why do I call my therapy practice Jupiter Center?

Pictured above is an ancient symbol for Jupiter (crudely drawn by yours truly). I use this symbol as a kind of branding for my therapy practice. You may have noticed it on the cover of this book and my website and wondered what it is. Now you know. The symbol and the name "Jupiter" were chosen because they represent the principles of choice, power and control, when we have it, when we don't, and when we make mistakes about these two situations. Confusion over these issues leads to many of our painful or problematic circumstances and feelings. It turns out that ancient ideas about these issues are really captured by the symbol for "Jupiter" and what it stands for.

Let's break up the symbol to its more basic parts so you can see how this fits together. Look back at the Jupiter symbol. Notice how there is a kind of backward "C" sitting on top of two lines that form a kind of cross. The backward C stands for *soul*. The crossed lines stand for *matter*. The C sits on top of the cross, which means "*soul dominating matter*." This is what the symbol for Jupiter stood for, soul dominating matter.

"Soul dominating matter...." A modern interpretation might be "mind over matter," or in my own words, "mind working with matter." I love this idea. We are the product of circumstance, to be sure, and this is where matter comes in—the physical aspect of our lives. We didn't choose our birth parents, our race, ethnicity, gender, time in history to be born, or the birth order among our siblings (if we have any). If this is what completely defines us, then we are nothing but circumstance. This cannot be true. And it isn't true. We have a mind, or a spirit or a *soul*, if you like. Our mind gives us the freedom to choose how to respond to circumstance. This is where "mind over matter" comes in. We are actually right now the product of both our physical circumstance (matter) and our personal choices and responses to the physical world (mind/soul). We often have little or no control over circumstance, but always have control over how we choose to respond to it. Therapy clients who are willing to do the needed work to make real change in their lives is constant proof that this is absolutely true.

I doubt this will be my last book. I do not intend to stop writing my thoughts about being a therapist anytime soon. On the other hand, you never know when your "time will come." While putting this book together, I was taking some pictures and slipped and fell on an icy rock ledge on the shore of Lake Superior. I missed hitting my head on the large rock behind me by just a couple of inches, and so suffered only a bruised shoulder and arm, rather than a serious concussion or worse, which might have ended any attempt at finishing this or any other book or thought.

There's a pretty famous guy in family therapy circles named Carl Whitaker. I owe a fair portion of my therapeutic style to many of the things he seemed to think. I am glad I know about his thoughts, ideas, and his style of therapy. Although it might have been nice if he had written more about these things, I am glad I had the opportunity to learn about them as I was pursuing my education as a therapist. Even now, more than ten years after learning about him, I still use his ideas and even some of his sayings in my work with clients in therapy. If he hadn't written about his ideas about therapy, I would not have been able offer the benefits of his ideas to my clients.

I have no reason to expect I will ever be as famous or important as Carl Whitaker in the world of family therapists (or any other world). Still, in case I have had interesting and useful contributions and observations from my work as a therapist, I want to be able to say

I put it down to paper. I wanted to know that I had put into a single place something that described what I have learned from my clients and myself as a therapist, a therapy client, and a person. The stuff in this book is the culmination of many years of various writings, workshops, presentations, and handouts, along with some new material to tie it all together in one place.

I frequently receive calls from prospective clients who can't see me because the timing or logistics don't work—perhaps our scheduling doesn't match up, I am not in their insurance network and they can't afford to pay out of pocket, or I have a client waiting list that is too long for them, and they find help elsewhere (which is a good thing). These prospective clients might find me online, or as often as not, are referred to me by previous clients or professional colleagues who know enough about me to think I have something to offer to the clients they refer to me. In any case, for those clients, and anyone else that might have heard that I have a philosophy about therapy that is worthy of their consideration, I hope they can find in this book helpful ideas from what I have learned working with clients in therapy. The same can be said for therapists and other mental health professionals who might be interested in new or different ideas about how to help their own clients solve problems in their lives. In fact, several of the chapters in this book are modified versions of handouts I have used in presentations and workshops for mental health professionals and social service agencies.

For those of you who follow my blog at jupitercenter.com, many of the chapters in the book will look familiar. I thought about merging all the previous writings that came in multiple parts, and in fact have done so in a few cases where the whole series was not too long. When I put the book together, though, it seemed fitting to leave many of my previous writings as multi-part chapters (i.e. Flexibility, Parts 1, 2, and 3). Like the writings they are based upon, I want the chapters in this book to be both self-contained and easy to read in

5-10 minutes at a time so they are fully digestible, without length being a hindrance. If, having read the first part of a series of chapters leaves you wanting more on the subject, and you end up reading all the parts in one sitting, great, but they are written so you can more easily stop along the way, have some food for thought, and continue onto the next part at your leisure.

If you are interested in finding out what kinds of things I (might) have written after publishing this book, or things I have written but didn't include in the book, please feel free to check my website, jupitercenter.com, where I tend to upload blogs, handouts, articles, and workshop outlines as I create them, and as I have time. It is also likely that this book will either be updated with new material, or another volume will be published when I have accumulated enough new thoughts and ideas to make it worthwhile. If I do update this book, or put together another book, or if I ever publish my memoir about my childhood, Twelfth Child, I will note it on my website.

A word about confidentiality: in the following chapters there are, not surprisingly, numerous examples of clients in therapy struggling, coping with and overcoming different mental health issues. I offer them to illustrate points, to add some interesting ideas, to make the whole enterprise of working in therapy become more real for you, the reader. None of the examples use the names of actual clients. I have also taken the (necessary) liberty of changing certain elements of the situations or client information so that I am not violating the important duty of confidentiality to any therapy clients. So, while the examples are often based on some aspect of a client's struggle or a therapy intervention that actually happened in some form, I have been very careful not to be too specific to any one person's situation. So, if you think you see yourself (as a former or current client) or someone you might know (who is a former or current client), I am glad you can relate to the example, but be assured that I have added, removed, modified, and likely all of the above, some parts of actual client issues to make the situation different to some extent than it really was. I also often have many clients with similar patterns of situations and issues, and give the example as if this one thing happened to this one particular client, when my description is actually a composite of these many different but similar situations among many but different clients.

The caveat for mental health issues: seek help when needed!

I hope you enjoy and find useful some of the ideas and tools offered in my book. If you think anything in this book might be valuable to someone else, great. After all, it is your book and you are free to give it to whomever you like. Please keep in mind, though, that many of the topics in this book cover mental health issues that can be serious, deep, protracted, and even life-threatening (e.g. depression). Even if you think the examples given in this book sound very much like the situation you, a friend, or family member are currently experiencing, everyone is different, everyone experiences things differently, everyone's reaction to circumstance or the guidance of a loved one could be unanticipated. If either you or someone you know is suffering from a mental health issue, I strongly encourage you to seek the help of mental health professionals, educated and qualified to provide the help you or they may need. I say this with all the sincerity I can muster, because I myself have found the need to do this, for myself and others in my life, on many occasions.

Thank you for reading my book!

PART ONE:

HOW THERAPY WORKS

Several years ago, I was teaching a "Healthy Relationships Class" to prisoners at Faribault Prison in southern Minnesota. This was the first time I taught any kind of class in a prison. During one of the first classes, maybe even the first one, a prisoner asked me how I could understand anything about their lives or how they ended up where they were (in prison). To be honest, I really didn't prepare for this question, so I didn't know what to say at first. After a brief pause thinking about it, I suggested we were not so very different. I told them this story.

I started my therapy career working for a nonprofit named Reuben Lindh Family Services that helped families involved in the child protection system. During that time, I spoke with a mother who had lost custody of her children. She told me the story of one of her many children, a boy. Her husband thought this child was the product of an affair. The boy was not treated well. One day, Dad went for a walk with the boy, came back and said the boy had died on the walk, had "fallen" down a sewer. The boy survived, thanks to his screaming in the sewer and the neighbors who heard the screams and fetched him out. For ten years after that, dad took the boy down in the basement so no one would hear his cries as he beat the boy. Child Protection stepped in. By then, the boy had already started to get high, to drink plenty. By sixteen, he'd dropped out of high school and was committing serious crimes to support his habit. Here's the thing, this mother telling the story, she wasn't a Reuben Lindh client. This mother was my mother. I was the boy in the sewer. During my teenage years, I turned things around in my life. I found a good foster home. I stopped using drugs. I went back to high school, graduated with honors. I went to college, graduated Summa Cum Laude from the University of Minnesota, then went on to law school and then graduate school. Along the way, some of the people I knew died, went to prison, or both.

These experiences growing up, and my ability, with the help of others, to escape a life of limitations based on my origins is what prompted me to become a therapist, to do for others what others had done for me: offer hope, encouragement, care, a way out of troubles and struggles. Looking back, I ask why me? Why did I break free of my circumstance, the cycle of abuse, alcoholism, going nowhere, while others were not able to do so? Returning to these questions, finding the answers, asking the same questions of others, and helping them find their own answers, this is why I changed careers from lawyer to therapist, consultant, and speaker. I bring into my work a solid confidence based on this simple principle: if I can do it, so can you. If I can rearrange my life to suit my needs, so can you. Just because something is simple doesn't mean it is easy. It is sometimes still difficult for me to live my life without allowing my past misfortunes to dictate my future, despite having gone through years of therapy myself, years of "firewalking on Jupiter." I must continue to maintain focus on what's important to me and how I can respond to things in a healthy way to live a balanced life. When my life's challenges becomes more than I know what to do with, I will gladly seek the help of a therapist again. If you are willing to face things even when it is difficult, you can also make incredible changes. Whether you are an individual, a couple, a family, or you work for an organization that needs change, making better choices in how you address your needs will lead you to overcome even the greatest obstacles. I know this because I have lived it.

I continue to live it.

So can you.

WHAT IS "MENTAL HEALTH?" PART 1: THE MEDICAL MODEL OF MENTAL ILLNESS

During my first session with clients, I often suggest to them that while they are thinking about which therapist might be a good fit for them, they ask themselves this question, "How does this therapist define what constitutes 'mental health'?" I wonder to myself, if asked that question during an initial session or phone call with a client, would most therapists be able to answer it? I have my doubts. This, I think, is because the mental health profession as a whole seems stuck on the question, "What is mental illness" when we should (also) be asking "What is mental health?" Isn't the goal of therapy to get to a place of mental health? I think it should be. And you aren't going to get there if you don't know where "there" (mental health) is.

We all have a pretty good idea these days about what constitutes "mental illness." We see the commercials that ask questions like, "Where does depression hurt?" or suggest: "If parties make you nervous, anxious, fearful, you may suffer from 'social anxiety disorder.'" As a psychotherapist who takes payments from insurance companies so clients can see me who otherwise couldn't afford it, I am required by those insurance companies to rely on a book called the "Diagnostic and Statistical Manual of Mental Disorders, IV-TR" to diagnose and describe the problems of my clients. That's quite a mouthful. The shorthand name for the book is the "DSM." And it's a big book to boot. It's about 800 pages long, and contains groups of many different varieties of symptoms that are given names and categorized as mental disorders. The most well-known names of disorders include Depression, Anxiety, Attention-Deficit Hyperactivity Disorder (ADHD), Post-Traumatic Stress Disorder (PTSD), along with lesser known names of disorders like Obsessive-

Compulsive Disorder (OCD), Anorexia Nervosa, Bulimia, Schizophrenia, and Borderline Personality Disorder.

What do all these names of things have in common? They all describe a set of symptoms that cause problems in the life of the person who has those symptoms. The symptoms are grouped together and given a separate name if it seems like there are patterns of symptoms that people share. For example, lots of people with depression lose interest in doing fun stuff in their lives, and they often also lose weight, can't sleep, feel tired a lot, and have difficulty making decisions. Not everyone who suffers from what the DSM calls depression suffer from all of the nine symptoms listed in the DSM for depression. In fact, to be diagnosed with "depression" according to the DSM, you only have to show five of the nine symptoms (and one of the symptoms needs to be either "depressed mood" or "lack of interest"). Each of these names of mental disorders has a numeric code, which therapists, doctors, and others use as a kind of shorthand for whatever diagnosis we make about a client's mental health. For instance, depression starts with the number "296." Generalized Anxiety Disorder is "300.02." ADHD is "314." Don't ask me where they came up with these numbers. I have no idea.

Now you have a little insight into how the mental health profession uses the DSM to define "mental illness." Oh, and before I move on to "mental health," I want to mention the fluid nature of all of this. Note that the name of the DSM includes the Roman numeral "IV" and the capital letters "TR." That means that the current version of the DSM approved by the American Psychiatric Association is in its fourth revision, and not just the fourth revision, but the fourth revision that also has had a text revision. That's the "TR." "Text Revision." So, the names of mental disorders, the symptoms included, and the ideas about their cause and their treatment have changed many times. And version "V" will eventually take over, with different names, symptoms, causes and suggested treatment. It's all very fluid;

so don't get too stuck on what it says right now. In fact, the fifth version is out now. I am still using the fourth version because I am not yet required to learn the new version and am putting it off as long as I can. I imagine that once I do learn the fifth version, there will be yet another "TR."

In the next chapter, I'll delve into what constitutes mental health for most clients, and offer some insights into the various ways to move away from an "illness" (or deficit or problem) concept of therapy to a "health" (or strength or solution) concept of therapy.

WHAT IS "MENTAL HEALTH?" PART 2: BEYOND MENTAL ILLNESS

In the previous chapter, I described the current model of "mental illness," which seems to be the dominant focus of the mental healthcare profession. Rather than focusing on what constitutes a "healthy" mental state, the medical model and insurance driven services have led the mental health profession to identify "what is wrong" with a client's mental state, address that problem, and if the "problem" is removed, we are to assume the client is no longer "suffering" from a "mental illness." Focusing on the removal of symptoms of "mental illness" is not an adequate way for either the mental health professional or the client to determine whether the client has achieved mental "health." I will now offer some insights into what amounts to a healthy mental state, with or without reference to issues of mental illness.

In its briefest (and therefore necessarily incomplete) form, the best way I can describe the ideal of mental health is a state in which a person is able and willing to address every aspect of their inner life, regardless of whether they experience difficult feelings, including fear, while addressing those aspects of their inner life. This is the opposite of running from aspects of your inner life that make you uncomfortable. I used the word "ideal" in my description of "mental health" because no one can ever address every single aspect of his or her inner lives. We are just too complicated for that. We also evolve, and that evolution of our inner selves never stops, so there are new experiences, memories, concerns, issues and relationships to contend with, which all present new challenges. So, let's put "mental health" on a spectrum or a continuum; at the least healthy end is "avoiding all aspects of our inner lives" and at the other is "addressing all aspects our inner lives."

Avoiding (inner life)<————————————>Addressing (inner life)

Let's call this the "mental health spectrum" (so I can refer to it later and you'll know what I am talking about). This is not the kind of continuum in which the middle ground indicates a good balance. In this continuum, no matter where you are on that line, moving toward the right is a sign of increased "mental health." There is no point at which we can say, "This is good enough," and leave it at that. Strangely, if we are not increasing our capacity and willingness to address our inner experiences, our emotions, our inner conflicts, we do not merely stop on the line, we automatically begin to move back toward the left, toward escaping, avoiding, dismissing, discounting, denying and repressing aspects of our inner selves that make us uncomfortable. Part of this is our tendency to focus mostly on what is right in front of us, part of it is our tendency to deny what is difficult to consider, part of it is the frail nature of memory.

There is no such thing as coasting once you've reached a certain point. A client once told me, "you can only coast in one direction" and then he made a hand gesture indicating "down." I see this phenomenon again and again in therapy. A client or a couple or a family will make progress in dealing with emotional issues, they will have achieved notable personal growth and attained their therapy goals more or less. They then leave therapy, and several months or a year later, I get a call, and they come back, having fallen back into behaviors that help them avoid addressing conflict within themselves and in their relationships. They left therapy and then forgot that they needed to continue to address their inner lives or they would go back to old patterns eventually.

Alcoholics Anonymous reveals this fact in its 12-step program. After completing most of the steps, the Tenth Step of A.A. says, "Continued to take personal inventory, and when we were wrong promptly admitted it." There is no end to the work of the tenth step. It's continual.

Imagine cleaning house. If the house is really cluttered and messy, it can take a great deal of effort to clean it all up and arrange things how you want them. Once you do that, though, you can't just stop cleaning. If you do, things will get very messy again, and you'll be right back where you started. You have to continue to pick things up, put them where they belong, and do a little cleaning every day along the way to maintain that state of cleanliness. Mental health is very similar. We are either growing, or we are regressing. There are multiple reasons for this, but that is a topic for another chapter or even its own book!

Maintaining good mental health can require a fairly significant attitude adjustment about how you want to live your life. The further you are on the left of the mental health spectrum (toward avoiding your inner life), the greater your attitude may need to change. Also, a person might feel a strong urge or need to stay on the left of the spectrum. Someone might be in an abusive relationship and want to get out, but there are children involved, financial distress, and years of patterns that seem inescapable. A person might have been raised with very little confidence in themselves, or in the possibility of change, and therefore has come to believe after many years of avoiding themselves, their feelings, the reasons their relationships are difficult, that they do not have the capacity to make serious changes in how they approach themselves and their feelings. A victim of trauma may be afraid of new trauma. These are all real concerns. Yet, these concerns do not need to prevent movement on the mental health spectrum toward the right, toward a greater capacity and willingness to address and make changes to their inner struggles. It might just mean the road is longer or more difficult toward getting there and they need added support and resources.

So, what are the benefits of "mental health" as I've defined it here? Why go through all this trouble of addressing scary or painful or seemingly endless inner strife and struggle? Is it worth it? One way to answer these questions is with another question: what happens if you stay on the left side of the line, continuing to avoid the issues in your inner life that need to be addressed? What is the price of avoidance? It isn't free, that's for sure. Drug addicts continue to use drugs to escape, with all the trouble that comes with addiction. Victims in an abusive relationship continue to be abused. Past trauma continues to haunt its victims, controlling their decisions and causing problems in their current relationships in ways they do not understand and cannot control. Family childhood issues like mistrust, honesty, secrets, denial, feeling unwanted, impossible expectations, are projected onto current work or home situations that make life difficult without it having to be so difficult. If a person is unable or unwilling to address serious issues of their inner selves, the behavior they use to avoid those issues (e.g. alcohol, drugs, gambling, workaholic, unstable relationships, etc.) can itself be highly destructive. Even if people are not engaged in highly destructive behaviors of avoidance, those issues will continue to have a negative impact on their lives until they are understood and addressed.

The greater your ability and willingness to address all of these kinds of mental health issues, the greater your flexibility in dealing with new issues as they arise, and the more you are likely not to fall into patterns of avoidance, which allow these issues to disrupt your lives, your moods and your relationships.

Perhaps an even greater benefit of growing over time toward the right side of the line is the assurance you will gain in your ability to cope with whatever life may throw at you. Personal struggles can really bring about new strengths, including the capacity to stay strong in spite of difficult circumstances. For instance, risk-averse behavior can help you avoid the negative consequences of those risks, but it can also keep you trapped in a life of limitations. If you have engaged in a course of personal struggle that leads to personal growth, you will take the risks and achieve the benefits of those risks, to reach the short-term and the long-term goals you have always wanted.

This is also something I see with my clients. When they have really begun to address inner issues they had been avoiding, people also begin to do things in their lives they had not previously thought they would even try (changing careers, going back to school, getting promotions, finding new and more meaningful relationships). This is because they have not only made strides in dealing with whatever inner struggles they had been avoiding; they have also begun to have a much stronger sense of their own value, their abilities to get what they want, because they are less afraid of what will happen if they don't—they know they will be able to deal with disappointment and setbacks better than before. A person able to deal with the issues deep within them also becomes more able to deal with whatever issues are going on around them. And this is proven to be a significant benefit of mental health every day in what I see my clients achieve.

Mental health is not defined by the absence of fear. We are all afraid sometimes. Mental health is defined by our capacity and our willingness to face our inner feelings, thoughts, attitudes and perceptions, in spite of fear. We need to move past our fears so we can make choices that bring greater meaning and happiness to our lives. Once we see the benefits of addressing the issues in our inner lives, we will not want to stop. We will see ourselves more able to cope with change and adversity when it arises, because we will understand and have greater control over our reactions to those changes. We will feel stronger in our capacity to adjust our thinking, perceptions, and understanding of new challenges without losing any sense of ourselves. We will know that we can remain strong internally no matter what happens around us, but this can happen only when we stop running from ourselves, when we embrace a new kind of mental health.

HOW IMPORTANT IS YOUR PAST IN THERAPY?

Clients are often (justifiably) concerned about getting stuck or dwelling on their past for months or years as part of the therapy process. Sometimes clients have a concern that therapy might encourage them to rely on their past as "an excuse" for whatever their issues might be in their current lives ("I can't get my life together because, when I was a kid, all this bad stuff happened to me..."). This chapter will explain that this is not how I practice therapy and is not the experience clients have in therapy with me. If you read the first part of this book, with the snippet about my childhood and what I have done with my adult life, you know I expect more than that from myself and want more than that for my clients.

Sometimes this concern is bolstered by popular culture ideas about therapy—think of the image of Sigmund Freud with the client lying on the couch going on and on about her relationship with her mother. We hear about folks who have been in therapy several times a week for years on end with little progress (Woody Allen comes to mind for me when I think about this). But, sometimes this concern is the result of a client's actual experience in therapy, where they may have worked with some other therapist for years, going around and around about their family and childhood histories, with little progress. Or, perhaps they saw a friend or family member have this experience, and want to avoid it. These are valid concerns. I want clients to avoid getting stuck in therapy. I use specific tools and ideas to help prevent clients from dwelling on their past, while also helping them understand ways their past might continue to influence them now so they can put a stop to it.

There are modes of therapy that do focus intensely on childhood development issues as a way to explore deep-seated "psychological neuroses." One approach is called *psychodynamics,* and *psychoanalysis* is the therapy process it uses. This is the main kind of therapy we think of when we think of Sigmund Freud with his client lying on the couch for years. I understand the concepts behind this mode of therapy. Psychodynamic therapy can be useful from time to time with certain clients. However, I do not make the assumption that going through a detailed history of a client's childhood is always relevant to a client's needs in therapy. Sometimes it is, but often it is not. Even when it is necessary to help a client understand some basic connections between their childhood experiences and the decisions and feelings they have as adults, that doesn't mean I need or want to know everything about a client's childhood or their parents and other family members. It all depends on how a client's history affects their current situation.

So, here's the question I ask myself when trying to decide if childhood and other historical experiences are relevant to a client's therapy process: "Is there some way learning more about the client's history would help us solve the client's current issues?" In other words, how is the past connected to the present? When clients tell me they think they "dwell" on their past or are stuck in the past, I tell them that they might want to ask themselves the same kind of question I ask in therapy: "Is there a purpose to having these thoughts, these questions, these memories? Is there some reason I might be having these thoughts and memories now, based on my issues, needs and goals? Will it help me attain my goals in my life or avoid making unhealthy decisions by figuring out something from my past, and is this the reason I am thinking of these things now?" If the answers to these questions are either "maybe" or definitely "yes," then it's probably worth pursuing these thoughts and memories and the feelings that go along with them; don't push them away, see where they go, write about them, talk to friends and family about them, discuss them with me in therapy. If, however, you really can't see a reason you are having these thoughts and memories, you might then be "dwelling" on the past, which might lead you to avoid or justify what is happening in the present.

I ask all clients limited and basic information about their personal history in the beginning of the therapy process simply to rule out the need to spend additional time on the client's past. More often than not, clients do not need to spend much time on their childhood histories in therapy, although it may resurface from time to time. Only when they make the distinction I suggested above (by asking themselves if there is a purpose to revisiting their past), can they begin to distinguish memories that keep coming back because they are the result of unresolved issues from those that have no value at all. By facing the past, neither running from it, or dwelling on it, clients learn to live in the present without being overly bothered by their own histories.

The balance is to think about the past when necessary (to understand its influence and avoid repeating mistakes) without spending more time than is really necessary. I also recognize that many clients are not bothered by their past, and do not need me to create any reason for them to be bothered by their past. For those clients, we don't spend time discussing their past once we've ruled it out as not particularly relevant to that client's needs in therapy.

If there is a purpose to thinking about and remembering parts of your past, you are not dwelling on the past; you are simply trying to learn from it. If there is no purpose to it, and this part of your past is best left in the past, then learn how to let it go, without denial, so you can live the life you have right now uninterrupted by useless interference from past issues that no longer affect you.

WHAT DOES "I DON'T KNOW" MEAN IN THERAPY?

I hear the phrase "I don't know" quite a bit in therapy. I hear it more from some than others. It is maybe the most common answer to any question I ask when I am first getting to know teenagers, which makes sense in their case (more on that later). I tend to give teenagers the benefit of the doubt because they so often genuinely do not know what they know. So when in doubt, they say "I don't know." Fair enough. With adults though, I am not as willing to accept the answer quite so easily, passively. Don't get me wrong, it's not that I jump on anyone because they tell me they don't know how to answer my question. That would be disrespectful. Sometimes it is also a needed opportunity for me to reexamine my own question to make sure it makes sense, is understandable, and is asking something a client is pretty likely to know. I find it helpful to try to restate a question as many times as it takes for a client to know what I am asking. The point of this chapter, though, is about adults who say "I don't know" when the question is pretty clear, when they are likely to know the answer, and their response of "I don't know" is therefore probably not really or completely true once they have a chance to really think about it.

Why do people say "I don't know" if they actually know at least some part of how to answer the question? Why do they repeatedly say, "I don't know" even when it seems like they do know? Are they lying? Possibly. Not usually. When people say, "I don't know," I presume it is only part of the answer they want to give, and try to imagine finishing the response for them. I say to myself, "does she mean, 'I don't know... [...how to answer that question] or [...how to say what I think or feel] or [...what you really want me to say] or [... how to say what I want to say without offending you or making my partner sitting next to me in therapy really upset with me]."

A therapist friend of mine (who is a Buddhist and a pretty astute guy all around) once told me about a situation in which he asked a client something like, "How do you think your mother might respond if you told her how you feel about...." The client said, "I don't know." My friend then asked something like, "What would it be like if you did know?" This exchange seems strange, funny, and even a little ridiculous. It has a point, though. My therapist friend and I tend not to trust someone's assumption that they do not know what they do in fact (at least partially) know. Or maybe a better way to put it is to say clients know much more than they think they know. They mistakenly assume that they have to "completely know" or completely understand everything about a question in therapy to answer it properly. This is never true. There are very few questions in any context I ever know how to answer completely or with complete understanding. In fact, I find that questions I don't know how to answer fully are often the most interesting to consider, for myself, and with my clients.

Another approach I take when a client has a really hard time answering a question is very simple and effective. I say, "Okay, so you don't know how to answer that question. That's okay. But I think it is a good question for you. And I want you to figure out how to answer it. Let's not accept 'I don't know' as a final answer. I want you to think about the question and possible ways to answer it for yourself after you leave today." Sometimes, if it seems like a question worth really exploring, I will even write it down on a piece of paper and hand it to the client. I might even tell them that anecdote about my therapist friend, and will ask them to imagine what it would be like if they did know how to answer the question.

Let me give you a few examples of important questions to which clients have said "I don't know." "What might be an ideal version of the kind of person you are?" "If you could have one thing change in your marriage more than anything else, what might it be?" "What do you want your ideal partner to want from you?" "How do you think it might feel if you stopped engaging in self-destructive behavior (excessive drinking, drug use, gambling, cutting, tolerating an abusive relationship) for six months straight?" I like all of these questions, depending on the needs and circumstances of the client. My point in listing them is to show you the variety of the kinds of questions that come up every day in sessions with clients. They might also tell you why I am reluctant to accept the answer "I don't know." If a client is willing to consider what it would be like if they did know, they can more easily imagine their own growth and find encouragement to move toward it. These are all global, big picture, existential, life changing questions, so asking clients to ponder beyond "I don't know" is kind of obvious, I suppose.

Then there are the more trivial, mundane, immediate questions that clients will answer with "I don't know." First, let's get back to teenagers, who sometimes say "I don't know" more than anything else when they are first starting to get to know me, no matter how trivial the question. "How was your day at school today?" "I don't know, fine, I guess." How was your weekend at your grandma's house? "I don't know, kind of a bummer." Why was it a bummer? "I don't know, it just was." And so on. Teenagers are an exception, though, because they do not really know themselves, and are in a fairly consistent state of confusion and internal transition. So, "I don't know" might actually be true in their case. Teenagers are also very guarded. For good reason. They are often not in therapy on their own accord. Their parents, a probation officer, school counselor, or their pediatrician probably instigated therapy, either against their will, or without their full support, at least initially. So, I tend to be much more tolerant of letting questions go when teenagers say, "I don't know." I mostly just translate it as really meaning; "I don't want to tell you about that." I assume a teenager is in a better position than me to know whether it is safe or acceptable for them to disclose an answer to any of my questions. As a teenager learns to trust that I am not interested in judging them or offering unsolicited advice or planning to disclose their answers to parents or teachers, they often come around to being more willing to talk, and I hear "I don't know" from them much less as sessions continue.

Unlike teenagers, adults come to see me of their own accord (okay, other than partners who come to satisfy their partner's request to come). So, when an adult voluntarily comes to therapy and then tells me "I don't know" to even the most basic questions, I assume they do know something about how to answer that question. A man comes in for a session; he tells me he just had a huge fight with his partner, proceeding to tell me all the details he can remember about the fight and how it made him feel. I listen carefully; discuss with him how he feels now. He is able to tell [answer? respond to?] respond to whatever I ask. Then I ask him to go back to the beginning of the fight, and tell me how his partner might describe the fight. He says, "I don't know." I ask him to pretend he has a videotape of the fight, and ask him to tell me how he contributed to the escalation in the fight. "I don't know, I just got mad when they said..." Clearly, the client isn't ready during this session to examine his own behaviors and responsibility for the fight. That's okay. No hurry here. Later in therapy, when another fight comes along, I will ask him to compare that fight to the fight he's just described. I will help him put together the pieces of identifying patterns. When he begins to see these patterns on his own, he will learn that talking about his own responsibility for the conflict doesn't mean it is all his fault, that he is a bad person, that his relationship is doomed, etc. As the client gains confidence in his ability to become self-aware, he will also hopefully gain some relief from no longer having to hide from what he knows, but doesn't want to see. He will then use this confidence, this relief, this acceptance of himself as part of the problem to seek out new solutions, even discussing them with his partner, or bringing his partner into therapy with him, ready at the start to discuss his part in the problem, as well as his perception of his partner's responsibility for the ongoing conflicts.

As you can tell, I generally do not trust when a client tells me "I don't know." It is rarely true, even though most of the time the client believes it is true. More importantly, challenging this response in therapy—with respect and patience—is almost always valuable for a client. When clients no longer trust their "I don't know" response and view it as a way to avoid an answer, they can look at why they are trying to avoid the answer. The reason behind avoidance is often the real problem, not the question itself. Addressing the reasons for avoidance helps the client figure out what they are hiding from, so they can eliminate their self-induced but previously unknown limitations. They can open up to new possibilities. Clients who refuse to accept their own "I don't know" answers will find better and more real answers, if not now, then later, when they are ready to say "I do know the answer, or at least part of it." This is the beginning of a genuine and confident path to self-discovery and self-acceptance.

ACKNOWLEDGING THE PROBLEM IS NOT ENOUGH

There's an old saying, "Acknowledging the problem is the biggest step." Most of the time, this turns out to be completely untrue.

Many of my writings and articles have been about the kinds of problems people bring to therapy including anxiety, anger, ADHD, boundary issues, etc. For each of these issues, I have also touched on how we deal with those problems in therapy—mostly by identifying the reasons people have those problems, and then identifying the specific sources of the problems in that particular client's life. So far, so good. But then what? What do we actually do in therapy to *solve the problem*? I mean, that's what the client wants, right? It is what the client wants. Even when the client isn't so sure.

Everyone wants to get rid of his or her problems. I know it doesn't seem like that sometimes with some people. But, no one wants a problem, unless it seems to solve some other problem that feels even worse. Take denial for instance. Denial is a problem all by itself, but if it covers up some other problem, like an addiction issue or childhood sexual abuse, then it seems like it helps solve the underlying problem by helping us ignore it (but of course it doesn't in the end, which is why denial is a problem). Once we work through the denial, we can begin to address the "real" problem, right? Yes and no.

There are usually four steps to solving a therapeutic problem:

1. Acknowledge the problem (by its consequences);
2. Identify the source of the problem (behavior, attitude, and perception);
3. Establish a likely solution (propose the needed changes); and

4.   Implement the solution (making the changes).

Which is the hardest? Step number four, implementing the solution. No question about it. The first, second and third steps often require the assistance of a friend, family member, spouse or a professional. The fourth step requires that the person with the problem take full control and responsibility of the problem and actually do the hard work, usually doing it over and over and over. It is not the hard work that's the problem. It's taking full control and responsibility for the problem that causes so much difficulty. It's also doing something different than what you are used to doing, what has become comfortable, familiar, or "easy" (which is why we call it change).

We often want to blame things outside ourselves for our problems, sometimes rightly so. However, solving problems always, always, always (really always) requires us to take control and responsibility for the problem. If we are stuck in blaming other people or "uncontrollable situations" for our problems, we will remain stuck in the problem. We can't change other people and we often cannot change circumstance. We can only change our emotional, mental, and physical behaviors.

This four-step process of dealing with a problem (acknowledge, identify, propose, and implement) often results in two stages of therapy. Stage one is "acute" meaning the problem is identified as quickly as possible, and temporary solutions are proposed to curb the consequences of the problem. The second stage of therapy occurs after implementation begins. This stage often amounts to helping the client stay on track, avoiding regression into old patterns, and confirmation that change is actually occurring as the result of the implemented solution. It can also lead to modifications of the proposed solution, as things get better. Sometimes this requires a trial and error approach. When a solution has been implemented over time but change isn't happening, it can be necessary to go back to the drawing board to think about other solutions that might be more successful. Both stages are rewarding, but the second stage is most rewarding because it is the one that is the hardest for the client, and the one that demonstrates how incredibly courageous and strong people can be when they decide to take control and responsibility for their problems. The second stage is also the only one that demonstrates real change over time, which is really the whole point.

PERMISSION

Therapy is about permission—really, an exchange of permissions between the client and me. They ask my permission, and I ask theirs. Although we are both asking for permission from the other, the kind of permission we seek is very different. A client asks permission to talk to me about their problems. They don't say it this way, of course. No client calls me and says, "Can I have your permission to tell you about my problems." Before a client utters a single word to me, they already know part of my job as a therapist is to listen to what they have to say about what is going on in their life.

In a way, getting therapy going is really this simple. I answer the phone, the person on the other end tells me they have some kind of issue that would benefit from therapy and they want to set up a time to meet with me. We find a time that works for both of us, and then when we meet, they start to tell me about their issues. They inherently have my permission to use my time, my office, and my attention to hear their problems. If this were all there were to it, though, I am not at all sure it would get very far, or do much good for the client.

So far, I have not asked them for their permission. But I will. I always do, in one way or another. And if I didn't, it is likely they would not give themselves permission to really feel safe to not only tell me their story, but also to openly question the ways they see their problems, see themselves, see their lives. And it is this permission they give themselves, a little later in therapy, that is far more important than the permission they ask from me to listen in the beginning. I always (implicitly if not verbally) ask a client for permission to let me try to understand them, to question them, to be with them in their confusion, their fears, their pain, guilt, anger, whatever. I do this again and again, reassuring them at all times that it is their decision, their right to decide whether I get to be included in the way they are experiencing their issues. It is vital that their permission be transparent and intentional. They must know they have the power to share (or not share) with me, to allow me to share with them, whatever is going on.

I want to do more than just listen. In fact, if this is all they want from me, I am generally not interested, not on an ongoing basis, not if it is the primary basis of why they want to be in therapy. Sometimes clients need to vent, or just tell a story, and sometimes this process can take a whole session, or even a few sessions. At some point, though, an exchange takes place, in which they include me enough in their experiences so that I can sort of imagine what they are going through, and then together we use that shared understanding to begin to map a new way of experiencing whatever the issue is, so they can find a way out of the problem at hand, a new way of seeing themselves as stronger, as more complete, as more capable than they did when we first began discussing the problem.

The permission I seek from my clients is necessary because, without it, their ability to trust me is very limited. What I mean here is a little tricky. A client might trust me very deeply simply because they believe that as a therapist, I have some kind of special ability, through education, experience and aptitude, to truly understand them, to help them, to guide them. And they would be wrong to trust me deeply based merely on these assumptions. Too much power for me, too little power for him or her. To trust me in that way would create a dependency on me that is illusory and not good for the client. A client's trust should not come at the expense of their own power in their lives. That kind of relationship is less like a therapist-client, and more like a guru-acolyte. No thanks. I don't want that for me, or for any client.

Instead, I want a client to think to themselves, "Do I really want to trust this guy? Why should I trust him? Does he seem like the kind of guy who can really help me? Does he know what he is doing? Can he really understand me and my issues?" Questions like these are not only appropriate, they are essential. By asking them, a client is considering whether they should give me permission to enter into their mental and emotional space, which belongs to them, is dear to them, and in which they are exposing themselves to great help, or great harm. Tread lightly here, I say. Any person should consider very carefully with whom they share such close and important space. This kind of permission should not be freely or easily given, no matter how difficult or desperate a person's situation might feel.

I learned the importance of obtaining a client's permission very early in my therapy career because my clients were often people who had every reason not to trust me, not to want to give me the very permission I now know is essential to successful therapy. Most of my clients then were struggling financially in difficult neighborhoods. Many were people of color–their families were often torn apart by the effects of systematic racism in schools, on the street, in the courts, the prisons, the grocery store, and the HR department at work. I became involved in their families when the county determined the parents had abused or neglected their children. Now the parents were struggling to keep their kids, or get them back. And here I was, tall, white, ex-lawyer guy, carrying a briefcase, looking exactly like a probation officer, a cop, a social worker, another part of the system, at their front door. "Hi, can I come in?" Now you can begin to understand why permission was vital. But it might not seem that way if you weren't paying attention.

I could have been at the door, asked to come in, and assumed there was no issue with permission. I mean, what were they going to say. If they said no, if they didn't let me do my "thing," they weren't going to get their kids back, but it wasn't real permission. As true as this probably was, if I acted like this, and I saw many workers in my field doing exactly that, I might have gained their apparent cooperation, yet would never have gained an inch of trust, and therefore would have accomplished nothing therapeutic, nothing worth doing, a waste of my time, their time, a wasted opportunity to connect and help, truly help.

I still remember some of the exact details of a living room in a house of a family I started working with several years ago when the issue of permission became central to my work with that family and through them, my career forever after as a therapist. I had scheduled the home visit with the mother of a family, all of whom were people of color, to meet with her and her husband and one of their children whose issues had come to the attention of the county. When I arrived, the mother let me in. She invited me to have a seat in the living room. I sat on the couch. We chatted for a little while and then she called to her daughter, who was the source of the county's concern. She came down, seemed curious, wondered if she was in trouble, again. I said no, and smiled. I handed them each a card, explained that I did not actually work for the county, that I was to be an advocate for their family.

Then the father came home. When he saw me on the couch, he was furious, asked what I was doing in his house. He was yelling at me, at his wife, swearing, fuming. He told me (summarizing), "I spend all day at work doing whatever my white racist boss tells me to do, knowing I have to do it because I need the job, the money, and I put up with his crap [he used a different word] day after day, and now I find a white guy sitting with my wife and kid in my house when I get home. No! Get out! Get out of my house! I will come to see you, in your office, downtown or wherever, but you will not come into my house! No! No!" I sat there, stunned, unprepared for this. Nothing in my schooling as a therapist or my scant previous work as a therapist had warned me that I could be subjected to such raw seething contempt. For the sake of the possible audience for this book, I am using tame language to describe what he actually said.

I started to cry. I just sat there on the couch and I cried. Not hard, not blubbering, not sobbing, just silent tears running down my face. I felt so terrible for him, for what he had to go through, for how I had unwittingly contributed to his pain, anger, mistrust, and deep sense of injustice. I knew without a doubt that I had made what I now consider the gravest error I can make as a therapist, I failed to make sure I had his permission—permission to work with him, to talk to him and his family in his house about their lives, to be in his space, to be a white person in the only space in his life where it felt safe to be himself, to be a person of color outside the purview of white eyes upon him. I apologized through my tears, stood up, said I would go, and I would let my employer know that they might prefer finding an advocate of their own choosing.

The father was as stunned by my tears as I was by his wrath. I did not plan to cry. It was not an act, although it was my decision to let it come out. I felt the pain there within me and decided to be honest about it, to share it, express it in the tears that naturally came. He stopped yelling at me, asked me why I was crying. So, I told him. I told him how sorry I was that I had not asked his permission to be in his home, thinking his wife's permission was enough, but now could see I was wrong. I began to leave.

His wife asked me to wait. Then she explained to him that I had previously called, arranged the meeting with her, reminded him that she had told him about the meeting, explained to him who I was, and that he had agreed to meet with me. He admitted to her, and to me, that he had forgotten, that he'd had a particularly difficult day that day at work. He then apologized to me for becoming so angry. I said I understood. He asked me to stay. We talked some. I explained my role. I said I would do my best to understand him and his family and to help reduce, if I could, the impact of the county's involvement on his family's life.

I worked with their family for nearly a year. After that year, when my role in their lives was coming to an end, we had a final therapy session at their house. During this session, everyone cried a little when we said goodbye, including the father. I had obtained their permission to share some small but important part of their lives. They gave me permission, not freely, and with the father, not easily, but they gave it sincerely, and in doing so made the decision that they could trust me. When they gave me permission to be with them in their lives, they also gave themselves permission to be much more fully present with me during our sessions.

Looking back, I can't say I did anything particularly "wrong." I didn't just show up at their door. I asked the mother about a meeting, and she agreed. I did assume that her permission was adequate, which seemed sound and sufficient. I probably assumed she'd call me back if her husband raised serious objections. What didn't occur to me was the power of his vehement denial of permission. I learned from him over that year how many times professionals had assumed they had his permission to enter into his life and the life of his family, when in fact they did not have his permission at all. They had only his tacit, pretended permission, his superficial cooperation. He had learned that with the county, the government, he needed to "go along, to get along." When I explained that I did not want this, that I either wanted him to learn to trust me, or not, and either was okay, he began to consider the possibility that I was asking to earn his trust, earn his permission. And that was exactly right. He became much more directive in our work, taking responsibility for what he wanted for himself and his family. He became invested in the process of therapy. He was no longer just going through the motions as he had in the past.

I could give other examples, but they would end up carrying the same message. Only when a client consciously, willingly, and intentionally gives me their permission to enter into their emotional and mental space, can they really trust not only me, but the process of our mutual participation in a process in which they become more powerful. This is because they are not giving themselves over to me. They are inviting me into a shared space they own, a space they define, a space they create. So, when that space is no longer necessary, when that space has helped them attain their therapy goals, they can close it up, say goodbye to me feeling secure with themselves. Along the way, they will also have given themselves permission to trust me and the process of self-exploration in a way that can never happen without such permission. In doing so, they will have helped create a space in which they can seriously question themselves, their stories of themselves, of their relationships, of their decisions, of who they are, and ask me to participate in this exploration of themselves. This will become a space for clients to explore the kinds of freedom and responsibility I explain in the chapters called Freedom and Responsibility, Parts 1 and 2.

Permission in therapy is always a two–way street, an exchange of permissions between me and my client. I give them permission to use my time, knowledge, skills, care, attention, and compassion. And they give me permission to connect and be with them as they share their troubles until we can together find a way out and satisfactorily resolve the issues that prompted them to come to see me.

FEAR AND SAFETY, PART 1: UNDERSTANDING AND RESPECTING FEAR

When I sat down to write tonight, I had planned to begin a series of chapters on my experiences working in therapy with people who have suffered childhood sexual abuse. I find I am not ready yet. I must first address something that prevents the topic from ever coming up in therapy before discussing what it is like when it does come to light. Like a funnel, before I get to the more narrow end, I think I need to first explore something at the wider end, something more general, something that is certainly part of the process, but comes at the beginning: fear.

Fear arises in so many shapes, so many varieties; it stops us in so many ways. Someone very close to me in my personal life said he thought fear was the most basic emotion—that all other emotions could be understood by considering how far they are removed from basic instinctual fear. Perhaps. I have heard professionals say the most basic human emotion is love. I have heard yet others say there is at the heart of things a struggle between fear versus love. Again, perhaps. Many of us seem to fear ourselves more than we love ourselves. At the very least, despite whatever love we may feel for ourselves, we can let our fears of what lies within us, within our memories, our past, our thoughts, feelings, our sense of who we are, what we have done, what has been done to us, keep so much of it hidden from our present awareness. Sometimes we lie to ourselves with such vigor and constancy, we believe our lies. Most of the time it is not at all this simple. To have a memory within us does not mean we are aware of it, or doing anything intentional to keep it hidden. It might just not be accessible.

Suppose it were possible to have no fear. It isn't, but suppose it were. Imagine all the memories you might be able to access. Reading this, you might be thinking, I don't have any obvious fear. I can't say if you're right, I don't know you, and even if I do know you, I am not you. I will guess, though, that fear keeps very many things hidden from your present awareness. I won't go into all the possible reasons this might be. The list is too long. Besides, it's also possible you no longer fear something you feared when you repressed or otherwise blocked your access to a memory. Now, you may not even remember having that fear, or the memory you blocked due to the fear you once had, but no longer have.

I'll get to the point though. I respect fear. I trust it. Think about that for a second. I am saying I trust and appreciate fear. Weird, I know. But there is a reason we fear things. Fear is always in some way related to managing the potentially unmanageable, controlling the potentially uncontrollable. Always.

Let me offer a few examples to show you what I mean. If you are driving at a slow easy pace, listening to a favorite song, maybe daydreaming about what you'd do if a big bunch of money dropped in your lap, you have no present fear. You're all good. Then an unexpected turn in the road comes. Your easy pace is a bit too fast, and you realize it a little too late. In a panic (fear), you hit the brakes, slow down, glide the turn, adjust your speed to accommodate this now less pleasant road, and fear slips away. You feared losing control, then lost the fear when you gained control.

You go to a meeting. You are prepared. You have your thoughts aligned for what you need to say. Your part of the meeting is minor, and the stakes are not high. No big deal. No fear. You can manage this meeting half asleep. On your way down the hall to the conference room your colleague catches up to you, leans in and says, with what you note is an irritating bit of delight, "Hey, did you see that email?" (you didn't), "The director is out today, so you're in charge of the meeting." Now all eyes will be on you. Can you manage? Yes, but will you? Fear, anxiety, your mind starts going over all the possibilities of what is suddenly expected of you, all the things you can think might go wrong, all the potentially unmanaged things you will now be expected to manage. You think you still have it under control. You walk into the meeting thinking, "easy peasy..." There at the head of the table to greet you is the director's boss, the Vice President. So much for "easy peasy," panic (fear) comes back. You smile, hide the fear, again going through the process of how to manage the potentially unmanageable, control what might not be controllable. Once you know it is controllable, your fear subsides. Smiling back, the VP says she is taking over the meeting. Your worries are over. Relief. You slide back into a comfortable place of well-being, of safety, and maybe a little welcome boredom after your emotional roller coaster down the hallway.

Driving? Meetings? What does this have to do with therapy? Nothing specifically, but these situations do provide fairly tame examples of how fear arises and subsides, naturally, almost instantly, in response to what we perceive is a situation we might need to control, but might not be able to control. If we don't need to control something, no fear. If the thing we need to control is easy to control, no fear. If the thing needs to be controlled, and we might not have it within us to keep it under control (the car, the meeting), fear!

Therapy clients typically have something both more general and deep to fear than a curve in the road or a meeting—some aspect of their inner selves they carry with them all the time, all day, all week, every week, all year, sometimes for years. This fear prevents them from confronting the very aspects within their inner life that bother them. Some people have the capacity to either address these issues on their own in some way despite their fears. Many decide they either cannot do so, or that they would be able to deal with the issues causing the fears more completely, more effectively, through therapy.

These are people who have tried already in their own way to address the problems, whatever they are, to no end they find satisfactory.

If fear is related to perceptions that we will not be able to control what we need to control, therapy clients usually have the doubly difficult task of confronting something that tells them very specifically they do not have the capacity to control the feelings that come with the issue. I know this is pretty vague, but fear covers so many topics, really just about everything related to why a client comes into therapy. Take, for example, a guy with low self-esteem caused by a berating parent during childhood. He must bring himself to believe in the possibility that he can overcome his fear that these messages are true, that he is in fact "worthless," "a failure," "stupid," "irresponsible," and that he will always feel this way. A woman who's experienced trauma, of whatever kind, rightly fears having to relive the traumatic events in therapy, that the memories will come crashing down on her and she will re-experience the terror of those events, will become completely overwhelmed by them, as she may vaguely have recalled being overwhelmed when the original trauma occurred. With time and the capacity to distance herself from the trauma, the last thing most trauma victims want to do is go back into the heart of the trauma, and she may believe this is necessary for therapy. It isn't necessary, or even wise to push a client to re-experience the trauma as a horrible event in therapy, but most clients don't know this, or they don't believe it, and want to simply stay as far away from the traumatic experience as possible, because they are afraid of their perceived limited capacity to experience the event in their present state.

The point is that therapy clients, people who decide they either cannot or do not want to try to address by themselves without professional help the things within them that cause them to be afraid of some aspect of themselves, must first overcome their fear that they will not ever be able to address the issues within them even if they do go to therapy. Usually, this comes as a kind of, "I have nothing to lose" mentality. Trying and failing to address the issues in therapy ends up looking like a better alternative than not trying at all, and it is worth the risk of failure to take the chance on putting an end to whatever is troubling them. With this minimal "benefit of the doubt," clients who come to therapy have at least a small opening to the possibility that they are strong enough, with my help, to confront their fears, and the things within them that lie beyond their fears.

The therapy clients I meet have to overcome issues that tell them they do not have the capacity to move through the very issues that are causing them fear. Yet they come. Talk about courage! In the next chapter on fear, I will discuss ways clients find to remove the fears that prevent them from resolving their issues and explain why I trust and respect fear, despite its sometimes-devastating effect. Fear, it turns out, is an essential part of the therapy process because it prevents us from moving into an area of ourselves precisely because we are not yet ready to be there, we are not yet safe, strong enough, confident enough to experience the feelings, thoughts, memories that will come with addressing the issue. Therapy provides a place of safety, so that in time, gently, fear subsides enough to allow the kind of exploration clients need to make to resolve their struggles. When safety comes, clients learn they are stronger, more capable, less prone to becoming overwhelmed, than they thought.

FEAR AND SAFETY, PART 2: OVERCOMING FEAR IN THERAPY

In the last chapter I explained why we fear parts of our inner lives. In this chapter, I will explain why I respect this fear, and what I do to help clients overcome it to resolve their issues.

I trust fear. I respect fear. I understand fear. Fear is natural, it comes on us without thinking we should be afraid. It's just there, when we need it. So, I don't want to do anything that would cause someone to ignore fear when they should be paying attention to their fears.

Most clients have been pondering their issues for a long time, either on their own, or with a previous therapist. For whatever reason, a new client has some kind of conviction that not doing anything is not a good idea, that doing nothing hasn't worked very well, that ignoring their issues, most likely due to fear, cannot continue. Some level of confusion about their issues is troubling to them. I'd like to say this confusion is in all cases based on fear of themselves. I think this is probably true, but I don't trust absolutes, so I will just say I find it very common that there is some barrier between that client's present awareness of their issues, their situation, their thoughts and feelings, and whatever it is they say they don't understand, can't articulate, still struggle with, find unresolved. This barrier is often some kind of fear. A fear of becoming overwhelmed by the thing they don't understand, or can't remember, or if they do remember, still bothers them. That fear may be very well placed. I prefer to leave it intact. I trust the client's sense of what they can handle.

We work together to dismantle the fear, bit by bit, as we grow to understand why it is there, what part of themselves they need to build up to be able to manage the issues they fear. If I don't respect and trust a client's fear of their history, their memories, their ability to manage whatever it is they are struggling with, and they try to resolve too much too soon, before they are ready, they may experience the very thing they initially feared, becoming overwhelmed. It's better to play it safe. Take it slow. Let the client determine when, how, under what circumstances they are able to safely see, understand, remember, articulate, the events and the meanings of those events they have previously kept hidden.

In therapy, the opposite of fear is not courage; it is safety. All my clients have courage. A client without the courage to face their internal struggles doesn't come to therapy, or if they do, they might come to a single session, engage in a one-time inquiry to find out what therapy is all about, but they won't come to a second or a third session, not unless they are able to muster courage they didn't previously possess, which almost never happens. Courage is not the issue. All clients have courage, or they would not ever have decided to come to therapy. Fear is the issue. Fear is usually well placed. When a client has been living with some set of issues for years, even decades, who am I to say they should conquer their fears quickly. If they've waited this long, unless there is some pressing need, better to make sure they are ready to finally come to grips with this thing they've been carrying around for so long untended before we delve into the things they have been holding back for so long due to their fear of it.

Courage will come as fear recedes. Fear recedes as clients become aware of their ability to trust themselves, to trust me, trust the process of therapy, trust the benefits of opening up (very often one of the first benefits is a relaxing of the tight feelings of fear that keep so much of their inner life in check). None of this can take place if the clients do not experience their capacity to manage their part of the process. The opening up of a safe place in therapy has a lot to do with permission (see my previous chapter on the topic of permission) because it gives the client power and control over the process, how fast or how slow it moves.

I cannot always be certain if a client is moving as fast as they feel safe moving, or too fast, or too slow. So, I ask.

I also watch for a client's revelations, discoveries, and insights. Are they realizing things about themselves that might have caused fear before, but do not cause fear now? If so, they are moving into new territory, shining the light of present awareness on what had previously been concealed in the darkness of fear. Clients become more powerful, feel more powerful, and see themselves as having the capacity to face things they didn't even know they feared. All in good time, their time, when they can manage it, when they find it isn't as overwhelming as they had feared. I do not pull my clients by the hand. I do not lead. I do not follow or push. I walk by their side. Their desire to overcome their issues, coupled with finding a safe place to do it, and to do it with someone else, to not be alone in their struggle, to have both their struggles, and their fears about those struggles validated, again and again, this is key.

When, on occasion, a client feels remiss, embarrassed, or apologizes for not revealing some past event or insight sooner in therapy, my instinct for all the reasons stated in this chapter is to assure them there is no need for their apology. I tell them they told me when they felt they were ready for me to know, for them to say out loud in therapy what they had not thought themselves ready to say before.

Sometimes clients do not have a choice. They feel the need, pressing perhaps, to share in therapy memories or a subject that they are not ready to cope with, and it becomes more than they can handle. They may then experience what they see as a setback. Maybe they need to seek medical help for a time to cope with the new revelation, memories, or the impact it is having on their present lives. Although I want to avoid this wherever possible, it is not always avoidable; therapy is not science and certainly not an exact science. We do the best we can to keep things as safe as we can. That's the best we can do. So when it does happen, when a client feels overwhelmed by their issues, I try to encourage her not be discouraged, but to take care of herself, to seek the help she needs, and try not to see it as a setback. We slow down, we review what we know, we may take a break for a while on that issue, reset the current goals. We do what is needed to once again make sure our therapy work feels safe, while also encouraging continued growth at whatever pace is needed to avoid her becoming overwhelmed again. There is no perfect formula here. There is my intent to keep her safe. There is her trust in her ability to move forward and growing trust in my capacity to be as flexible as her needs dictate.

I want to say a little bit about trauma here. In the last chapter I mentioned that it is not wise or necessary to force clients to re-experience trauma. What I mean is that, given sufficient time and the chance to build internal resources through a safe therapy process, a client who's experienced even severe trauma will be able to recall with clarity the traumatic events without re-experiencing the events as current trauma, with horror, or terror, or feeling he is trapped and cannot get out. This can apply to witnessing or being the target and victim of events such as attempted homicide, rape, brutal beatings. In these cases, the last thing I want to do is cause the person in therapy to re-experience these events in the same way he experienced them in the past. I want him to have the memory of these events without fear, without feeling overwhelmed, and this takes time.

Fear is real. Fear can be terrible, crippling. Fear can also be a tool that tells us what we can handle, and what needs to wait until another day. Facing our fears is central to therapy. Overcoming our fears is part of the process. Ignoring those fears is never part of the process. We must find strength and, yes, also build new strengths within us to make it safe to tackle the issues our fears kept us from taking on before we were ready, so when we do, we do so with success, with resolution, with self-respect. In this way, not only does our fear of ourselves diminish, our belief in ourselves genuinely becomes something new and great and long-lasting.

The Greek philosopher Socrates went to a place to pray called the Oracle of Delphi. Over the door there was a saying, "Know thyself." This is a theme in all of my writings, in all the therapy I do with my clients. Knowing yourself is an essential first step toward accepting yourself. The ultimate goal of first trusting and respecting fear and then overcoming it is to get to a place of acceptance and comfort about the things we fear, to embrace them as part of who we are, so what we do know about ourselves, our histories, our relationships in the past and present, are all knowable without fear, avoidance, denial, repression, and the other detrimental mental energy we have been using to avoid what scares us about ourselves. When you are ready, listen to your fears and then face your fears. Know yourself. Accept yourself. Lose your fear.

THE RELIEF OF HUMILITY:
"I AM JUST SOME GUY"

Several years ago, I started saying to myself "I'm just some guy" in therapy to remember I never know more about my client than they know about themselves. The phrase was also a reminder that there are other therapists who are just as good or better therapists than I am, and a client is always free to go find someone else. Then, I began reminding clients, "I am just some guy" if I thought it would help them realize that they had it within themselves to make changes in their lives, and I was just there to help out. Also, using this phrase in therapy helped to relieve myself of the burden of unrealistic and unnecessary expectations for my capacity as a therapist and helped avoid a lack of humility, which would cloud my ability to do what the client needs from me, rather than doing what I need to show that I am a good or great therapist.

I believe in humility. I do not believe in humiliation or modesty, both of which are forced and rarely genuine. When we experience humiliation, someone or something outside of ourselves makes us feel small or unimportant or flawed. When we display modesty, we are often forcing ourselves to discount or diminish our own capacity in order to impress others that we are not full of pride. Modesty can be genuine, but humility is a more full form of modesty. Humility is genuine, whereas modesty often is not genuine.

So what is "humility?" Humility is simply a recognition and acceptance of our limitations as humans; including our flaws. Humility accepts our tendency to make mistakes, our limited understanding of others, limited control over outcomes or people, the limits of our capabilities as imperfect beings. Humility has two great benefits when we allow ourselves to experience it genuinely. First, it keeps us honest with ourselves about what we can do by reminding us of what we cannot do. Second, it offers a profound and lasting relief by reminding us that, since we can't do "everything," we do not need to try to do everything. If I can't make a client achieve one of their goals in therapy (and of course I can't), and I remind myself of this limitation, it relieves me from feeling responsible for whether they do achieve the goal. Back to the honesty piece, by reminding myself that I can't make a client reach a goal, it also reminds me that they have to reach those goals themselves, which actually helps the client become stronger.

Once I was in a meeting with several other therapists. We call these meetings "consultations," where we discuss issues our clients are having and how we might want to help them with their issues (don't worry, we don't give out names or other client-identifying information). I had suggested another therapist think about "firing" her client who had missed several appointments in a row with not very good reasons. The other therapist was surprised, shocked even, at the suggestion, asking me, "What will the client do then, if I fire her?" I said, "Your client either will or will not find another therapist." This might sound cold, or even callous. Don't worry; I don't fire clients easily or for missing a single appointment. I even feel bad when I do have to let a client go for this kind of thing. But that's not the point. The point is that I really do believe that "I'm just some guy." I consider myself important in my life. But my client might not, and maybe should not. I am not that big of a deal in the scheme of things. There are thousands of other therapists out there. The client needs to find solutions that work for them, and I have just one set of solutions. That other therapist's client might be missing appointments because they aren't getting what they need and don't know how to tell that therapist. By "firing" (terminating the relationship with) the client, that client will then have the opportunity to seek for themselves another therapist that is a better fit for their needs, whatever they may be.

In saying these kinds of things to myself, I remember that my clients have the power to make change in their lives. Sure, I want to help, and do help them make changes. But I do not and cannot make the changes for them. And when I can't help them, its time for them to find someone who can, or do it on their own, and they are in a better position most of the time to make that decision for themselves. I have to accept this limitation in what I do, in who I am, in my role.

When I say to myself "I am just some guy" it reminds me of my limitations, which is good for me. When I say "I am just some guy" to my clients (and I do actually say this sometimes in therapy!), it reminds them that it is within their power, not mine, to make changes in their lives, which of course is good for them.

A THERAPY OF EXISTENCE, PART 1:
A PRIMER ON EXISTENTIALISM

In my first year of college, a philosophy professor joked, "if you are ever at a party and want to sound really smart, tell someone you are an 'existentialist.'" We all laughed, even those of us (like me) that didn't quite understand why this would make us seem smart, or what it meant to be an "existentialist." It was a long word with a lot of syllables, so it sounded smart to me (if you don't know this already, I was starting college at a bit of a deficit because I had dropped out of high school for a year, and then struggled really hard to graduate from high school on time, so I missed a lot along the way).

Once I began to learn what "existentialist" meant, I realized the term probably has almost as many meanings as the number of people who describe themselves as such, and many of the most famous people called "existentialists" would deny the attribute. So, I better define what it means when I use the word. Keep in mind that I am going to try to explain in a few pages what it has taken countless writers over a century to explain, so this is going to be very limited, and incomplete. But, then again, it's just a chapter in a general self-help book, so we shouldn't expect it to be much of an exposé. For a much more involved explanation, I encourage you to visit Stanford University's online Encyclopedia of Philosophy and do a search for an article on Existentialism.

In its most basic sense, existentialism is a philosophy of human life that basically says, "We are who we make ourselves become." One of the most famous proponents of "existentialism" is a French guy, named Jean Paul Sartre, who described this with the phrase, "existence precedes essence." By "essence" he meant, more or less, "what kind of person we are." So, "existence precedes essence," can be explained by saying that we existed (were born) before we became who we are. This might seem obvious. At least it seems kind of obvious to me, at this point in my life. When I first heard it, though, back in that philosophy class when I was 18, I was blown away. It might help to understand that I was raised in a pretty strict Catholic upbringing. My dad took it very seriously, and we were expected to do the same. And for many years, I did. I went to church several times a week for a while as a kid. I went through catechism. I attended a Catholic school for four years, from Fifth to Eighth grade. In this kind of environment, you hear things like "he was always meant to be a priest," or "you were blessed to be given the gift of [insert any number of talents or skills]." In other words, in the Church I was raised in, a person's essence definitely preceded their existence in some really important ways, like what you were supposed to do in your life, what kind of person you would end up being, what kind of special talents or limitations you had, all tending toward the belief that a person's essence was predetermined, meaning you had no choice about who or what you were at some very basic level.

Existentialism turned all of this on its head. It rejected the whole idea of being born with predisposed traits that would determine who you would become. Instead, it suggested you focus on who you want to be or better yet, how to make the kind of choices that will lead to you becoming who you want to be within whatever limits might be beyond your control (like genetic attributes, etc.).

Existentialism also has the reputation of being kind of a downer, a bummer, pessimistic, using words like "dread," "anxiety," "angst," "nausea," and "absurdity" to describe the normal mood of living an honest life. Some of this reputation is deserved because a lot of existentialist writers looked at some very tough aspects of human "existence," but it is not the whole story, or I couldn't very well use it as the basis of much of my thinking about the value and the process of therapy. Therapy can't be too successful if it is a complete downer.

A basic premise of existentialism is that we are born with brains that want to understand the world using "reason" (or "logic" or "rationality"). We want to make sense of the world by making the world make sense in our heads. But, the world doesn't make sense.

Fundamental aspects of the world are random, or at least they appear to be random to us, and are therefore unpredictable, sometimes in very scary ways. Tomorrow your best friend might be diagnosed with an aggressive form of cancer and find out she has 3 months to live. She didn't do anything wrong. She is a good person. She might even have small kids who really need her. This doesn't make sense. Yet, there it is. You can't make any sense of it. Yet, you try. You reason it out, you try to give it a meaning it might not have, an explanation that doesn't work. Your friend is going to die, very soon, and there is no reason to it at all. It just is. See what I mean about the reputation of existentialism as being a downer? It kind of is, so far. Be patient, though, it gets better (less pessimistic).

I have just described one part of the existential notion of "absurdity." Absurdity to an existentialist is basically trying to make sense of things that do not make sense. When we are born, to whom we are born, when we die, how we die; these are all questions about aspects of our world that are completely beyond our control (assuming we do not kill ourselves). Trying to lend meaning to a thing that cannot have meaning leads to absurdity. It leads us to believe something that simply cannot be true, no matter how much we might wish it were true. Even if there are ultimate reasons for these events, we do not know them, we do not understand them, and the result is the same: trying to figure out the reasons will get us nowhere.

So, now you have an idea of what "absurdity" means to existentialists. This attempt at figuring out the riddle to the absurd, if pursued with any level of frequency or vigor, can lead to a kind of anxiety. Like a dog chasing its tail, we look at our impending death with increased "dread" because we realize that our life's supposed meaning looks much more fragile if death is completely unpredictable, might be final, and makes no sense at all. We are prone to conclude that our life cannot have meaning if, in the end, we just die and that's it, nothing more. If we get stuck here, focusing on the irrationality of our birth and death, we may end up in a place of "nausea" about our life, a resignation into pessimism.

If I left it here, and said, "well, there's existentialism in a nutshell," you'd be right to suggest it has little use, especially to a therapist trying to help people feel better about themselves and their lives. But I encourage you to let it sit with you, just like this, for a little while. Let the possibility that the fact of your life, when it began, when it ends, by itself, is something you had no say in, didn't control, didn't ask for, do not choose. The circumstance of your birth was a matter of completely random luck, good or bad. The same is mostly true about when and how you will die. You might live longer if you don't smoke. You might also die in a car crash when someone else loses control of her car no matter how healthy you live your life. Yes, this sucks in an almost unbearable way, but there's no point in denying it. It just is. Bummer. There's more though. The next chapter will show how this is actually a really great starting point for making huge changes in your outlook and your life. At least, that's what it was and still is for me, and is for a large number of people, including clients in therapy.

A THERAPY OF EXISTENCE, PART 2: EXISTENTIALISM IN THERAPY

In A therapy of existence, Part 1, I described some of the basic tenets of existentialism, but didn't get into any detail about how these concepts might be useful in therapy. That will be the topic of this chapter.

So far, the discussion of existentialism might imply that an existentialist must believe there is no life after death, and even that existentialists are all atheists or agnostics (lack faith or doubt faith in God). This is not true. One of the first people considered an "existentialist" was a guy named Soren Kierkegaard, who was until his dying day a devout Christian. Throughout its history, existentialism has included both secular and theological thinkers. What they all have in common is the value of accepting that there are things about life worth recognizing that will never make sense to us, no matter how hard or how often we try to make sense of them, and the best we can hope for is to gain a better understanding of our existence, as it is, right now.

Giving up on the pointless exercise of trying to make sense out of things about life which will never make sense is extraordinarily liberating, freeing, a huge relief, if you let it be. So, let it be. Let it sit for a minute. If you stop trying to make sense of why you were born, why you will die, how and when you and everyone else you have ever known or ever will know will die, you will stop spending energy on something that can never and will never make any real sense. You have your life, and even though that doesn't make sense, it is there. Now, use it. Use it how you want, not based on some kind of idea of how it should be, but on how you want it to be.

At the risk of seeming like I am trying to sound like I am smart, I will do as my professor suggested back in college, and tell you, "I am an existentialist." Let me change this just a little though. Instead, I will say I "adhere to a philosophy of existence." Specifically, I believe that a substantial part of my essence, and your essence, are the result of choices you make in your life, after you were born. I prefer the term "philosophy of existence" to "existentialism" because it seems more open to variance, and less pretentious somehow. We are of course limited by the genetic endowment given to us at birth (nature) and by the irrational and unpredictable parts of our lives (nurture), things like our upbringing, culture, social class, race, gender, etc., but beyond this we are completely free to live our lives as we see fit. Existentialism says to me, "I exist, now what?" Talk about freedom! How can this be pessimistic? It is so full of possibility.

Even though there are some really important parts of our lives that do not and never will make sense (see above), there are other parts of our lives that make sense because we can make them make sense (what we want to do with the lives that have been given to us for whatever reason). I feel bad for so many people who spend so much of their mental energy trying to make sense of parts of their lives that they cannot possibly understand (e.g. why they were born), so that they never end up being able to pay attention to the parts of their lives they might actually be able to understand if they changed their focus (who they are becoming based on the choices they make every day). Paying attention to our choices, and taking full responsibility for the meaning and the consequences of those decisions on who we are becoming is another tenet of a philosophy of existence.

One of the criticisms of existentialism, which is well deserved in some cases, is that it leaves wide open a person's morality, how they decide right from wrong, without the structural restraints of religious or social influence. If we are fully responsible for making whatever decisions we want to make in our lives to become the kind of people we want to be and live the lives we want to live, what is to stop us from doing things others would consider really awful? Wouldn't there be some risk that we would become selfish, bullying, lying, cheating, socially reprehensible? In some cases, I think the answer has to be yes. In fact, to tell you the truth, one of the most prominent early existentialist thinkers ended up supporting Nazis. It doesn't get much worse than that.

So, how do you limit your sense of right and wrong if existentialism is at least partially valid? Let's just say for now that it puts the responsibility for doing what is right squarely on you, and no one else. And that is a good thing, I think. I have touched on part of the answer to these questions about morality in the chapters "Selfishness and love," "To the weak I became weak," "The DEA and CIA—making better decisions," and in little places all over in other chapters. I happen to have a very positive attitude about what lies at the core of most people. I truly believe that most people want to do the right thing, and know what the right thing is, without having to be told by someone else. The more I work with others in my therapy practice, the more I believe this is true. If we give ourselves permission to make the choices we think are right, while being aware of who we are, we will become better people. How to give ourselves permission to act in accordance with our own sense of right and wrong based on who we think we are, is the topic of the chapters "Freedom and Responsibility," Parts 1 and 2.

Now let me bring this a little closer to home. Existentialism is a set of ideas that changed the direction of my life forever. If I didn't need anyone else's permission or approval to be who I chose to be, to live how I wanted to live, then I could stop worrying about the Catholic Church and my father looking over my shoulder, and make the kinds of changes that made sense to me. I could look back at the teachings in the Bible as guides to my own personal integrity, rather than a rule book I had to follow "or else." Until first hearing about existentialism, I had lived my life with a nagging feeling that I wasn't supposed to be alive at all, brought about by things my parents said and did when I grew up. Existentialism gave me permission to be, to exist, to live. And now it was going to be up to me to decide what to do with all that life in front of me, the life that had been given to me, and now was mine for the taking, the defining. I would now find the part of my essence that existed at that and other points, and then begin to create the parts of my essence that didn't yet exist. I am still doing it now, several decades after someone first talked to me about existentialism. I encourage you to do the same, now and for the rest of your life.

PART TWO:

CHOOSE YOUR FEELINGS

One of the most important things I think I do as a therapist is to remind clients that their feelings are almost never all "good" or all "bad." When I discuss feelings with clients, I do not merely ask, "How does that make you feel?" I ask, "What does that feeling tell you?" "What do you think is the purpose of that feeling in that situation?" "Why do you think you ended up having that feeling as opposed to a different feeling?"

We often have far more choice over how we respond emotionally than we think we do. We can make choices about how to feel, when we know why we feel our feelings. We can say to ourselves, I am not going to let that person's insults hurt me no matter what he says (I actually used to say that to myself when I was doing depositions back when I was a trial lawyer). We can also say, I want to be sensitive to this person, because I love them, and if they are in pain, I want to let myself feel pain too.

I do not subscribe to the notion that "my feelings can't be wrong!" Yes, they can. How can a feeling be "wrong?" It's just a feeling. Well, feelings do not exist by themselves. They don't exist in a vacuum. Feelings exist because of other things going on with us. Feelings are based on other things, like perceptions, interpretations, our own insecurities, our attitude, our values and beliefs, our personal history, and so on. Think of it this way. It might not be "wrong" to feel hurt. If you are feeling hurt, that doesn't harm anyone, does it? How could it be wrong? The problem comes in when the person feeling pain doesn't need to feel that kind of pain, but might just be used to feeling pain in response to certain things, and then reacts in accordance with that pain, which leads to other unwanted consequences (like hostility, defensiveness or isolation). Besides, there is a difference between useless pain and useful pain. *Useless* pain doesn't do any good, it doesn't need to exist. It just makes us feel bad. Isn't this feeling (useless pain) a bad thing? *Useful* pain prompts us to react to what is causing it, change it, remove it, take action to get out of whatever situation keeps the pain going. Useful pain is good thing. Useless pain is a bad thing. So, when a person is experiencing emotional pain, I want to help them figure out if what part of it is useful, or useless, what part is good, or bad.

Guilt is another feeling that can be the result of misperception or a pattern in relationships in which someone believes they have done something they should not have done when this is not necessarily the case. Feelings based on inaccurate perceptions or interpretations can lead to low self-worth, and can keep us trying to make changes to ourselves in order to satisfy someone else's expectations of who or how we should be. Feelings that are the result of inaccurate perceptions can also make us respond in certain ways that are detrimental to ourselves and the people in our lives. Misplaced guilt can keep us in unhealthy relationships that we'd be better off ending, it can lead us to end good relationships that do not need to end, or it can prevent us from making good but troubling relationships better by addressing the sources of our doubts.

On the other hand, no matter what your feeling might be at any given time, even if there is some part of it that is the result of personal insecurity, or a history of self-doubt, guilt, or even trauma or abuse, that feeling is trying to tell you something, if you are willing to listen to it. Feelings *always* serve a purpose. They inform us about how something in the external world affects the way we see others and ourselves. When we look for the purpose of a feeling, when we try to find out why we are having a particular feeling, what caused it, an attitude, a perception, an interaction, our own personal values, we learn more about ourselves. We learn more about how the world affects us. In its simplest terms, negative feelings like shame, guilt, loneliness, anxiety, and sadness—these all tell us that we need to make changes to whatever circumstances are causing the negative feelings. Positive feelings like joy, contentment, satisfaction, and relaxation— these all encourage us to follow, get closer, repeat behaviors that have caused us to have those feelings.

When a client describes having a feeling, and then makes a negative judgment, not just about the feeling, but about themselves for having the feeling, I try to remind them that having the feeling, whatever that feeling is, can be helpful, if we look for the purpose of the feeling—what is that particular feeling trying to tell my client about themselves and their situation. A common occurrence is when someone judges himself or herself after they get angry with someone they love. They might criticize themselves in the session. "I was arguing with my boyfriend, and he didn't seem to be listening, which made me really mad and I walked away. Now I feel so stupid for getting so mad over what started as a minor issue. Why do I do that? What's wrong with me?"

This idea that all feelings are sometimes good, healthy and appropriate, and sometimes not good, not healthy, and not appropriate, is an ongoing theme in my writings, just as it is in my therapy sessions with clients. The following chapter, "Choose your anxiety: Focus on what you know" is intended to help sort out whether the anxiety you feel is based on wanting to understand how to control what can or cannot be controlled, so you can make choices about where to focus your anxiety, reduce it, and even eliminate it when it does nothing for you. The chapter, "Choose your guilt," discusses the difference between healthy guilt (which comes from within) and unhealthy guilt (which is derived from what other think or feel). The other chapters in this part of the book address the issues of choosing many different varieties of your own feelings, rather than allowing circumstance or other people to choose them for you, including feelings of anger, hurt, anxiousness, loneliness, and other feelings we commonly have, all of which tell us something, and can help us lead better, more meaningful, and less painful lives, if we know what to look for and what we want to change.

CHOOSE YOUR ANXIETY: FOCUS ON WHAT YOU KNOW

As just explained in the introduction to this part of the book, this chapter is the first part of a series of chapters that begin with the phrase "Choose your (insert feeling)." These chapters are based on the concept that our entire range of human feelings are all designed to provide us important information about our experiences and situations; information which can be crucial for telling us how we need to respond in order to obtain what we need. Anger tells us someone has intruded on what we think is an important boundary (see chapter, "Choose your anger.") Guilt tells us we ourselves may have done something we think is a violation of our own sense of right and wrong (see chapter, "Choose your guilt.") Whatever the feeling, I always try to help clients find out what part of it is legitimate, reasonable, and useful. Then I try to help clients find out if there is also some part of that feeling that is problematic because it is misplaced, intrusive, limiting and based on an inaccurate perception of themselves, someone else, or an event or situation.

Anxiety is no different. Anxiety tells us there is something we need to control in order to be safe, satisfied, or to obtain something important in our lives, without which, we think we will not be okay in some way. Anxiety can be highly useful and informative, motivating us to take action where necessary and can also become downright crippling, or at least a major source of unnecessary interference in our lives, preventing us from sleeping, focusing on immediate needs, and even leading to physiological problems like serious muscle tension, headaches, chest pain, etc. The anxiety a student feels before a test can both be a powerful motivator to study and be prepared for the test, but taken too far, can lead a student to freeze during the test, or avoid studying for it at all. This chapter will discuss what can be done when anxiety becomes a problem because we think we have to know something to solve a problem, but the thing we think we need to know might not be possible to know and we might not actually need to know it after all.

Racing or "obsessive" thoughts are often the result of trying to make sense of things that cannot make sense. We ask, "How can this be?" when we feel someone has betrayed us. When someone wants to end a relationship that we do not want to end, we try to figure out how it is possible that they are not interested when we were so interested. We will likely never actually know for sure. It isn't possible for us to get into their heads. We can listen to what they have to say, if they are willing to tell us, and then decide to take it at face value, or not, and then leave it. When we cannot just leave it at that, our minds go around and around and around, *why, why, why*, like circling a thing we simply cannot reach. This is a form of intense anxiety that clients often feel in their lives that brings them to therapy.

Once we have identified that this is part of the problem, I often suggest: "focus on what you know, rather than focusing on what you do not know or cannot know." It often turns out that they do already know all they need to know to move on. They just don't know that!

I hope this suggestion doesn't lead you to believe I think this kind of anxiety is easy to deal with or that I think it actually solves the entire problem with a simple sentence. The anxiety leading to these kinds of racing thoughts can be the result of literally years of pain, anguish, mistrust, insecurity, etc. I recognize this fact and yet still suggest focusing on what you know, rather than what you don't know, as a starting point to containing and accepting the very real possibility that much of what a given client might want to figure out about a certain event or situation, especially one dealing with other people, cannot be figured out, no matter how hard or how often they think about it. I suggest they put the need to know aside for the moment, to focus instead on what they do know, and then decide whether what they do know is in fact enough. It often is. And when it is not, there is usually some underlying thing driving them to think about what they do not know, and we need to also identify this for what it is, and deal with it. We might need to do this repeatedly for months in order to help the client re-orient their reaction to their anxiety, by not automatically giving into it, trusting that it has merit when often it does not, or is at best misdirected and therefore until redirected pointless.

Consider the following examples of this kind of anxiety. A woman in a relationship wonders if her partner is thinking of leaving. Her partner assures her countless times he does not intend to leave. The anxiety about leaving persists. She goes over the "evidence" again and again—little things said about dissatisfaction about their lives, irritability, how he has been spending his time, or their money, who he has been talking to lately, his criticisms about her. Every time they have an argument, she wonders if this is when he will tell her he is leaving, has found someone else, or is just fed up with her.

A man is highly anxious about losing his job. He fears an imminent layoff. This fear has been present for nearly two years. He is stricken several times a week with thinking his boss is unhappy with him and will announce any day that he is being replaced. He watches as his boss walks by his office without saying "good morning." Recently, his boss and another manager invited a co-employee to go out to get a bite to eat for lunch, but they did not invite him. He was recently omitted from a training event that others were asked to attend.

A young woman just out of college had a decent job, but lost it in the last recession. She has found temporary work since, but hasn't found another "good" job. She panics during interviews, has trouble sleeping several times a week, feels dread nearly every time she pulls up to her computer to do job searches or print out another resume and cover letter.

In each of these examples, the person suffering from anxiety had some reasons to believe the thing making them anxious might actually happen. And it if did happen, they would have a serious problem (losing someone they love or financial distress or a failed career path). The common problem among these examples is that the person is trying to predict an outcome that cannot possibly be predicted, no matter how long, how many times, how hard they try to predict it. They are each trying to know something they cannot possibly know. Can anyone ever be absolutely sure his or her partner is completely faithful and is never ever going to leave him or her? We can certainly believe this very strongly, but can we ever know it for a certainty?

Same thing with employment. We cannot ever know for sure when or if our employer is going to let us go, no matter how many times they assure us we are doing a good job and our job is safe. Every state in the United States has laws allowing employers to terminate employment relationships "at will" (translation: any time for any reason not otherwise prohibited). When we interview for a job, unless we have the inside track (a previous connection), we cannot know whether we will be hired. So, what can these clients all do to relieve themselves of at least a significant portion of their anxiety, an anxiety that is not helpful at all? They can focus on what they know, or can know, about their current situation, rather than focusing on what they do not know.

The woman thinking her partner plans to leave can seek validation in ways that are not accusatory or destructive. She can consider how her partner has demonstrated commitment in ways that are more than just words. He works his tail off to make enough money so they can avoid putting the kids in daycare. He rarely goes out without her, and when he does, he is good about telling her where he is going, and with whom. His finances are transparent. He has offered to show her his phone records if she wants to see the bill. And if she needs more demonstration, she can ask for it in ways that are reasonable, not accusatory. The employee worried about being fired can recall that he just received a promotion. His "numbers" are good (he works a lot of hours and gets a lot done). His performance evaluations have been generally very positive. Although the economy is sluggish, his employer is doing well, making money. The woman who fears never getting a good job can focus on how many second interviews she's gotten. She graduated from school with honors. She has a very high recommendation from her previous employer, whose company went bankrupt, so she can easily explain her current employment situation.

The first step in this process is to take a look at some basic "facts" in whatever situation is causing us problematic anxiety. This is usually fairly quick, and not too difficult. It can be done (and redone) in a few sessions or less. A harder change in focus is trying to figure out why each person had become so focused on something they cannot know. What drives that anxiety internally? Is there something that predates the situation within that person that led them to become so anxious? Did the woman worried about her partner leaving suffer from insecurities, low self-worth, or bad relationship patterns before she was in the current relationship? Or is there something about the relationship that needs to be addressed to make it better, more secure, some unresolved conflict or interactional pattern and she hasn't been able to identify what that is or how to address it with her partner? Is the man worried about being laid off too focused on the importance of his job? Is he overcompensating for feelings of inadequacy in other areas of his life, putting all his eggs in one basket, his job? Is the college graduate suffering from a related fear that she will never get the approval of her parents if she can't find a job as easily as her older brother did who is now doing great in his career?

Whatever the answers might be to these more internal questions, each person can work out the anxiety by first identifying what they can know, what they do know right now, what they can change, what they can "figure out," so they don't get trapped into a never-ending circle of trying to figure out what they will never figure out. In this way, they can become unstuck, make changes that need to be made, use the anxiety as useful information telling them that they need to change something, while recognizing they will never be able to know or change things beyond their scope of knowledge or control. Once clients learn how to do this in one sphere of their lives, they are often able to find ways to do this in many other areas as well.

CHOOSE YOUR GUILT

I came up with the phrase "choose your guilt" to describe to a client how to deal with a situation in which someone might feel two kinds of guilt. The first kind of guilt is a healthy way of deciding right from wrong. The second kind is not really guilt at all, but is instead a misinterpreted sense of responsibility for someone else's feelings which can be experienced as guilt.

Guilt is painful, and can really feel deep and awful. So, we often run from guilt, not wanting to feel it. But not all guilt is bad. Guilt can be a tool. Just like a burn tells us not to touch a hot oven to protect us from hurting ourselves, guilt is an emotional pain that teaches us important lessons about doing the right thing, and not doing things we know are wrong. Guilt is an emotional punishment, which is sometimes a good indicator of our own values.

When we run from guilt to avoid this awful feeling, we can confuse ourselves about when guilt is trying to teach us right from wrong and when the guilt is actually not our guilt, coming from inside us, but guilt handed to us from the outside, from another person or perhaps from lessons we were taught as children that we no longer believe.

Have you ever felt guilty because you thought you "should" feel guilty? Have you ever felt guilt, not because you actually thought you did something wrong, something that seemed to be inconsistent with your own sense of right and wrong, but because you thought someone else believed you had done something wrong? Imagine wanting to leave an unhealthy relationship. You know the right thing to do for you or maybe for your children as well, is to leave. But you stay. You stay out of a sense of guilt for causing what you know, or believe, your leaving will do to the other person. You stay because you fear the guilt you will feel when you see how much pain you've caused by your leaving. Is this guilt? Or is it something else? It is the feeling of failing to take care of your responsibilities to someone else. Yes. True. Does that make it guilt? No. It doesn't. You are only guilty, truly guilty, if you do something wrong. Leaving a relationship in which you are being hurt, verbally or physically abused, frightened, controlled, or in which others are being subjected to relentless fighting, this is not wrong. And if it is not wrong, then you should not feel guilty. You are not responsible for causing pain to someone else if you are leaving the relationship because of that person's very own actions.

Leaving a person you committed to stay with, in marriage, or in a long-term relationship, can be wrong if you are leaving for the wrong reason or leaving in the wrong way (leaving out of boredom, not facing your own issues, or leaving by having an affair). But leaving is not always wrong. And it isn't wrong just because it might cause the other person pain. The same holds true for responding to others by taking care of yourself, in any situation. If you need to do something, take action, ask for something, make some kinds of changes that get you what you need, this is not wrong. It doesn't become wrong if in doing so, you also cause someone else to feel pain. Their pain alone doesn't make your decision to take care of yourself wrong. Their pain alone should not cause you to feel guilty if what you are doing is not wrong, but is good.

So, how do you "choose your guilt?" How do you choose when the guilt you feel is a healthy tool that tells you right from wrong and when it is an unhealthy sense of misplaced responsibility? Pretty simple, actually. Just ask yourself this, *Am I feeling guilty because what I have done or am thinking of doing feels like it violates my own sense of right from wrong* (e.g. breaking a promise without reason, lying, deceiving)? *Or does it feel guilty solely because it might make someone else feel something they do not want to feel or I do not want them to feel?* Remember, if the only reason you feel guilty is because of the way it might make someone else feel, that is not sufficient reason to feel guilty. You are responsible for your actions, to be sure. So if something feels wrong because you believe it is wrong for you to do it, then go ahead and feel guilty and think long and hard before you do it, or do it again if you've already done it. If it doesn't feel *wrong to you*, but you still feel guilty because of the way it might make someone else feel, then it might not be wrong at all. So, choose. Which is it?

Choose your guilt based on what *you* think is right or wrong, not based on what someone else thinks is right or wrong for you.

CHOOSE YOUR ANGER

Let's think about "anger management." I can't say exactly why, but I've always had some kind of attitude problem with the concept of "anger management." Many clients (mostly men) tell me they have tried, without success, to control their anger after participating in an anger management course. I have a sneaking suspicion that the failure of such programs is due to an unspoken message that anger is basically a bad thing, and the road to a better life is to get rid of anger wherever possible.

Isn't it true that anger is basically a bad thing and it would be a good thing if we could just get rid of it as much as possible? No. Anger is not a bad thing. Anger is sometimes not only appropriate, but necessary and good. Anger is an energy that, when used in a constructive way, can help us find our way out of all kinds of problems, including oppression and depression.

What if anger isn't the problem, what if anger is actually a good thing sometimes? If so, what can we do to make sure it doesn't get out of control, but it also doesn't get stuffed down (which can actually make things worse in the long run)? How do we deal with anger so that we can use its positive benefits without letting it be destructive to our relationships and our own good feelings about who we are?

A couple of years ago, I heard a guy on the radio, a psychologist, say he thought anger was a "moral feeling." I liked that idea a lot. It made sense to me. I've been using the idea in my own life and with clients ever since. Over the years, I have given this idea my own interpretation. By "moral feeling" I do not mean that anger is a "right or correct feeling." Instead, we tend to feel anger when we feel like someone has violated our sense of what is right and wrong for us. Think about what makes you angry? Isn't it usually the case that you become angry with someone else when you think they have done something wrong, especially when they have done something wrong to you or someone in your family—when you feel insulted, cut off, ignored, when someone is rude to you, or treats you unfairly. Someone doesn't let you into a lane when you are trying to merge: you think they should, and it makes you angry. The guy at Best Buy tells you they don't sell the product you came to buy, and then you find it online, and it was right at the store you just left: you're irritated because he shouldn't say anything if he doesn't know (or better yet, does what it takes to know before you get to the store). These are trivial examples, and don't justify outrage, but they illustrate that anger is often justified, even at a relatively mild level.

When dealing with anger within myself and with my clients, I start by asking if the anger is justified, because sometimes it is justified and sometimes it is not. When it is justified, it can tell me something about my interpretation of another person's actions, and whether I need to do something to let that person know their actions bother me. This is a primary and legitimate path to changes in your relationships. It is also often a way to begin to exercise a feeling of power over having your needs met. One of the most common elements to a long-term struggle with depression is the belief that it is not okay to assert needs that arise out of anger. Fear of anger can be a very damaging and limiting way to approach relationships and the world. I am not touting anger as always appropriate or the best way to deal with a situation. I am merely saying that anger can be a very important tool in our range of feelings to tell us what we need and how to get it. Anger is an energy that, like fear, when appropriate, motivates us to take action to make changes that are necessary for us to improve our lives.

The way people experience anger seems to have four distinct features, each of which can lead to problems that need to be addressed. Here they are:

1. *Triggers* (someone or something outside of us causes us to feel anger);
2. *Frequency* (how often we feel anger—from almost never to constant irritability);
3. *Intensity* (how angry we feel given the trigger—from mild annoyance to irate);
4. *Expression* (how do we let others know we are angry—from firm speech to punching a hole in the wall).

The specific way I help clients in therapy deal with each of these features of anger is too varied to cover in a single chapter of a book, but the process is the same for all of them. First, I ask the client to put aside the idea that anger is either all bad or all good (never okay or always okay). Second, they need to put aside the idea that their anger is immediate, automatic, or that they can't help it when they become angry. Yes, they can, although this can take some time. There is no such thing as "automatic anger." Anger is always a choice. I know this might sound wrong. But I really believe it to be true.

Let me repeat, anger is always a choice. We can choose what kinds of things make us angry (triggers), and the same thing can be said about frequency, intensity and expression of anger. Think about how many times you've made an almost unconscious decision not to let yourself get angry about something that might have made you angry. A guy cuts you off in line at the store and clearly knows he is doing this. You know it's rude, inconsiderate, but you are having a good day, you are not in a hurry, and you just let him be a jerk and go on your merry way a few minutes later. You "pick your battles." You decide not to let yourself get angry because you don't like the way your anger will affect you. This is often a good decision. However, avoiding anger too often because we are overly afraid of conflict or we have low self-esteem (we doubt whether we deserve to be treated with respect or dignity) can lead to other problems like anxiety, depression, or a continuation and worsening of low self-esteem. If we do not let ourselves feel or express anger in situations where it is appropriate and might prompt positive change, we can become stuck in a pattern of seeing ourselves as powerless, vulnerable, a victim without the capacity to make things better for ourselves.

The more aware we become of the reasons things make us angry, how angry they make us and how we express that anger, the more we will be able to make conscious choices about anger so we can use it to our advantage, rather than letting it become destructive to ourselves and our relationships. For instance, when we can pinpoint why a particular situation made us angry when looking back it seems like it shouldn't have made us angry, we may find that we are "generally irritable" because of some unrelated stressor we are not dealing with and when we do remove the stressor, the irritability will begin to dissipate.

A client was irritable with his wife and kids for several months, becoming increasingly angry. He learned through therapy that his irritability was due mostly to having a contractor working on his house who was cutting corners, and he is mad, but afraid to confront him because he wants to just get the work done. He is afraid to tell his wife because he doesn't want her to think he isn't doing a good job monitoring the contractor, so he is irritated with her too. After he finally confronts the contractor (allows himself to be angry with the contractor), gets better performance, he becomes less irritable with his own family. This kind of example may seem obvious, now that the whole story has come out, but when this is part of a pattern of years of stuffing anger, it can be somewhat difficult getting at where the "real" source of the anger is coming from, because we need to break through barriers of denial and self-doubt (like "I don't really have a good reason to be angry at the contractor, I am probably wrong about him cutting corners," etc.).

We can choose to understand our anger so we allow ourselves to become angry when someone really has violated our sense of right and wrong. Anger helps us demand what we legitimately need at the risk of conflict, rather than always assuming anger is not okay, trying to stuff it, and then letting it come out in ways we never intended. When we make anger a more conscious decision, in the moment, or thinking about it later, we can learn how to use it to our advantage and how to prevent it from cropping up where we think it serves no purpose for us. Learning to distinguish between appropriate and inappropriate anger helps us to ensure the anger stay where it belongs, with whom it belongs, so we can more easily let it go because we've expressed it where necessary and we don't need to hang onto it as resentment.

I have watched many clients over the course of several months become sufficiently aware of anger so that they can put it aside most of the time, without fearing it as a bad thing. We do this by focusing on exactly what was happening in the moment the person experienced the anger, and how they interpreted and responded to the situation, on an emotional and a rational level (what were all of their feelings and thoughts right at that moment), and then how that led to their response. Over time, they learn to do this themselves almost automatically, and then can make better decisions about their interpretations of the kinds of things that made them angry and ask themselves if something else is also playing into their anger. With these skills they can make better choices; they can choose when to be angry, how angry they should be, and how they want to express that anger, without fear, guilt, shame, or self-doubt.

SHAME, PART 1:
THE VALUE OF SHAME

There is valuable shame and there is destructive shame. The first part of this discussion of shame will explain how shame can be a helpful and important part of self-discovery. The second part of the discussion explains when shame is destructive, and how to eliminate that kind of useless shame.

If you've spent any time in therapy with me, you know I think this: all feelings have value. They tell us things about ourselves, our situations, our relationships with other people and to the world as a whole. Shame is no different. Shame tells us that we should not like certain things about ourselves when we notice these things. Shame is a tough pill to swallow, but avoiding shame where it is appropriate is even worse.

Let me explain how I think about shame. I'll start with a rehash of guilt (see the chapter "Choose your guilt" for more details on guilt). Physical pain we call "pain." Emotional pain we call "sadness." What do we call "moral pain?" We call it guilt. We feel guilt when we do something we believe is inconsistent with our personal moral values. Guilt is about some specific thing we've done. Guilt is about a single act. Shame is like guilt, but spread over time, over several acts, acts that form a pattern. This pattern, when we notice it, tells us that we keep doing something we know is wrong because there is some aspect of who we are, our very character, that we do not like. Guilt is the snapshot of moral pain. Shame is the movie. Guilt is about the thing we did wrong. Shame is about what makes us do that thing.

Just because we did something wrong, and feel guilty about it, doesn't mean we should necessarily feel shame about it. We don't want to translate a "bad" act as meaning we are a bad person because we did the act we now feel guilty about. This is where I think some therapists often want to go when they try to dissuade their clients from judging themselves with shame. If this were all they were trying to avoid, that would be fine, and I would agree whole-heartedly. Sometimes, though, therapists try to help clients avoid feeling any kind of shame at all, as if shame can never be appropriate, valuable, or valid. But it can be all these things, and when it is, paying attention to it is an important opportunity for self-discovery. Ignoring shame when it is appropriate, like ignoring any deep-seated feeling, comes with a price.

How can we ever hope to attain meaningful personal growth and self-improvement if we are not willing to consider the certainty that there are parts of who we are that we do not like, that we do not feel good about, that we wish were not there? Even Alcoholics Anonymous acknowledges the importance of learning about our negative personal traits, so we can get rid of them! The fifth step of A.A. deals with things we have done that are wrong: "Admitted to God, to ourselves, and to another human being the exact nature of our *wrongs*." The sixth step takes these wrongs and bundles them into "defects of character." "We're entirely ready to have God remove all these *defects of character*." In other words, we want to remove the parts of our character that led us to do the things we now can see we shouldn't have done. Sometimes, a regrettable act, when repeated, tells us of tendencies within ourselves for which we should feel shame. By the way, despite being in A.A. for over thirty years, I do not actually believe you can remove character defects permanently by asking God to remove them, nor do I think this is necessarily what the sixth step means. I interpret this phrase to mean that once we are aware of our character defects, we can try to avoid allowing those defects to let us repeat our past "wrong" behavior.

If we grab a hot pan from the oven and burn our hand, we think twice about ever doing it again. If we do something wrong, and then feel guilty about it, we can console ourselves by thinking it the product of a mistake in judgment, promising ourselves (and maybe others) that we will avoid making the same mistake in the future. If it never happens again, we can chalk it up to a simple transgression and (mostly) forget about it. If it keeps happening, there is a deeper issue, it's more than just a mistake. The first time someone is convicted of driving while intoxicated, the law takes it seriously (as it should) but allows for the possibility that it won't happen again—we might call it "a lapse in judgment." This describes the circumstance of the act. The second DUI begins to look like a pattern, and will require some kind of serious intervention—we are more likely to call it "alcoholism." This describes the person doing the act, not just the act or circumstance.

I have character defects that I have felt shame about in my life. I am a drug addict. When I was using drugs, I dropped out of school. I stole stuff and sold drugs to support my habit. I lost my job. I lost good friends and damaged relationships within my family by doing harmful things to them. I felt not just guilt for doing these things, but shame for being the kind of person who could do these things, again and again. I know I need to never use drugs or drink again. If I do, there is a very good chance I might do some of these things again. I also have a temper, which a long time ago occasionally erupted into violence. This is a character defect that I still possess. I must stay vigilant and remember the shame I felt after realizing the harm I had done with my violence toward others to avoid anger when it is not helpful or appropriate. I must keep in check the anger I sometimes still feel, so it doesn't ever get to the point of violence again. This is the value of shame in my life and I cannot afford to ignore it.

I will probably always have a tendency to become more angry than I should and to abuse drugs or alcohol if I take the opportunity. Neither makes me a "bad person." They make me an otherwise good person who has tendencies to do "bad" things when left unchecked.

So, I have to be vigilant in my work to keep these tendencies (and others) under control. This has become a natural and permanent part of my self-awareness and personal growth. This is my way out of shame—change! Instead of continuing to feel shame about my drug addiction, I feel pride at being sober for all these years. Instead of feeling shame about my anger, I feel proud that I have never spanked or hit my son (who is now an adult).

Clients spend huge amounts of energy avoiding shame. If they spend energy trying to avoid shame defined by outside sources that are not applicable to them, I encourage and applaud the effort (we'll be getting to that in the next chapter on shame). Unfortunately, denial of actual negative character traits that should result in shame will keep them stuck, and the energy they expend toward that denial ends up being a disruptive and destructive force in their lives. The process of self-discovery carries with it the necessary task of not only looking at that which we like about ourselves, but also looking at, taking seriously, and promising to minimize (even if we can never eliminate) those parts of ourselves we do not like.

Fear of shame, avoiding shame, even if the shame itself might be valuable, brings people to therapy and does them harm because it creates so much anxiety or depression. In fact, depression and anxiety might be the main thing most people think is the problem, when they are really symptoms of something deeper: shame or the avoidance of shame. The avoidance of shame can also lead people to do other things more destructive to themselves than the shame itself could ever be—drinking, drugs, gambling, and instability in work, relationships, and life.

Facing shame, to put it in its place, contain it, and learn from it is usually an important part of work toward ending many instances of anxiety and depression, as well as helping to keep permanent abstinence from drinking, drugs, gambling, and other forms of energetic and destructive avoidance. Facing real shame, healthy shame, shame about our character defects, our patterns of behavior that are inconsistent with our sense of right and wrong, is more than anything an indispensible tool to teach us what we need to do and not keep doing to become the person we want to be.

SHAME, PART 2:
DESTRUCTIVE SHAME

In the first part of this discussion of shame, I have tried to point out that not all shame is a bad thing, that it serves an important part of self-awareness and personal growth. There are reasons to avoid some kinds of shame, though, and that is the focus of this part of the discussion, destructive shame.

There are two kinds of destructive shame. The first kind of destructive shame happens when shame is internalized from an outside source, which might be both inaccurate and damaging. I dealt with this a lot in the prison system. Many of my clients and students there recalled having been told over and over again as they were growing up things like: "You will never amount to anything," "You think of no one but yourself," "You are going to be just like your (dad, brother, uncle) who rotted away his life in jail." Racial epithets hurled at some of them and other acts of overt and covert racist discrimination over the years were internalized in ways that became self-fulfilling prophecies that they adopted without necessarily even realizing they had. They began to see themselves as worthless because it seemed to them most of society thought they were, from a very early age.

Female clients often feel shame about their bodies because they were sexually abused or because they do not look like their sister, mother, or the woman on the billboard draped over a car. Rather than saying, "I am not as fit or healthy as I'd like to be," they say "I feel ugly, and I have always felt ugly for as long as I can remember." Female clients even sometimes feel shame about themselves precisely because they have done well at something when they thought they weren't supposed to. I have had a number of teenage female clients who were both depressed and anxious because they were doing so well in school they felt ashamed of it. They had internalized the message that girls aren't supposed to be smarter than boys. And these girls weren't misinterpreting the social cues. They were just making the all too common mistake of internalizing destructive social cues.

Men in therapy often talk about feeling shame for their sexual desires, fantasizing about women other than their wives, even though they haven't acted on any of these thoughts, do not intend to, and otherwise have solid good relationships with their wives. Men also carry shame if they conclude that they will never be able to achieve their career aspirations. The problem here is when those aspirations were set, not by them, but by someone else along the way—a parent, sibling, mentor, spouse or societal expectations. The shame becomes permanent because they are trying to satisfy expectations they did not themselves create.

The second kind of destructive shame occurs when a person feels shame, not about one or more character defects, but about themselves entirely. A client might legitimately feel shame about something they did that says something about who they are: "I am ashamed that I was too afraid of conflict and an unknown future as a single parent, so I did not defend my children when their father hit them as they were growing up. Looking back, I feel very selfish for my decisions then." Okay, fair enough. She can work with this to make amends where possible, to instill in her children now her desire that they not make the mistakes she did, by being involved in their lives, pointing out when she thinks any of them may be repeating patterns she helped create. If, though, she says, "I am a horrible person. I stood by and watched as my husband beat my children. I have no excuse, and do not deserve to have a relationship with any of them." This is destructive, limiting, and inaccurate shame. It is taking shame too far —by allowing shame about one aspect of herself to define her entire person. It is destructive because it is so painful, all encompassing, and because it allows for little change, if any. It might also put the burden on her children to make her feel better about herself, without really addressing meaningful change. Then her children might feel shame if they are not able to help her reduce her own shame—the children become responsible for the shame she feels.

In all these cases, my approach is to help clients identify the source of their shame. If their shame comes from an external source, we review its accuracy. If it is not accurate, I ask them to "externalize" it by actively rejecting it. The man who thinks he is lazy because he is not as wealthy as a sibling begins to tell himself that he never really wanted to be wealthy. He shares this feeling with his wife, finds out that she has always thought he worked too hard, that she doesn't want the kind of life his brother has with his family. Relief and an improved marriage replaces shame, eventually.

If shame doesn't come from an external source of expectations, I ask clients to explore the source of the shame by describing some aspect of themselves they really do not feel good about. Then we come up with strategies to minimize or eliminate the thing about themselves that cause them to feel shame. The wife who has had a long-term affair might spend time in therapy digging into why she started the affair in the first place, and then how she was able to hold both the marriage and the relationship outside the marriage for so long. When she understands these parts of herself better, she might be able to understand the initially legitimate needs she sought to have met outside the marriage, so she can decide whether it might still be possible to meet them with her husband. If so, she might save the marriage. If not, she may need to leave the marriage to get those needs met in a different relationship as an alternative to repeating the behaviors for which she has felt such long-term and deep shame.

Whether internal or external in its source, shame that becomes so large it causes a person to define themselves as altogether "bad" is the worst kind of destructive shame. How can one change, grow, become a "better" person if they are just plain bad to the core? They can't. And that is the problem. I'll call this kind of shame, "enveloping shame" because it almost covers the whole person. This is a highly destructive, debilitating kind of shame. Fear of enveloping shame is probably the reason so many people spend so much energy trying to avoid shame at any cost. They fear the shame they already feel for some part of who they are will become so large it will define how they feel about themselves as a whole, and they will then become completely trapped and overwhelmed by it. So, they avoid it. Who wouldn't?

With enveloping shame, I first try to help a client address the source of the shame they already feel. When they see where this shame is derived, whether accurate or not, internal or external, from just one part of who they think they are, they often begin to feel some relief from their fear of shame. Often, this can lead to further discovery of why they spent so much time believing they were somehow bad to the core due to this more limited shame. When they identify the source of this issue, they know how to combat it as the feeling comes up again. They might have come to believe they were not supposed to feel good about themselves from an early age, and they found something within themselves to feel shame about, and then applied that feeling to the whole of their person. Perhaps they were the product of an affair, or were adopted, or felt unwanted, a burden to their parent. Perhaps they were sexually abused and told it was their fault. We then try to find other positive, accurate, believable and helpful messages to replace the messages that told this person they were bad. The reasons for enveloping and destructive shame are many and varied; the process for addressing it is the same: identify, externalize, remove, replace.

Shame has its place. We can learn much from our shame. We lose so many opportunities for growth and change when we run from shame. Face the shame; identify its source and level of accuracy. If external, reject it. If internal, learn from it, and change. This is the value of shame. Shame can be destructive, too, when it comes from an outside source or when it becomes overwhelming, describing not just some part of us but who were are at our core. Separating out valuable shame from destructive shame is one of the most difficult, and therefore also one of the most rewarding parts of therapy and self-discovery, because it so often leads to such meaningful and positive changes in the way we think about who we are.

EXPECTATIONS AND RESENTMENT

Resolving conflicts in relationships is one of the main reasons clients come to see me for therapy. The difficulty is often related to resentments. Resentment is mostly the result of:

1. Having an expectation about something from someone;
2. Disappointment at not getting what you expected; and
3. A continuing belief that the person "should" have met your expectation.

Resentment, then, is at least partially the result of not accepting that your expectations were not met, and hanging onto the belief that those expectations should have been met. The solution: acceptance.

If you are clear in your expectations, and the other person continues to fail to meet them, there is a good chance that you will change your expectations pretty quickly if you are honest with yourself about whether there is any point in maintaining those expectations. Note that this statement includes situations in which you have every right to expect whatever you wanted from the person.

Recently, I made plans with a good friend. He had asked me to get dinner with him on a Saturday night. I was also invited to a party that evening, but turned down the invitation because I'd already made plans with my old friend. A few hours before we were supposed to get together, he called to cancel. I had a right to expect him to meet with me, unless there was a good reason he couldn't. He did not have a good reason. In fact, in the past few years, he often cancels without good reason. Was I angry? Yes, a little. I was irritated. Did I resent him? No. Why? Because I know this about him. I accept that he is fairly unreliable. I cater my expectations so they are in line with what I know is likely behavior. So in the moment I could let myself feel disappointment and irritation, but not hang onto resentment. I had prepared myself for this exact scenario. If that other party I missed had been an important event, I would not have allowed myself to miss it on the chance that this friend would cancel. I appreciate the friendship, even though I know he is not reliable. I accept the downside because I value the friendship for other reasons. Maybe this is an obvious or trivial example, but it shows how we can avoid resentment up front by modifying our expectations. Note, though, that I am not saying we shouldn't have expectations, or that we should always be willing to let those expectations go. Having unreasonable expectations, in the face of what we know to be different, though, sets us up for unnecessary and detrimental resentments.

The more we modify our expectations so they are in line with what we know about how a person is likely to act, the less we will be disappointed. The less we are disappointed by the behavior of others, the less we will end up resenting them afterward. Let's take a more extreme example, one that resurfaces in therapy quite a bit: resentment toward a family member who continues to try to control us. Bill (not his real name) has a father who wants Bill to be someone other than who Bill believes he really is. Now a man, Bill wants to be able to stop being judged by his parents because he has chosen a career path very different from the path they had expected him to take, and they remind him of this in various ways nearly every time he sees them. He goes to dinner at their house. His father talks to him about his job, with what clearly appears to be disappointment and judgment. He leaves their house, once again resenting his father. What should he do? Accept it? Yes, and no.

Bill can accept that his father tends to be judgmental about Bill's choices, and stop expecting his father to change his tune. Bill thinks his father "should" be less judgmental of him, which might very well be true. But it's not likely to happen. So no matter how much we can agree that Bill is "right" about this situation, continuing to want, hope, believe, and begrudge that his father is in the wrong isn't making things better for Bill. Bill can tell his father to stop being judgmental, to leave him alone on the issue, but having said it, Bill can learn to accept that his father may never change his attitude, and also stop hoping to get his father's approval.

This brings to mind a simple tool for changing your own expectations in a way that doesn't compromise your sense of what you consider important—the Serenity Prayer (modified to make the point in this chapter):

God, grant me the serenity to accept the things I cannot change [how other people act], *the courage to change the things I can* [my expectations about how other people will or should act], *and wisdom to know the difference* [balancing my expectations with how I know other people really are, as opposed to how I think they should be].

I am not trying to be preachy by offering a prayer as a mental health tool. I offer the prayer in part because I use it often in my own life, and I find it very helpful for just this kind of thing. If you don't like the "God" part of the prayer, just leave it out.

Wanting to get our needs met in an open honest way in our relationships can be an important part of our own integrity, and can lead us to obtain what we need in a very healthy way. However, when we have made it clear what we want or need, and another person continually doesn't do that for us, continuing to seek that very same thing is pointless, and breeds resentment, which we carry within ourselves as an unnecessary and heavy burden. To the extent possible, then, let go of "being right" or making conclusions about how others in your life "should act," so you can accept how they "do act." Once you do this, you will be in a much better position to decide whether the way someone acts is something you can accept, even though you don't like it, or if you cannot accept it (which is certainly a good decision sometimes, as in an abusive relationship), make the kinds of changes in that relationship so you can accept the behavior. This can include increasing distance, avoidance, or even cutting off the relationship, when the behavior is very extreme. When it is not clear how to communicate and resolve these kinds of expectations, it can also be a good idea to seek the help of a professional, either for you, or for you and the other person, to see what is really at the heart of the continuing conflict, disappointment, and resentments.

Resentments, like all feelings, tell us something useful if we are willing to pay attention. Just don't let them continue to build. Resolve your resentments, by either changing your expectations that have lead to the resentments, or changing your relationship that leads to the resentments. Resentment is a telltale sign that you have expectations, rightly or wrongly, that are not being met and are tied to some kind of need that is also not being met. Find out what those expectations are, what those needs are, and be as open as you can about them. And if after that, you find yourself still disappointed and resentful, consider acceptance. Say the serenity prayer, change what you can, which is yourself.

AUTHENTICITY, PART 1:
BEING WITH YOUR SELF

"Being authentic" has become a frequently cited goal in discussions between therapists and other healers. I am often confused by what other practitioners mean when they talk about wanting to "be authentic." This is just not obvious to me. So, I want to take a crack at explaining what it means to me to "be authentic."

A couple of years ago, I was working at a clinic in Lakeville. One of the office staff told me she'd been looking at the clinic's "return rates" for the therapists there. I asked, "What's a return rate?" She told me it's the percentage of clients that come back to a therapist for at least one additional session after their first session. She then told me that I was one of the therapists that had a high return rate and she wanted to know if I could tell her why. I thought about it, and said, "Maybe it's because I am 'WYSIWYG' (what-you-see-is-what-you-get). I try to be real. Maybe clients can tell that I am being real with them and they like that and trust it." She smiled, said she appreciated my thoughts and the conversation ended.

Maybe, then, "authenticity" is the same as "being real." But what does that really mean? What is "being real?" How can we know when we are "being real?" Speaking for myself, I can say I know I am being real when I can feel a sense of myself as different than the role I am fulfilling in a relationship. When I am in therapy with one of my clients, I am constantly asking myself, *Where is the "me" in the role I am playing as a therapist with this particular client?* Am I aware of "me" as I am also aware of my client? Am I aware of "me" as distinguished from my awareness of how I might appear to my client as "the therapist"?

The "me" that is not the same as the "therapist" I am being with my client is not always easy to separate, but it can be done. How? By looking for the "me" that feels the same when I am playing the role of therapist with a client, and playing the role of father to my son, and the son to my mother, and the friend of a friend. "I" am in all of those roles in all of those relationships and "I" is different than the roles because the "I" doesn't change, but the role does, depending on the context and the nature of the relationship.

The most prominent role to be played for finding your "I," your "me," your "self," or your "essence" is the one you play when you are completely alone, when there is no other person to whom you must project an image. However, being alone by itself does nothing. Even when we are alone, we sometimes become so immersed in what we are doing with our bodies or minds that we feel little or nothing of ourselves. I lose myself while gardening (which is one of its greatest benefits–it is so engrossing). I also lose myself when composing music or editing photos (some of my other hobbies). That's okay. Creativity often requires immersion in a thing or an activity. Sometimes, though, we aren't as much interested in "immersing" ourselves in creativity. Instead, we are simply avoiding ourselves or avoiding the fact that we are at that moment alone and don't know what to do with ourselves. If we can learn to "be with ourselves" when we are alone, we can begin to be "with ourselves" when we are also with others. And this is the crucial piece to finding authenticity.

Finding "me" in these roles is only part of being authentic. I can be internally aware of all of this, but I am only authentic when I allow "me" to change the role according to how "I" help define it. Michael Kinzer as therapist is and should be very different than anyone else being a therapist. Michael Kinzer as father should be very different than the father next door, because Michael Kinzer is a very different person within his role as a father.

Summing it up, then, authenticity can be described as being "with yourself" when you are either alone or with others in a way that makes you aware of your "self" and sharing that awareness so others can also experience the "you" that is not completely defined by your role you are trying to play. I suggest to clients that they ask themselves "Where am I in it?" (the IT is the context and the role) and then let others see this.

Of course, none of this answers the next question, which is: "Why does authenticity matter—what's so great about it?" That is what I write about in the next chapter.

AUTHENTICITY, PART 2:
WHY AUTHENTICITY IS IMPORTANT

During the first chapter on authenticity, I explained what the word and concept of "authenticity" means to me. I left unanswered the question of why "authenticity" is important. My aim here is to take a shot at trying to answer that question.

When we are not authentic or "real" with others, we must hide within ourselves to create the space necessary to appear to be what we think others want us to be. We also create "perceived holes" within ourselves, hoping that things outside ourselves will fill these holes (another person's view of us, work, sex, alcohol, etc.). The more we hide within ourselves, the more likely we are to be disappointed, hurt, lonely, and fearful about the part of ourselves that feels empty–the "holes" or spaces within us left empty by the failure of others to meet needs we can in reality only meet ourselves. If we hide within ourselves, but create an image of ourselves in the likeness of what others want, we also make it more difficult for others to know what we really need from them. We will in essence be asking them to guess what we need. And when they guess wrong, or even worse, don't guess at all, we might end up hurt, angry, or resentful.

If you can "expand" your "self" or encourage the authentic part of you to grow closer to the exterior boundaries between yourself and others, allowing them to see you as you really are within yourself, you will be more able to clearly ask for what you want for yourself and they will be able to see what you really want from them. Put it this way, most of the time we think about what we want other people to think and feel about us, to do for us. That by itself is not a problem. There is nothing wrong with wanting others to like us, to like to be around us, to have a positive image about us. So far, so good. The problem comes in when we pretend that we are what they want us to be so we can get what we want from them. We might continually hide from others and ourselves because we become convinced that what we are isn't good enough, or is somehow not what we "should" be. This can lead to poor self-worth, self-loathing, denial of ourselves, loneliness, depression, and anxiety.

Being authentic helps us get what we really want and avoids the pitfalls of hiding within ourselves and pretending to be other than what we truly are. So, why aren't we always authentic–it sounds like a no-brainer? For one thing, to be authentic with others we must allow ourselves to lose control over getting what we want from others. We must allow them to decide whether to give us what we want, or not. Being authentic in our relationships always carries the risk that who and what we really are is not what others want from us and they may then reject us. If I ask someone "will you do this thing for me?" They can say "no." I then have to deal with the hurt that "no" might cause. In addition to telling me "no," they might say or imply that I shouldn't have asked in the first place–that not only are they not going to meet my want or need, but it was inappropriate for me to even ask them because I am not being who they want me to be for them (of course, they aren't going to say that to you, but that will be the reason they say no). Talk about rejection! If, on the other hand, I am not authentic, and I don't directly ask for what I want, but I invite them to engage with me in a way that makes it likely that they will want to give me what I want, they will not be able to directly say "no" and I will not have take any responsibility for asking. There are other risks involved with being authentic; such as offending others, making ourselves more raw and exposed to others and therefore feeling vulnerable, creating expectations that others should also be authentic with you, and coming across as "overbearing," "arrogant," "pushy," or "too blunt."

Don't let the risks of authentically engaging with others discourage your willingness and desire to be authentic. There is one more reason authenticity, while sometimes tough, is so important: you cannot achieve meaningful personal growth or fulfillment in your life if you are not trying to be authentic. You will remain stuck if you expect others to fill needs within yourself that only you can actually fill. Trying to fill the empty spaces within yourself by encouraging others to fill those spaces for you is simply not possible, so you will keep trying to fill those places, with no success, continuing to feel that emptiness. Being authentic allows you to know you, be you, understand you, fill your own empty spaces and gain further understanding of yourself and others when they too can see the real you.

FREEDOM AND RESPONSIBILITY, PART 1: CHOOSING NOT TO BE FREE

In the chapters, "A therapy of existence," Part 1 and Part 2, I showed how the school of philosophy called existentialism starts out pretty bleak, focusing on death, unpredictability, and the absurdity of trying to figure out why we are alive; but also pointed out how we can use these ideas to end up in a more satisfying place that gives us ideas about how to justify having what we want in our lives. This and the next chapter will take that idea a step further, first by discussing why we often avoid the very freedom a philosophy of existence says has been there the whole time, and then by explaining how we can exercise our freedom in spite of the barriers that have held us back our whole lives.

What do we want? All of us? Can there even be a single answer to such a broad question? Some of us want wealth. Some of us want a quiet peaceful life. Some of us want fame. Some of us want our children to grow up healthy and happy. Some of us want more than anything lasting love. I could go on, but you get the point. We want different things, very different things. So, how can we describe what we all want when what we want is so different from one person to the next? There is one thing we must have in order to get whatever we want: freedom. We cannot have any of these things—wealth, peace, success, love—if we don't have the freedom to choose what we want to focus on in the first place. We want freedom. And then we want whatever else freedom can help us obtain.

Before getting to the main point of this chapter, let me stop for a moment and pay genuine respect for limitations that this chapter is not intended to cast aside. There are many situations beyond our control that deprive of us of the freedom we might want. Social circumstances and injustice, such as poverty, racism, sexism, all other forms of bigotry, exploitation and oppression by those in control of opportunity can seriously limit our ability to reach life goals. There are also real physical barriers to having complete freedom to do what she choose: chronic illness, disease, disability, brain injury, horrific trauma, and all other manner of unfortunate and debilitating circumstances. Neither this chapter nor anything else I will ever write can eliminate these very real and often insurmountable limitations. I do not want to write anything that would discount any one person's experiences or circumstances that prevent them from making the kinds of progress in their lives that they might otherwise have obtained if that limitation hadn't existed for them. Even with these kinds of limitations, there may be modes of freedom that can be achieved by learning how to work within them, if escape from them is not realistic or possible.

So, assume a person has it within their grasp, despite whatever limitations might exist for them, to obtain what they want, but they have not obtained what they want. Here I am talking about how we could have freedom in our lives, but we reject freedom. We walk away from it. We see what we want, know how to get it, and then don't. This might seem absurd. Okay, it is. And yet it happens all the time. Half of what I do in therapy is try to help my clients find the space to give themselves permission to go get what they want. They have, for all kinds of different reasons, come to believe that they cannot possibly exercise the freedom that sits right in front of them. Why? Why would someone who is stuck in their lives in a place that feels like crap or is at least very dissatisfying, and who has the ability and the opportunity to change things for the better, decide not to do so? Why would someone who has freedom stay in a kind of prison of his or her own making?

Why do women whose men beat them stay for so long? Why do talented, energetic, thoughtful people stay in jobs that require none of their talents, when they could search for jobs that would offer great personal reward and better pay? Why does a 35-year-old man sit in silence while his father tells him he is worthless? Why does a 40-year-old woman about to leave a family gathering, exhausted by the tension and unresolved conflict, decide to stay after her mother berates her for wanting to leave early? Why does a client, and then another, and then another, come in for their first appointment with me and tell me they have struggled with severe depression or anxiety for the past 10 or 20 or 30 years, and they have not been able to leave it behind, take action to eliminate it?

Why do they all deny themselves freedom? If freedom is so great, so plausible, so attainable, why don't they want it? Do they want to be stuck? Can they not see the freedom they could have if they reached for it? Yes, but that is only usually part of the answer. The main reason people do not exercise freedom in their lives is that freedom comes at a very high cost, which most people absolutely do not want to pay. The cost of freedom is responsibility. That might sound silly, unimportant, hard to believe. You might ask, "That's all there is to it?" Yes. I think it is true. And I am not alone. Responsibility as the high and sometimes forbidding price for exercising freedom is a theme that runs throughout existential thought. And I see it all the time in therapy. We really quite often don't want to do anything that will leave us on our own, isolated in our decisions, breaking us apart from what we know, radically changing relationships with people in our lives. We'd rather stay in the crowd, surrounded by what is familiar, even if the familiar becomes confining, limiting, stifling. Fear of responsibility can run very deep, stretching out for the entirety of lives of countless people.

Responsibility sets us apart. It makes us different than we were, different from how others expect us to be. And that expectation is a very powerful pull in most people's lives. So powerful they would rather obey unwritten rules in their families and with their friends than take action to remove themselves from detrimental situations. Think of how many decades it has taken for the Catholic Church, its clergy, and its parishioners to begin the monumental task of putting a stop to the rape of children! What kept silent those families, those clergy, those who knew, saw, and did nothing, or acted to cover it up, knowing how wrong they were to do so? In all the years I've been doing therapy I regularly, without fail, hear clients tell me they were sexually abused, they told an adult family member, they were hushed. They kept silent. Maybe it continued, maybe it didn't. They didn't tell anyone else until 10 or 20 years later; when they found a therapist, me, or someone before me. On the other end of that trauma, I could recount plenty of examples of therapy clients telling me they were the adult a child came to, telling them about some kind of abuse, and they did nothing, or blamed the child, in order to avoid choosing the freedom to put a stop to the abuse. They aren't bad people. They are people afraid of freedom because then they'd risk conflict, radical change, family strife, and they would be the ones responsible for all of that, or so they think. I can easily come up with dozens of less horrible but still puzzling examples of how people refuse to give themselves permission (freedom) to stop destructive behavior or leave destructive relationships at home or at work because they fear being responsible for the change it would bring and the risks it entails.

What is so frightening about responsibility? To be honest, I am not completely sure. The fear of responsibility strikes me as bizarre in the abstract—far removed from how I want to live my life. Uncertainty I can understand. I have, as I think we all have, had circumstances that were a "mixed bag" (a bad relationship that might improve, a bad job where we stick it out because we think the boss might get canned). We wait to see if things will get better without having to make dramatic change. Okay. Makes sense. For a while.

Responsibility, total responsibility for our own lives, requires us to hold ourselves, and no one else, accountable for the outcome of our decisions. If we try and fail, it is our failure and there is no one else to blame. If we don't trust ourselves to have what it takes to "make it happen," we will not want to exercise freedom and the seemingly inevitable and awful responsibility of having failed because we were inadequate. We fear responsibility when we are convinced that standing on our own will be worse than staying in a situation in which we can hold someone else responsible. This is not just about blame. It is about self-concept. It is about not wanting to be wrong. It is about not wanting to see our existence as completely belonging to us, and no one else. Some people experience this idea as a terrifying kind of loneliness or alienation. If they do not believe they have what it takes to handle this kind of responsibility, they shy away from it. It feels safer to be in the middle of the herd than on the edge, where you are exposed.

The woman at the family gathering mentioned above; she stays after her mother berates her because she believes her mother's accusations about her selfishness and inconsideration might be true. She fears that if she leaves, her mother might be right, that she will lose family connections because she sets herself apart. The women whose men beat them stay sometimes because they so completely buy into the idea that they are not capable of living on their own, or that leaving will constitute a terrible abandonment of the very man who just beat them. The priest who stays silent knowing the man in the room next door at the rectory has raped children because he fears the repercussions of standing up for what he knows is right. The new client who has been depressed for 20 years and has done little to eliminate it rightly fears that he will need to re-examine the possible dysfunction of many relationships in his life that support his continued hopelessness.

We deny ourselves freedom to have what we want in our lives because we believe we either cannot obtain it and do not want to fail (self-doubt) or we have accepted as true the admonitions of others about what we should not try to obtain (social pressure or external guilt). In all cases, we fear taking action through freedom that will result in having to then take responsibility for making a bad decision. To avoid that potential consequence, we take no action, walk away from freedom, and stay stuck in whatever ails us.

By focusing on the origins of self-doubt and external pressures to stay frozen, by examining the origins of the story of ourselves we tell ourselves now, but with the courage to consider the possibility that the story is warped or just plain wrong, we can begin the process of seeing ourselves differently enough to give ourselves permission to exercise the freedom we have always had. We can begin to hope and believe in the possibility that when it comes time to take responsibility for our decisions, we will be able to say to ourselves that we did it, we achieved our goals, we made the right decision, we are who we thought we were, not who someone told us we were. This can take time, a long time in fact. Once we begin, though, we will eventually be free, be fully responsible, and be fully ourselves. We will answer to ourselves because we are no longer afraid of who we are or what we want. We will live our lives in freedom and responsibility.

Where do we start? How do we "begin to believe" that we will succeed if we exercise freedom? If we have been stuck in our situations and stories up to this point, what can we do to rid ourselves of the fear of responsibility that keeps us stuck? The answer is complicated. Many of the chapters I've already written speak to this, at least indirectly. In the next chapter, I will take on the topic more directly.

FREEDOM AND RESPONSIBILITY, PART 2: HOW TO CHOOSE FREEDOM

When I write these chapters, I have to try very hard to find a balance between two extremes. On the one hand, I want to tackle meaningful topics surrounding the suffering and struggles that come with mental health issues. Naturally, this means the issues and the answers are very complicated. On the other hand, the purpose of the chapter is to give clients and others usable tools to think new thoughts about struggles in their lives or the lives of those they know. In finishing these chapters, I hold myself to the task of balancing complexity on one side and oversimplification on the other side. When it comes to how people experience their lives, this is never easy, and sometimes probably not achievable in a chapter format. I can think of no issue that makes this balance between complexity and simplicity more challenging than the topic of this chapter: how can a person overcome their fear of taking responsibility for the direction of their life when they have been stuck in thinking they are better off following the direction others have suggested, expected, or demanded. Yet, I will do my best to describe in a few pages the process of how a person moves toward choosing their own definition of "right" and "wrong," "saint" and "sinner," "leader" and "follower," "winner" and "loser."

Part of my job as a therapist is done before I say a word. Clients contact me to set up an initial appointment because something has gone seriously wrong in their lives. And that is not all. They have recognized that something has gone wrong. Usually this wrong thing in their lives has become progressively worse over several years. It is the recognition that something is amiss and they don't know what to do with it that brings them to therapy (okay, other than court order or the threat of divorce or some other dire consequence pointed out unmistakably by someone else). I use this scenario, this recognition of a thing gone wrong, right away in the first session. I begin to look for ways this person has been telling themselves the thing that bothers them wasn't bad enough to do anything about it, until now, until they decided to come to see me. I ask them to look at their own struggle about coming to terms with the need to change, and why they may have avoided that process.

I ask clients to begin to doubt themselves, their decisions, and the story they have been telling themselves about their lives, their relationships, and the person they think they are. I am guessing this process sounds surprising, even a little scary. It can be scary, but I also try to tell clients over and over that I will stay with them in the process of re-examining whatever they told themselves that made it seem okay until they realized they had a serious problem and needed help. Part of the reason it is a scary process for some clients is that they have allowed their fear of questioning themselves to keep them on a path that led them right to the problem they now want my help in removing from their lives.

A man stays in a relationship for years as his partner drives away friends and family out of possessiveness until he finds himself isolated, lonely, depressed and feeling very guilty for abandoning his family and friends. And now I am asking him to do the very thing he's been avoiding: "Question yourself." "Why did you continue to let this happen when you knew you didn't want things to go this way?" In asking him this, I have begun to turn his thinking away from completely and only blaming his partner, toward sharing responsibility in his problem, so he can then begin to think about how to use that responsibility to make real changes for himself. If this translates to a kind of self-doubt, this is okay in the beginning. It is an important tool to start the process of questioning assumptions people make about their own lack of power in their lives.

After going through therapy, clients talk about how safe it felt for them to go through this self-examination process. I consider this feeling of safety the most important part of doing therapy. It seems to work; my clients generally do feel safe, which makes me feel good. I guess they know that I wouldn't ask them to do anything I haven't done myself or wouldn't do if I were in their situation. Probably the most important part of my involvement in this process is suggesting with kindness that they give themselves permission to question themselves. I ask their permission to ask them questions they've often never really asked themselves. They give me permission. In giving me permission, they are actually also giving themselves permission to doubt what they had always believed about themselves, their lives, the people and ideas that populate their lives. The process begins with permission, permission, permission.

The depth of the questions I ask people to begin directing toward themselves depends on the depth of the issue, which is usually but not always a function of how long the problem has existed that brought them to therapy, or the length of time they have carried the messages that told them not to make any changes. A single traumatic event can freeze people in their lives. In most cases though, a self-concept that includes great fear of exercising freedom and taking responsibility is the result of many years of messages from important people and institutions that tell them they will fail if they do—that they are essentially inadequate in some fundamental ways, or that their decision to act on their own to find themselves will violate some rule or code of conduct, or will constitute an act of betrayal to a family expectation.

I tend to be a rather assertive person. I take this for granted. I have lived my life fairly strongly in accordance with the principles of freedom and responsibility for so long; it can be difficult for me to remember what it was like at the beginning, when I first started reading about existentialism, when I first started a serious investment in my own therapy process. I sometimes forget how hard it is for others to choose to be free, and then begin to evolve toward ever increasing freedom in their lives and relationships. I must remind myself to patient with them, just as I was patient with myself long ago.

Clients will tell me a story about an encounter that has led them to feel very low. It might be an argument with a spouse, a parent, a colleague, or the cashier at a restaurant. Someone treated them badly, and they didn't resist, they "took it," they allowed themselves to be scolded, diminished, and treated with disrespect. I will ask them to review the story and imagine what it would be like for them to have responded differently, with defiance, insisting on respect. Some cannot imagine themselves doing this. Some can imagine it, but still have difficulty even retelling the story with this new perspective. I suggest a way to deal with it that is calmly, rationally, but emphatically insistent on the respect I suggest they deserve. I am told over and over, "That's easy for you to say." And it is, I suppose, not necessarily "easy," but easier for me because I have been doing it for so long. I need to remember that they might have spent years feeling they didn't deserve respect, which might be why, even after months of therapy in which they question this conclusion and can see how destructive it has been, they can still only barely imagine demanding respect from others who might react very negatively to their newfound resistance to bad treatment.

The messages some people carry that they should not take responsibility for the ultimate decisions in their lives can become so powerful they do not even see them as messages; they see these messages as a set of simple truths. I once heard a story on the radio about a guy whose parents discovered he was gay when he was a teenager. They solicited the help of a "repair" therapist, who along with his parents convinced him that his sexual orientation was a mental illness that could be cured (something some mental health practitioners still apparently believe). This poor boy endured three years of weekly therapy in which the therapist and his parents reinforced the message that there was something deeply wrong with him. He said he managed to satisfy his parents and the therapist by refusing to act out on his feelings for other males, but kept to himself that the attraction was still there. They thought he was "cured." Off to college, his parents warned him that they would cut off payment of his tuition, room and board if he became involved with a man. He ended up in a psychiatric ward due to the pressures of not being allowed to be himself. In his late twenties now, he can look back at nearly ten years of buying into the message that he was flawed before taking the plunge to question everything he'd been told. Fortunately, the hospital stay was a wake up call to his father, who said he'd rather have a gay son than a dead son. The gay son is now married, to a man. Making what was in his life the extraordinarily difficult choice to evolve toward freedom and responsibility led him to shed the pressure and messages to try to be something other than who he is. He is now free to be who he knows he really is.

When we examine the origins of the messages that lead us to conclude that we lack what we need to successfully exercise freedom in our lives, we can begin to separate out those messages in our daily lives. The most important part of this process is to move toward being able to recognize these messages and how they freeze us away from freedom in the moment they are happening, so we can see their immediate effect. At first, this is very difficult, and requires consistent reflection back to a situation in which we acted on these old messages and made choices that were not truly ours, but were the result of acting out on a message from someone else about who or what we should be. Once we begin to recognize these exterior messages in the moment, we can reject them on the spot, intentionally and knowingly refuse to act on those messages, and then choose to act based on freedom to be ourselves.

When a spouse tells my client that she or he does not deserve to be married, my client can take a look at the statement as fitting within some scheme of self-doubt in which she has been accepting this kind of teardown for years. She can then imagine what it would be like to respond to it by outright rejection, insisting on self-respect. If she spends enough time and energy in her therapy sessions and outside of sessions imagining herself responding in a way that cancels her self-doubt and demands self-respect, she can begin actually acting on these new beliefs. She might still be afraid that responding this way could result in increased conflict, even divorce. She might then have to ask herself whether the risk of divorce is part of taking responsibility for being free of verbal attacks that damage her self-worth. Hopefully, if the marriage is important, my client and her spouse will find a way to make the marriage a source of support for each of them to exercise freedom to be who they are, rather than staying stuck in a spiral of self-doubt and contempt.

When a person can, from moment to moment, separate messages about themselves which are supportive of who they are and supportive of freedom they want to exercise from those messages which keep them stuck in fear that they will fail if they try to do what they want, be who they are, they will be on an upward spiraling path that leads to more freedom, less fear, more responsibility, more freedom, less fear, more responsibility and so on. They will become involved in a process of proving to themselves the value of the new messages that support them, and the damage of the old messages that kept them stuck in self-doubt, insecurity, and feelings of inadequacy. I have watched numerous clients take this path, with amazing results. When they complete therapy, they do so rightly believing they no longer need my support and assistance in staying in this process. It does not end when therapy ends. It continues for the rest of their lives. Freedom and responsibility become a new way of life for them, in which they involve others in their lives to complement their choices, as they complement the choices others make, so they too can feel free to be who they are, to become who they decide they want to become. Getting onto this path and learning to stay on this path can take anywhere from several months to several years. Sometimes when clients are on the path of freedom and responsibility, they fall back into old patterns, listening to old messages, making choices out of fear of inadequacy. When they do, they sometimes call me for a few "maintenance" sessions. They come back a few times because they have become accustomed to the benefits of freedom and the relief of being responsible for themselves and they don't want to return to their old ways of being stuck without freedom or responsibility.

What I have written here about freedom and responsibility comes in part from the basic tenets of existentialist philosophers. I incorporate their ideas into the therapy work I do with my clients. I believe in its effectiveness because I see it work so well for my clients. Before becoming a therapist, I saw and felt how these existentialist ideas of freedom, responsibility and choice worked in my own life, starting with reading existentialist texts, and then spending time in therapy myself doing exactly what I just described in this chapter. I will continue to find ways to be more free and to enjoy taking responsibility for my life, including its successes and its failures, as I continue the process of becoming who I am, who I want to be. As I continue to learn more about freedom and responsibility, I will share what I learn with my clients, friends, family, and in all the relationships in my life. In doing so, I will be better for it, and I hope so will the world.

I hope you will do the same.

LONELINESS

Everyone knows that being alone and feeling loneliness are not the same thing. Sometimes when we are alone we feel lonely, but sometimes we don't. We can also feel lonely when we are not alone, when we are with someone we care about, who cares about us. I am sure most of us have felt lonely even when we were surrounded by people we know and like. So, what is loneliness? Where does it come from? What can we do to not feel lonely? These are some of the deepest and most troubling questions of human existence. I'll take a shot at providing some insights, knowing that I will only scratch the surface, and will want to come back to this topic in the future as I continue to reflect on loneliness.

First things first. In a way, we are completely alone. Always. We live inside ourselves. We cannot escape this sometimes-painful condition, no matter how hard we try—and boy do we try. This idea, taken to the extreme, is called "solipsism," which is the belief that we can only really know that we, our self, exists. For more on this idea, feel free to read up on René Descartes. For this discussion, though, solipsism goes to show the power of the limits of being completely subjective, completely "in our selves." If it is true that we cannot "know" that anyone else exists, how can we even make a connection with other people? We connect with others by imagining what they are like, what it would be like to be them. Think about this for a minute. I know it is kind of weird to think about, but it is worth the effort. Everyone you know, have ever known, you have only really imagined what he or she are like. You can't actually know what it is like to be them. You can only really know what it is like to be you. Oh, hey, I guess now that I've said this, that makes me a "solipsist." Okay, I can live with that.

When we try to connect with others, we listen to them, talk to them, watch what they do, how they act. We get to know them. All the while, we imagine why they do what they do, why they act the way they do, say the things they do, why they like some things, don't like other things. While we are doing this, we pretend for moments at a time what it would be like to be them doing what they are doing, saying what they are saying, eating what they are eating, being sick, laughing out loud, as them. This is the only way we can really get to know someone, understand them, and connect with them. Because we can never be anyone but ourselves, we have to kind of pretend that our friends, spouse, colleagues, children, parents—they all experience things in the way we do. Of course, we can't know this because we will never be them. We can approximate with our imagination. It mostly works, but not always. We misinterpret things they do because we don't have all their memories, motivations, genetics—their minds are not our minds, so it is a best guess.

Imagining what it would be like to be someone else takes an enormous amount of our mental and emotional energy and we do it all the time. It occupies so much of our attention, we barely notice we are doing it. If you take some time to think about this, you will see that it is true. It has to be. There can be no other way for us to understand each other while also being individuals "trapped" inside our self.

At this point, you might be wondering, "What does any of this have to do with loneliness?" In a word, everything. Loneliness is the state of being in which we find ourselves wanting to be connected to others but realizing we are not connected to others. It can be pretty awful, as you know.

Our desire to be connected might be directed toward a single person, a lover, a family member, or a friend. Or, we might want to be connected to no one in particular, just anyone, everyone, someone, and yet we feel disconnected. We don't just feel alone, we feel isolated, disconnected. This is why being alone by itself doesn't necessarily mean we feel lonely. I am writing this chapter in a one-room cabin way up in the north woods of Minnesota. Just my dogs and me. I am completely alone, have been for several days. Yet, at the moment, I do not feel lonely in the slightest. Why? Actually, because I am wondering, imagining, believing myself capable of knowing how you, the reader of what I am writing, will feel, think, and use the ideas I am writing. I feel connected to you, whoever you are. I imagine my mom reading this, or one of my clients that suffers from loneliness. I ask, "Will they like it, or will it be confusing?" In other words, I do not feel lonely because I do not feel disconnected.

When I worked in the prisons, I remember talking to guys about "seg" (short for "segregation," which means being in a cell by yourself all day every day for weeks on end). It is a cruel punishment, intended to cause loneliness. It works, which probably explains why prisons use it, because prisoners hate it. They get so lonely, they sometimes feel like they are losing their minds. They find ways to cope. They focus on memories of connection from the past, imagine future connections they will make when seg ends. Either way, they placate their desire for connection by imaging being connected, or they suffer from sickening loneliness.

Clients who suffer from severe depression often feel terrible loneliness. Some have given up entirely the idea, the hope, and the belief that they can actually find others with whom they connect in any meaningful way. Nothing touches me more deeply as a therapist as imagining how isolated they must feel, how lonely they are. It's not that they don't want to be connected to others. They usually do. If they did not, they might actually be isolated, but not lonely. In order to help them out of this painful place, I try to find out if they have given up on connection because (1) they don't think others can understand them, (2) they don't think they can understand others, (3) they don't think others have any interest in being connected to them, or maybe (4) they are so preoccupied by the reasons for their depression, they have no emotional energy left to make connections. But, in all cases where there is loneliness, there is a desire to be connected, but a lack of connectedness.

Loneliness has three components: (1) we are always alone within our self, (2) we want to be connected to others, and (3) we do not feel connected. What's the solution? I could say it is being connected, which is true. But if the solution were that simple, loneliness would not be one of the worst and most common ailments of the human condition. In order to move from disconnection to connection, we have to locate the barriers to being connected, which vary greatly between people and situations. For some, the barrier to connection is lack of community. Think of displaced refugees or recent immigrants —disconnected from their people and not feeling connected to the majority of the people that now surround them due to differences in language, culture, shared experiences, values, religion, life goals, and so on. For many people suffering from loneliness, the barriers to connection are interpersonal, based on lifelong family dynamics that encourage isolation. Some find it difficult to make or maintain connections with others because they have come to believe that the connections they have made do not have sufficient meaning or power in their lives to justify their continuation. So they allow the connections they have been able to make to fade, diminish, and deteriorate, until there is a slow creeping isolation. I see this with clients who lose a significant social connection after a geographical relocation, retirement, a death or divorce, or some other major life transition to which they have had great difficulty adjusting.

Once the barriers to finding connections are identified, we can begin to think of ways to break them down. Often, this might mean the clients take risks they haven't taken in years, reaching out to old friends, family, and social groups. It might also be an opportunity to try new things, new activities, and new-shared interests with people they haven't met. There are tools for this that didn't exist ten years ago —Internet sites that offer group activities for strangers with common interests. I joined a photography group that inspired me to start that new hobby and gave me a chance to meet others who shared that interest. Clients find all kinds of creative ways to test their isolation by reaching out in new directions. When they do, some of their fears and beliefs that they cannot be connected wash away slowly.

If we allow ourselves to become discouraged by the fact that we are born alone, die alone, and live our lives within our selves, we will become isolated. When this feeling of discouragement and isolation is coupled with the deep human need for connection, we have the recipe for loneliness. If you can accept that you are alone, without this having to mean you cannot find connection, you will find ways to be connected, knowing the limits of being an individual. We can understand each other by pretending what it would be like to be each other, while also recognizing we are not anyone other than our self. We can find satisfaction in others imagining what we are like, wanting to understand us, be connected to us, just like we want to understand them, be connected to them. In this way we live life mostly alone, but not mostly lonely.

"TO THE WEAK I BECAME WEAK"

"To the weak, I became weak." 1 Corinthians 9:22. You won't often see me quoting scripture here, not because it doesn't have something to offer, but because over the years, I have become unfamiliar with it. This quote, though, remains one of my all time favorite quotes. I am not going to pretend I really know what Saint Paul meant by it. That's not my point. I like this quote because of what it means to me. It involves what appears to be an inconsistency, but really involves one of the most striking paradoxes in human interaction. In order to allow yourself to be truly connected to someone, to empathize with him or her, to have compassion for them, to love them deeply, you have to make yourself vulnerable with them and to them. You have to allow yourself to be exposed to them.

The quote doesn't say, "To the weak, I am weak." It says, "To the weak, I *became* weak." In other words, we are making a choice to be vulnerable, to meet people where they are, where they need us to be. Loving someone involves a paradox because it involves two things that at first seem completely inconsistent, but they are both true. In order to allow ourselves to really feel love for and from someone, we have to allow ourselves to be vulnerable to being hurt by them. We have to allow ourselves to be open to them, which could result in being hurt by them. Yet, this is the only way to be connected to them at a deep level. So, to get that connection with someone we really care about, we have to make ourselves vulnerable to be hurt by the very person who can hurt us the most.

Choosing to be vulnerable, to be weak, often comes up with couples in therapy that deeply love each other, and yet have become so defensive and closed down because they each fear the possibility of being so hurt by the one they love the most. My job as a therapist in these circumstances is to encourage them to be as open as they can be despite their fear of each other, so they can reconnect, begin to build that trust, and then live the paradox of vulnerability and love.

Love is not important in the absence of fear. Love is important because it allows us to do things despite our fears. There is in this another paradox: when we do things despite feeling "weak" or "vulnerable" or with fear, this does not make us weak. It makes us strong, stronger. When we decide to be weak, to be with others who may feel weak by being weak with them, we are coming from a place of strength by making that decision, and then we and they become stronger in the process. I see this process repeated in myself, with my clients, and with those in my life that I love. That is why I love this quote. It is a contradiction, and yet so important and true.

PART THREE:

SELF-DISCOVERY

Part Three explores the process of self-discovery that comes with therapy. Every therapy session should involve some level of self-discovery. In this part of the book, I focus on the bigger picture for clients—how their perceptions of themselves and their lives change over the course of therapy, not just the process within or around each individual session. I start this part of the book with a discussion of the way clients can begin to see their depression or anxiety (or both) as a kind of coping skill that is no longer helpful, a way to deal with something in their lives they feel ill equipped to handle. Through a process of self-discovery, clients learn that they have sold themselves short in terms of their capacity to overcome and complete tasks in their lives, and in doing so, have also often greatly exaggerated the difficulty they thought they faced. This can take a long time to recognize, which is why these discussions are in Part Three of the book.

Meaningful self-discovery is not simple, easy, or quick. Unlike the movies about therapy and self-discovery, a single insight, no matter how deep, important or necessary it might be, must be accompanied by a recognition of its effect, its usefulness, the way it can help a person shift their fundamental understanding of themselves, the way they are in relationships, and what they want in their lives. Near the end of Part Three, you will find a discussion of the interplay of Identity and Personality. Identity is about how you view yourself in the world. Personality is about how you respond to the world. Understanding how these two most vital aspects of your person influence the way you feel and think about yourself is at the deepest end of self-discovery. It is about seeing yourself from an "outsider's view." Imagine watching yourself have conversations with others and being able to see how your tendencies sometimes work and sometimes do not work, and then think about how this might change the way you think about yourself. Over time, and with a good amount of courage and diligence, knowing your identity and personality are just some of the fruits of self-discovery.

DEPRESSION AND ANXIETY: TWO SIDES OF THE SAME COIN

Therapists and therapy clients know that depression and anxiety often go together. I'd even say depression and anxiety are flip sides of the same coin. The difference between depression and anxiety often comes down to how we respond to certain kinds of problems, either by slowing down (depression) or speeding up (anxiety) or both (feeling anxious about slowing down when we think we need to be speeding up). I'll get to the "flip sides" of depression and anxiety a little later, but first, let's answer the question: what's "the coin?"

Depression and anxiety can both be good coping mechanisms for dealing with a challenging situation. They become problems when we either slow down too much for too long or speed up in ways that feel uncontrollable. We slow down or speed up when we confront something that challenges our belief in our own capacities to deal with the challenge. The slowing down or speeding up can be unhealthy when the task seems to be too difficult to deal with at that time. If we have an issue or problem we need to resolve or overcome, but don't believe we have it within us to do it, we may slow down to get ready. This is depression. If you add a sense of urgency to this circumstance—that the thing to be resolved must resolved right now —you may end up feeling overly worrisome or anxious despite also believing that you are not ready or equipped to address the issue. This is anxiety.

So, the coin that binds depression and anxiety together is a task or set of tasks that are difficult and may seem impossible to complete, address or resolve. A common example of this kind of task in therapy might be initiating or finalizing the breakup of a relationship that you know you need to end, but you don't because you don't want to deal with the likely conflicts involved, or the aftermath (being alone with grief, and maybe also guilt or regret). Another example might be hoping for the approval of a parent who's never given it to you, yet you continue to try, and continue to set yourself up for failure. Whether the task ends up causing depression, anxiety or both, depends in large measure on whether the person confronting the task believes they have it within them to deal with it. In either case, a person heads into depression or anxiety when they begin to feel overwhelmed by the task. This might be due to the enormity of the task at hand, or a pervasive sense that they cannot face the task regardless of what others might think, or perhaps most confusing of all, not being able to identify the task or issue that is causing the anxiety or depression.

Depression is a kind of slowing down in most cases. People struggling with depression often sleep more, or want to sleep but can't, and end up fatigued either way. When we suffer from depression, we might lose interest in the things that used to excite us. We become withdrawn, not attending to our social connections. We might eat more, or less. We might isolate from most of our world. We might start thinking about death. Depression is serious business and can be deadly. So, what causes such a disastrous mood to take over people's lives? In many cases, it seems to be a creeping belief that "I am not capable of doing the things I need to do." This may not be a conscious thought, but can be a powerful limiting factor underlying our seeming inability to do what we know we need to do. It can last just a few days or weeks, or can drag on for years, always lurking in the background, wearing us down, making it difficult to see what is really possible—overcoming the challenging tasks that caused the depression in the first place.

We all have self-doubts. All of us. Within reason, self-doubt can even be a good coping skill—it can teach us about our limitations and therefore the areas of personal growth we might need to meet a new challenge. When taken to an extreme, though, self-doubt can really become a debilitating problem, telling us that we are far more limited than we really are. We can engage in cycles of failure brought about by negative self-fulfilling prophecies which in turn can be brought about by low self-worth: "I generally do not get what I need, so I don't ask for what I need, so I don't get what I need, which confirms that I am not worthy of getting what I need..." and the pattern continues, keeping us stuck or in a downward spiral of resignation and despair.

Sometimes depression knocks on our door because we've convinced ourselves that we must obtain a goal that is actually unobtainable and we therefore end up living lives with continual and important disappointment. Think of Sisyphus, the guy from Greek mythology whose version of hell was having to keep pushing a big rock up a hill that gets more steep until he has to stop, let the rock roll back down, and start all over. The example above, about wanting the approval of a parent who simply isn't going to give it to you because it's not in their nature or they are dead, is just like Sisyphus. Who wouldn't be depressed if this is their goal, their challenge?

Anxiety occurs when we are confronted with a challenging task or issue that we believe we are not adequate to complete or resolve, coupled with an overriding sense of urgency to complete the task or resolve the issue right away. So, we fret about it. We worry. We can't stop thinking about it until we have dealt with it. With anxiety, the most common problem is trying to control an outcome we cannot fully control. Like depression, anxiety often starts out as a good coping skill, motivating us to overcome our fears, our distractions, our procrastinations, and deal with something important. Anxiety compels us to reject our tendencies to follow the path of least resistance and do the difficult thing because it simply must be done. Anxiety starts to feel overwhelming when the thing we think must be done either cannot be done or even if it can, we are not able to do it because of some perceived inadequacy.

Anxiety is about control and power. We want the power necessary to control situations, people, and the future, and of course we nearly always have either no such control, or limited control. The funny thing about anxiety is that when we realize we don't need nearly as much power or control as we thought we did, we are able to meet our needs just fine, and with far less anxiety. For more thoughts about anxiety and control, see the chapter: "Anxiety and two powerful mistakes."

Conquering depression is definitely possible, but it requires new thinking about our capacities and the importance or feasibility of tasks that fuel the depression. Clients are often able to rid themselves of depression after years of struggle by reassessing their abilities to put an end to self-destructive self-fulfilling prophecies, to put an end to cycles of failures that can be avoided by ridding themselves of the belief that an impossible task is worth pursuing. Sometimes dealing with depression requires us to find new capacities and beliefs about ourselves so we can complete the tasks. We realize that by limiting our tasks to those we can actually accomplish, we are able to do what needs to be done, and we find a new confidence in ourselves. Sometimes dealing with depression requires us to walk away from tasks we thought were absolutely necessary to complete, but then realized they could not ever be completed or resolved, or it simply wasn't necessary after all. We stop allowing others to dictate, intentionally or not, what we must "prove" to gain their acceptance, and we accept ourselves as we are.

Not surprisingly, ridding ourselves of problematic anxiety often requires the same kinds of change necessary to eliminate depression: a change in belief about ourselves, our ability to meet challenging tasks, and the actual importance, or lack of importance in completing those tasks. If we review our sense of "urgency" it is often not the task that requires urgency, but our own insecurities that make us feel a task or issue must be addressed, when in fact it may not be necessary, or at least not immediately so. Where does the sense of urgency come from? Has someone else, recently or a long time ago, set us thinking we must deal with certain things quickly, or completely, or with the standard of perfection as the only acceptable outcome? Do we believe we cannot do something because we have told ourselves we cannot, maybe over and over again, for years? Identify these causes of both our urgency and our self-doubts and you will begin to figure out how to put aside the worry, the seemingly uncontrollable repeated thinking about an issue, a problem, a task, and then you will be prepared to face the task or issue head on, and without so much urgency, and anxiety.

Clients usually know before we meet for the first time that avoiding the difficult task or issue will not help them get rid of their depression or anxiety. In fact, it is the failure of this tactic—avoidance —that often brings a client to come and see me. Avoidance can actually make things worse because it confirms their feelings of inadequacy or insecurity about their ability to face the task or issues, while also increasing the urgency of actually dealing with the issue. There are times when we need to be patient in dealing with a difficult situation. For instance, grieving the loss of someone close can often involve a stage of denial, which allows us the time we need to gear up for facing and accepting the loss. That's fine. Taking time to deal with an issue becomes a problem, though, when denial is prolonged into a semi-permanent state of avoidance. I firmly believe that we must address difficult tasks or issues to overcome them. There is no such thing as "getting over" or "moving on" from a problem. We must "move through" the problem, as we increase our ability to believe in ourselves, and distinguish between tasks we set for ourselves and those that we have allowed others to set for us.

In therapy with clients, no matter what specific issues the client tells me they have come to resolve, they almost always bring with them a pocket full of coins (other unrecognized tasks or issues) with some level of depression and anxiety on either side of each one. As we discuss, identify, and begin to resolve the issues, clients nearly always learn new and more effective ways of viewing themselves and their tasks. This way, clients wind up having much more confidence in their own abilities, both to complete necessary tasks, and to identify when to let go of tasks that do not need to be completed. We don't need to get rid of all of the coins in a client's pocket. Once we get rid of a couple coins in therapy, most client are well on their way to being able to get rid of the rest on their own, which is another way of saying they have learned how to rid themselves of problematic depression and anxiety.

ANXIETY:
A STORY OF TWO POWERFUL MISTAKES

Why do we have anxiety? We experience anxiety when we want control over outcomes that are important to us. In this sense, anxiety itself is not a problem. A professor back in graduate school had a saying about anxiety: "Without anxiety all rabbits would be dead on the railroad tracks" (If they didn't jump like mad off the tracks when they heard the train, they'd get hit–and be dead). Just like rabbits, we need anxiety to motivate us to take care of important issues, to avoid certain kinds of problems, to make us aware of potential dangers, to get us thinking really hard about things we need to do and not do.

In fact, like anger and conflict (see my other chapters about those issues), anxiety is an inevitable, and often just plain necessary, part of life. So, anxiety is not good or bad, and we need to be sure to separate what's normal and healthy anxiety from what becomes a problem to deal with in therapy. Anxiety becomes a problem when it is no longer helpful and is harmful to the person experiencing the anxiety. This kind of harm can come in many different "flavors"—as in "panic attacks," which have a fairly specific set of prescribed attributes including a number of physical symptoms, but which may be related to any number of different triggers, or apparently no identifiable trigger at all. There are forms of anxiety and fear about very specific kinds of situations, which are called "phobias." Most people are familiar with the more common phobias, including agoraphobia (fear of leaving your house or being in public), arachnophobia (fear of spiders), and social anxiety (fear of social situations).

The most common form of anxiety among my clients, and perhaps most therapy clients, is given the name "Generalized Anxiety Disorder," which essentially means a lot of worrying about a lot of different topics that the client finds difficult to control and which comes with a variety of other symptoms such as sleeplessness, fatigue, irritability, edginess, etc.

Anxiety seems to be the result of one or both of two kinds of mistakes about control: (1) I think I *must* be able to control something over which I *actually* have no control; or (2) I do not have control over something that I think I *need* to control. The most common mistake is the first kind, and its most common flavor is when someone thinks they must have control over another person. Of course, in most circumstances, we have no control over others. And even when we do (as in a parent controlling their child), our level of control is far less than what we often think it is, or should be. So, when we convince ourselves that we must have control over someone else, but in fact we do not and cannot have that control, we stew about what will happen without that control. An example is when we do not want our primary relationship partner to act in a certain way (to not leave us, to stop gambling or drinking or smoking, to stop yelling at the kids so much). We try to control them, we cannot control them, and we worry about not being able to control them.

The second kind of mistake is less common, and is sometimes more difficult to identify in therapy, but is often just as much of a problem. This mistake involves thinking we do not have control over something we think we really need to have control. A simple example is a social phobia—we are afraid of social situations because we cannot control what others think of us, we aren't sure what we should say or do, who to talk to, and in the end we might get rejected no matter what we do. The mistake is actually often two mistakes. First, we think we need to control what others think of us, when in fact we do not. The chance of rejection is often far less likely than we tell ourselves as we are getting ready for the party. And if we do get some kind of rejection, it is often no big deal. Second, we have more control than we think we do. We know how to talk, to smile, to dress more or less appropriately, to shake hands, make eye contact when we are supposed to, but we might tell ourselves that we are going to flub it up, that we don't know how to do these basic things. These basic things are probably 95% of what we need to do in a social situation to avoid gaffes and be a presentable and enjoyable participant. These things give us nearly all the control we need in order to avoid what we fear: rejection.

So, what can be done to eliminate these mistakes leading to anxiety in therapy, or outside of therapy? As in all things therapeutic, recognize the problem, where it comes from, which mistake is going on, is it one or the other or both? Why do we make this mistake, where did it originate: childhood, a past relationship, an addiction issue? When do we make the mistake? What situations or triggers cause us to make the mistake leading to problematic anxiety? And finally, and perhaps most importantly, when is our anxiety helpful (because most of the time it is) and when does it become a problem, harming us or our relationship with excessive and needless worry and avoidance?

After recognizing the source and causes of problematic anxiety, we can begin to re-think our *need* to control things or situations and our *ability* to control things or situations. One very basic solution to most (but not all) situations with anxiety is to know that what you have *most* control over is yourself, your reactions, your decisions, and you have least control over others. So focus on more on you, less on others. Focus on what you can control, not on what you cannot control. Or, as they say in Alcoholic Anonymous, "own what you own [your reactions] and don't own what you do not own [the reactions of others]." Sounds simple, and it can be, but that doesn't mean it's easy!

THE TRAP OF REGRET:
HINDSIGHT IS NOT "20/20"

You've no doubt heard the old saying, "Hindsight is 20/20." I take this to mean we see things looking back to our past much more clearly than we saw them when we were still in the past. A related saying is, "If I had only known then what I now know, I would not have (insert decision)." Either way, the meaning is the same; regret is the result of deciding our past decisions were mistaken and have led us to some place we wish we had avoided. Regret is based on wishing we had a "do over." We plague ourselves with the "what ifs" (what if I had taken that job in a different city, what if I had not broken things off with an old love, what if I had gone to graduate school, etc.). Living by this kind of life analysis can lead to serious and even debilitating regret.

I see this kind of thing with clients in therapy all the time. It makes sense in a way, which is probably why it is so common. We want to learn from our past. What better way to learn from our past than to review what we can now see were mistakes, so we do not make those mistakes again, especially if we are confronting the same kind of decision again. Okay, that actually sounds pretty healthy. If we are in the process of a breakup and we can look back to see where we've regretted break ups in the past, we can ask whether we will once again regret our current decision. We can ask the "what ifs" before we make a crucial decision. We can ask ourselves, "When I have hindsight about this decision I am making right now, will I later wish I had decided things differently?" Call this a built-in impulse control. It is worth repeating another saying here, "Those who do not learn from the past are doomed to repeat it." Fear of regret later for the decisions we are making now can actually be very reasonable.

Go ahead and learn from your past. Don't make big decisions in your life without reviewing how you now feel about similar decisions in the past. You might learn that your decisions are overly influenced by fear of risk, by avoidant behavior, by some insecurity that compels you to flee when over time that turns out not to be the right decision very often. You might suffer from the syndrome of "I always quit (a job, a relationship, a situation) before I get fired" and then realize you weren't really at risk of being fired, so you "quit" for no reason.

On the other hand, instead of overreacting, you might see that, when it comes to big decisions, you are too passive, you do not make decisions, but rather let life make its decisions for you, and then you later wish you had taken a more proactive approach. You stay in a job or relationship or an educational program long after knowing pretty well that you do not want it to continue and are really dissatisfied. Or maybe you don't so much make decisions, as let others make them for you, and then find yourself resentful of the person that "made the decision" (when you actually made it, by allowing them to tell you what to do). You stay in a job you hate for years because you are the breadwinner and your partner needs you to make the money. Reviewing years of decisions that you later regret is probably the best way to change these patterns.

Here's the problem, though—Hindsight is not 20/20. "20/20" is "perfect" vision. It means we see things at 20 feet exactly how the eye doctors think we should see things at 20 feet. With hindsight though, we often insert a level of clarity that is not really there at all. We take it too far. We think, "If I had known then what I know now, I would never have... (insert decision)." This is very likely completely untrue. Why? Because our decisions are not merely based on what we know in the moment, they are based on who we are in the moment. Who we are now is different than who we were back then when we made the decision we now regret.

A client named Jill (not her real name) tells me, "I cannot believe I ever married him (her husband) 12 years ago. If I had known what he was truly like when he asked me to marry him, I would never have said yes." Jill now finds herself living in resentment against herself, bitterness toward her husband Mark (not his real name), and daily almost overwhelming regret about her decision to marry Mark. There's a real problem here, but not the one she's identified. She is making a fundamental mistake about hindsight. She is inserting the person she is now at the age of 32 into the situation she was in when he asked her to marry him. But she was 20 then. She was not the same person. She was not in the same place in her life. She hasn't merely learned a lot about her husband along the way. She has learned much about herself, her life, how she feels about being a mom, about her career options, about wanting things she couldn't have known she wanted "back then." Maybe she has lost her mother to cancer, after her mother spent 30 years in a marriage she found miserable. Her career goals seemed unimportant then, but now seem to be slipping away, fast. I could go on with many other facets of the way her life has changed. The important point is this: Jill's hindsight is not 20/20. She cannot separate the Jill that exists at the age of 32 from the Jill that existed at age 20. Jill probably can't really even remember, except vaguely, what it was like to be Jill at the age of 20. Her reasons for marrying Mark at 20 were partly the result of needs she had then that she no longer has (financial, emotional, social).

Jill lives in deep regret because her hindsight is warped. Yes, warped. Hindsight is not 20/20. Hindsight is nearly always warped by failing to realize that we are not now who we were when we made a decision that we now wish we had made differently. I do the same thing, and am pretty sure you do too. I think we all make this mistake. We forget that we evolve as people as we move through time. The more time, the more we have changed. We enter into parts of our lives that are fundamentally different, not just based on knowledge, but also based on our changed identities, personalities, and priorities.

I can make the same kinds of mistakes about regret as Jill made. I might regret deciding to go to law school instead of graduate school for philosophy. I might wish I had known back in college that I would eventually find the practice of law unfulfilling, or worse. If I had only known that back then, I could have had a totally different and possibly better career experience from my late twenties to my early forties. This regret kind of makes no sense, once you factor in that I am now the person I am in part precisely because I went to law school, then practiced law for 13 years. How can I get around that part of who I am now to honestly and accurately review my past? I cannot. My hindsight is warped by the fact that I have spent half of my adult life steeped in the law. The best I can do is recognize this, and when reviewing the past, take that into consideration as part of my reviewing why I made those decisions. Like Jill, I also need to recognize that I was in a completely different part of my life when I made the decision to go to law school. My needs were different, and so were the needs of my family.

It is unlikely that every part of the 12 years Jill and Mark have been married were regrettable. It's more likely that Jill now knows with clarity that she is ready to not be married to Mark anymore, but thinks she should have known this all along. Not only is this a mistake, it is also unnecessary. We don't need this kind of clarity about our past to make good decisions for ourselves now. Sometimes, though, it seems easier to make difficult decisions by telling ourselves that we should have known all along, that the whole thing we are now rejecting was a mistake, bad, so we can remove it from our lives completely without fearing regret. Jill is ready to leave Mark because she can now see things about Mark that she finds intolerable. Part of the reason they are intolerable, though, is that Jill is different too. Jill finds things intolerable now that would not have mattered as much when she was 20. That is the result of time, growth, changing values, priorities, and perceptions. Those things are actually not about Mark at all. They are about Jill, all about Jill.

If we can remember that hindsight is not actually 20/20, that it is warped because it carries with it the trap of incorrectly assuming that we are now who we were when we made past decisions, hindsight can be a useful tool. Only in this way can we both learn from our past, while also avoiding misplaced regret that can haunt us and make us unnecessarily resentful of ourselves or others who participated in the decisions we can now see led us to a place we do not want to be. A better alternative is to recognize that part of the reason we have the clarity we now have is because we made the decisions we now wish we had not made. Jill can see she no longer wants to be married to Mark because she married Mark. I can see that the practice of law is something I no longer wish to do because I practiced law long enough to know this in my bones. Actually, I do not regret law school or having practiced law because it taught me so much about who I am now, and helped shape me. Jill will hopefully get to a place where she will be able to appreciate all that her marriage to Mark has taught her, given her, shaped her, led her to a place where she can say she no longer needs to be in that relationship. When Jill gets to that point, she will no longer have the regret, the resentment against herself and Mark, and the bitterness of thinking she wasted 12 years. That is my hope for Jill, for myself and for all of my clients, and it comes only in time, with balanced clarity about our past decisions.

THE CATSKILL EAGLE:
DIVING DOWN INTO YOUR SELF

This is one of my favorite quotes of all time:

"There is a wisdom that is woe; but there is a woe that is madness. And there is a Catskill eagle in some souls that can alike dive down into the blackest gorges, and soar out of them again and become invisible in the sunny spaces. And even if he for ever flies within the gorge, that gorge is in the mountains; so that even in his lowest swoop the mountain eagle is still higher than other birds upon the plain, even though they soar."

It comes from the book *Moby-Dick; or, The Whale* by Herman Melville. In my version of the book, this quote is on pages 454–455.

I first read *Moby-Dick* about 20 years ago. I can't remember if this couple of sentences stood out then. Probably not, but maybe. I just read the book again a couple of years ago. I am pretty sure it sticks out now because this time I am a therapist (I was still practicing law when I read it the first time). So now I see how true these lines are in many peoples' lives. I see how clients achingly "dive down into the blackest gorges" and then triumphantly learn to "soar out of them again and become invisible in the sunny spaces." As clients repeat this process, it is less important for them to have someone like me remind them of the sunny spaces when they are in the deepest gorges—they begin to trust that they have it within themselves to fly in both places, which makes them stronger than if they had just stayed in the shallower airs "upon the plain."

A friend once told me, "We do not just learn from experience. We learn from reflecting on experience." I use this line often in therapy. When we soar like eagles into the darkest and the sunniest spaces in our lives, we learn, we grow stronger, richer, more complex, more able to take on even the thorniest situations and relationship issues, and we also increase our capacity for gratitude, joy and peacefulness. We become better versions of ourselves. We swoop and we soar, as needed, by our choice, and the more we do, the less fearsome those dark places become, the higher and brighter those sunny places become.

Here is another quote from *Moby-Dick* that sums up an entire life of swooping, soaring, and reflecting:

> *"There is no steady unretracing progress in this life; we do not advance through fixed graduations, and at the last one pause: – through infancy's unconscious spell, boyhood's thoughtless faith, adolescence' doubt (the common doom), then skepticism, then disbelief, resting at last in manhood's pondering repose of If. But once gone through, we trace the round again; and are infants, boys, and men, and Ifs eternally."* In my version of Moby-Dick, this quote is on p. 525 (the whole page is great, but I wanted to keep the quote short).

We get to live our lives to the fullest extent possible by deciding to face whatever there is to face, by going back again and "retracing" all the parts of our lives we have lived, and then live them again, as needed, as wanted, without letting fear of our history, our choices, our regrets, our failures, our recriminations, our dilemmas, block us from all that we have already done with ourselves.

When we go back into our memories, we often find a blend of melancholy and reminiscences, of doubt, but also conviction, of a tear, and a smile. Sometimes we need therapy to become accustomed to this process of retracing, either for entire chunks of our lives, or for specific circumstances. Eventually, though, it becomes natural, a habit, just "flying" around within our histories and ourselves. When we are able to do this without prompting, without needing to be encouraged to do this, we have become the Catskill eagle. When clients become Catskill eagles, they don't need me anymore; they are done with therapy. Every one of them that got there look back and have no doubt that therapy was worth it, worth all the trouble. Now, they get to dive as deep as they need, and can fly up to the sunny spaces on their own. They know they are no longer "on the plain" but in the high mountains of their lives. I am so happy for them.

Denial:
Keeping Secrets from Yourself

"No one, no one is blinder, than he who will not see."
- U2, "I Threw a Brick through a Window"
on the album *October*

A therapist's diagnostic interview usually notes something about a client's observable "level of insight." On a form I used to use, there was a continuum for this question—a series of boxes from the left side to the right side that you could check. At the right side (the high end), you could check a box that said "Very insightful." In the middle, there was a box that said, "Some insight." At the low end, it didn't say "Little insight" or "No insight." Curiously, it said "Denial." I wondered why. I don't actually know the answer. I didn't create that form. I liked that part of the form though. The form seemed to assume that all of us have an inherent capacity for at least a minor amount of insight or self-awareness. If we appear to not have this capacity, the form indicates that this must be due to an intentional blindness about ourselves, otherwise called denial. I have found this to be true again and again in my work as a therapist over the past decade.

Denial often comes up in life as a very important defense mechanism—it helps us keep at bay feelings that would overwhelm us or put us "over the edge" without it. Think of the famous five stages of grief we go through when we suffer a great loss in our life (denial, anger, bargaining, grief, acceptance). See what I mean? Denial is first on the list. This makes sense in a way. When we learn that we are losing someone very important (a family member or good friend finds out they are dying of cancer and have only weeks or months to live) we need time to adjust. If the severity of this came upon us all at once, we might be stricken into a kind of paralysis (sometimes we are stricken and this can also be a kind of defense mechanism). Anyway, denial in this situation can be a kind of shield, or filter, which gives us time and a chance to "get our heads around" the news that we are going to lose someone very important. During this time, we find support, we reach out, we come to grips with the new awful reality. We eventually let go of denial (hopefully) as we find ourselves increasingly able to cope with the loss we have suffered or are about to suffer.

When denial is used to blind us from ourselves, though, it can be a very tough barrier to healing, growth, change, to reaching our goals in life and in therapy. I will now provide some common examples of the ways denial can wreak havoc in the lives of therapy clients (and others).

I have worked with many people in abusive relationships. They repeatedly tell me they didn't see how terrible things had become until some consequence brought it to light. Earlier in my career, I worked with parents whose children were taken away by the county child protection system. Often, a mother would lose her children temporarily, not because someone was physically abusing the children, but because the children had been subjected to witnessing the mother's boyfriend or husband abuse their mother. This is, of course, its own kind of emotional trauma and abuse of the children, which is why they were removed. Mothers would tell me the abuse was so incremental, over a long period of time, they could deny it at first. It was just a thrown plate, then a push, then a slap, then he pushed me down, then he punched me, pushed me down and kicked me, and so on, until the police were involved. Sometimes even then, she'd be in denial about how serious and severe the abuse was. We are at this point way past any kind of denial as a defense mechanism.

I won't try to pretend there is a single or simple answer to why women don't leave sooner. Denial is a part of it, though, and it serves the unfortunate purpose of helping her avoid having to make what for some other reasons feel like a terrible decision (he will hurt me worse, he is the father of my child, I cannot fend for myself, he doesn't mean it, he loves me and I love him, he will change and I will help him change, etc.). The point of this chapter is not about domestic abuse (there are many well-researched resources for information about that issue). This chapter is about the power and the danger of denial.

Denial also comes up in most cases of drug and alcohol addiction—not just for the addict either. In fact, when I work with families that are dealing with addiction, the addict might be fully aware of her addiction and its consequences, but the family pretends the problem is not a big deal. Here, the denial is like an unwritten rule. No one says, "Hey we need to deny that mom is addicted to prescription pain-killers." The family might even deny they are in denial. They might be able to say mom has an addiction issue, but be unable to identify why it is a problem, why it needs to stop, how it is affecting the functioning of the entire family, how every person in the family is actively engaged in "covering" for the addicted person. Denial here is used to avoid having to make very difficult decisions about how to appropriately address the addiction issue (e.g. commitment of the addict to treatment, separation, divorce, custody litigation, etc.). This is especially true if the addict doesn't seem willing to do anything about the addiction.

In my office, I have a statue of the three monkeys, representing the phrase "see no evil, hear no evil, speak no evil." I use it as a reminder to clients that they often have relationships that reinforce denial. I will on occasion when I think someone is unable to see this (due to their own denial) pick up the statue and hand it to them to hold while they explain how they are unable to resolve serious conflict in some relationship they are describing. Doing so can sometimes help the client give tangible weight to their denial, to see the reality of it.

In the addiction and domestic abuse examples, denial is a very powerful tool used to avoid the conflicts that would occur if the family members were honest with themselves and each other about how to respond to the addiction or abuse. Denial is also a very powerful tool for individuals to avoid their own inner conflicts. Therapy as a whole cannot be successful if a client is unwilling to explore their issues. Denial is a normal part of a client's difficulty at the beginning of therapy. Most clients come to therapy having learned to cope with their mental health issues by using denial as one of the ways they can manage the severity of their inner conflicts. Take someone who suffers from very low self-esteem. They might think of themselves as barely able to function in their lives. They get up, go to work, come home, make something to eat, do the laundry, go to bed, and so it goes. They constantly fear that their life's burdens will overwhelm them if they are asked to handle one more thing beyond the basics of every day life. This person uses denial to keep at bay all the unconscious messages that lurk within them; pressing emotional or mental health issues they need to deal with, but they don't feel strong enough to face. Denial helps them avoid the crushing defeat they might feel if they had to actually face the actual subject of their fears—their very own self.

In a sense, denial can be a way to keep a secret from ourselves. I don't want to know something about myself, so I ignore it, intentionally. I tell myself it isn't true even when I think it might be true. Denial is intentional. Sometimes, though, denial runs so deep and lasts so long we are unaware we are engaging in denial. I call this "unconscious denial." This is the point I am trying to make when I hand the three monkeys to a client, so they can see and we can discuss how they are telling themselves something they probably know deep down is not true, but are afraid to admit it or they have difficulty seeing it.

A long time ago, as I thought about how denial in my family and within myself had caused so much trouble, I wrote this (please excuse the drama of it, I was a college kid when I wrote it): "The greatest character defect in people is their capacity for hypocrisy—the fact that a person can look in a mirror and completely deny the image reflected." Denial can be a valuable tool when dealing with traumatic events or significant loss. The problem is that denial can also be used to keep us in dysfunctional and even destructive relationships or other behavior patterns by helping us avoid conflict that sometimes needs to happen. At the individual level, denial can allow us to avoid addressing those parts of ourselves and our lives that might be much easier to address if we had the strength, and sometimes the needed help of others, to face them directly. No one needs to fear their own mirror, and yet so much of the time we do. A simple thing to remember when you fear looking within yourself (as we all do) is this: you are stronger than you think you are. It is also wise to remember: it is okay to ask for help.

TRANSCENDENCE

In the chapter "Loneliness," I stated pretty strongly that we are alone, all the time, for our entire lives. Being alone and being lonely are two very different things. We can be alone, completely alone, and yet not feel lonely, when being alone is our choice, when we are not striving, and failing, to find connection. It is because we are alone and also desire to connect to other people that we feel lonely. By itself, there isn't anything wrong with loneliness. It is painful. Fortunately, most of the time, it is pretty short-lived, because we do something to connect. How do we do this? How can we become better at connecting, not only when we feel lonely, but just because engaging in the world feels really good? We can transcend.

We interact with the world all the time. We interact with other people, with physical things, with pets, with finances, with everything that is not us, whatever makes us, "us." We cannot leave the domain of our bodies or our minds. We are stuck within ourselves. And yet, we yearn for more than this. We yearn for intimacy, emotional connection, spiritual connection, social connection, and sexual connection. We can feel joy when we are in a community of our most important people, at synagogue, during family events, out on a date. We want to connect, connect, connect. It is in our nature to want to move beyond the borders of ourselves. This is what it means to "transcend"—to "move beyond." So, "transcendence" is the state of having moved beyond.

I do not know if it is possible to stay in this state all the time in a kind of perpetual "grace," but that isn't the topic of this chapter. I am talking about more transient, momentary, frequent and regular ways to transcend. Yet, finding healthy ways to experience transcendence is perhaps the greatest thing we can strive for in our search for mental health, for mentally healthy lives. If we are able to experience transcendence, it means we have the capacity to truly engage in the world in a way that lets us understand the world and ourselves from something more than a subjective viewpoint. Transcendence also lets us appreciate "others" in a way we cannot if we are stuck in our own selves, whether that other is a family member, a loved one, a dog, a tree, the stars, a raven eating your grass seed (see my chapter on Gratitude).

Some transcend themselves at church with the help of their community of like-minded believers. Some transcend themselves in music, or in all forms of creative pursuits, nature, prayer, and meditation. The form of finding transcendence is less important than the effort taken. The result is less important than the attempt. Transcendence in all its forms, wherever and however successful, is always an attempt to engage in the world, and therefore rejects and replaces the feeling of isolation, loneliness, alienation, separation that can and often does lead to harrowing mental illness.

Transcendence doesn't need to involve anyone other than yourself. Some of my most transcendent moments happen when I am walking in the woods by myself, when I feel connected to a beautiful sky, the rugged lines up and down a tree's trunk, the moon coming over the horizon, aspen leaves blowing in a sunny breeze, an unusually shaped rock lying on the ground. If I choose, I can find ways to move beyond myself in every direction I set my gaze. So can you, if you try, if you allow yourself to consider it possible.

Can we "try" to be connected, to transcend? Sure. Absolutely. Monks spend entire lives in meditation attempting some kind of semi-permanent transcendence. I consciously evoke a sense of connection during my walks in the woods. This chapter itself, and all my other writings, are an attempt to transcend myself, to go beyond myself, to reach you, who is reading this now that I've written it. I want you to come talk to me about it, about how it made you feel, whether it "resonated" with you, whether you got something useful out of it, whether you now feel that we understand each other better now that I have written it and you have read it. I don't even need to know who the "you" is, just that it might be someone who is curious about their own capacity to transcend themselves, to find new things in their lives, and share these experiences with me. If "you" do, you will undoubtedly be repaying me the favor of enriching my life with your experiences. You will help me transcend my own experiences by imagining what it would be like to be you reading my writings in whatever form, and then using it in some new way in your life that I hadn't considered or wouldn't know how it might feel to you until you told me later.

We also transcend ourselves whenever we "make a mark upon the world." When we have a child, we are in them; when we raise them, they are in us. When we make something for dinner for a friend or our family, we put effort into their sustenance; our gift of food is in them. When we create something, anything, we put out into the world some little message about who we were in the moment of creation. When we participate in our civil affairs, write a letter to our elected representative, when we vote, attend a town hall meeting, we share in the creation of our community's future. We become a part of them and they us.

Transcendence is important because human beings are designed to be connected to each other and to the world. Without feeling connected, we can lose our sense of direction, our sense of where we belong in the world, our belief that others will come to our aid if needed. Our sense of belongingness is a very important part of how we see ourselves; it's a part of our very identity. How we relate to others and how they relate to us can either support our sense of well-being or detract from it. The more we are able to consciously find connections with others, the more we are likely to feel comfortable within ourselves.

When it comes to problem-solving in therapy, I typically spend at least some effort encouraging clients to find new ways to feel connected to their world, through improved relationships, new communities, new artistic endeavors, volunteer activities, educational opportunities; whatever will help a client feel they have a direction that includes something that is beyond who they are now. This is the very heart of personal growth, and it comes so often, so powerfully, so recognizably with transcendence. In other words, a healthy outlook on life requires some level of positive feedback from our mental states, self-talk, activities and relationships now, but also requires us to move beyond our situations as they are now, to transcend not only the border of ourselves, but transcend into our future lives, our future selves, with the hope and belief that we have some capacity to move beyond whatever troubles us now, whatever limits us, or even whatever goals we have yet to create, yet to achieve. Transcendence is not just hope, it is hope in action. It is believing in the possibility of moving beyond who we are, what we are, right now, by noticing we can be more than this, and then taking action to make it happen, to connect, to reach out, to notice, to know, so that, even when it feels like it, we are not alone, and we never were, we never have to be again.

AGING, ENTROPY, AND AUTONOMY

As I approached my own 50th birthday, I thought it was a good time to address the topic of aging. People react very differently to aging. Some take it in stride, barely paying attention to it. Others panic at every birthday, counting down the time they think they have left before they are gone. Most of us are somewhere in-between, which I think is probably unavoidable—and so, a good place to be with it.

Let's face it, aging at some point has some serious drawbacks. We get tired more easily, stuff hurts more when we are active, our cognitive abilities start to fade, we have trouble remembering things, and we lose our youthful appearance. This is the part of aging that sucks. It is about entropy and is unavoidable, no matter how hard we fight against it (at the gym or the cosmetics counter). Entropy is a very interesting concept in physics that describes how energy in a closed system tends to move from a "higher-ordered state" to a "lower-ordered state" (a state with a high level of randomness in it). For us in this discussion of aging, entropy means that everything falls apart, including our minds and bodies. Think about a garden, or just any old front lawn. What happens if we stop putting energy into it— if we stop mowing, picking weeds, fertilizing, watering? It turns to a weed-filled prairie. We see this when an empty lot goes untended. The higher-ordered state of the manicured lawn quickly goes to a more random, lower-ordered state of grass here and there, and also lots of different kinds of weeds, bare spots, etc. Order moves toward randomness.

What can we do about entropy? We are always resisting its push. When we eat, we put energy back into our system. When we exercise we are increasing order in our bodies by using the food we eat to build more muscle tissue. When we stop exercising, our muscles atrophy, which is a kind of entropy. So, although we cannot avoid entropy entirely, we can slow its affect on our bodies. There is even research that says we can reduce for a time the impact of aging (and entropy) on our minds by exercising our thinking, doing puzzles, reading, teaching, staying active in intellectual pursuits, even listening to music.

The inevitability of entropy—that we are always falling apart until we die—means there is no point in either entirely avoiding the process through some kind of denial, or focusing on it so much, we miss out on the important parts of our lives that are happening all around us. We need to balance our struggle against entropy by exercising our minds and bodies and also enjoying our lives while we are here. It's just like the well-ordered front lawn. The presence of a few weeds has always been my way of identifying a healthy lawn. If it is all weeds, it's not really a lawn. If there are absolutely no weeds, I wonder how much chemical "weed-n-feed" has been doused on that yard to remove all signs of weeds (pretty to look at but you might not want your kids playing there).

Is there any advantage to getting older? Yes. With age comes expanded autonomy, at first external autonomy and then later, if we stay aware of it, internal autonomy. Autonomy means independent freedom of choice. How this changes over our lives will take some time to explain.

At first, there is freedom of movement. As children, autonomy begins so simply. As toddlers, we are allowed wobble on our little legs from the couch to the recliner. A few years later, our parents allow us to ride our bikes around the block, and then across the street, and then to our friend's house three blocks away. Later, the risks are a bit higher, curfews expand, we get our driver's license, maybe even rent a hotel room and stay out overnight at Prom. At college, we (hopefully) learn to balance our social lives against academic necessity. In our jobs, we are (hopefully) given greater autonomy as we demonstrate our ability to add value to the work we are asked to do.

All of these changes in our earlier lives involve what I am calling "external autonomy." External autonomy means our freedom of choice is granted by those outside of ourselves; as young children, by our parents; as we get older, by others who have authority to control our choices (from college professors to supervisors at work). Starting somewhat in adolescence, and then more prominently in adulthood, we begin to attain what I call "internal autonomy" which is not choices about what to do (behavior), but freedom to choose how we think and feel about who we are and the life we have (values).

The older we get, the less we concern ourselves with the opinions of others about who and what we are. This is a basic sign of maturity. Our identities (our sense of who we are) are pretty much fully developed by our mid-twenties. In the years before our mid-twenties, we try all kinds of identity experiments. Teens color their hair purple; college kids get a nose ring and maybe their first tattoo. Once we have a stronger sense of whether we are the kind of person who really wants purple hair or a chunk of metal bolted through our septum, we are ready to move to less physically apparent experiments with our identities. We change jobs to see what kind of work we want to do, and whom we want to work with. We might start our own business. We might go back to school for a career change. We travel. We express ourselves in ways we didn't earlier in life.

Internal autonomy can only be achieved by giving ourselves the freedom to make choices about how we want to live our lives. It is entirely up to us. And it seems to come only with some level of emotional maturity, with some aging, with some years of growing into ourselves.

At about the age of 40, I made the decision to stop working as an attorney, even though I had put three years into law school, tens of thousands of dollars in student loans, and 13 years of experience as a trial lawyer. It never occurred to me (as it did to others) that I was throwing all this away. I was just moving past it, into something else. My adult son later told me he thought I made the change from lawyer to therapist because I had given myself permission to stop proving to others what I could do (be a trial lawyer) and start doing what I really wanted to do (be a therapist). His was a keen insight into exactly the kind of progression I was making, from external constraints to internal autonomy. My personal values always tended away from material wealth and toward personal growth and introspection. My move from the practice of law to that of therapist was a natural corollary to creating internal autonomy—allowing myself to rearrange my life around the kind of person I thought I was.

I write about age too because a large percentage of my clients struggle with anxiety about age, death and terminal illness. They deserve to have their fears about such facts of life validated. Death and the often slow and painful process of getting there due to medical complications and disease are legitimate concerns for all of us. Likewise, how can we not feel some deep level of concern watching our older relatives lose their youthful energy and abilities as they slip into elderly states, knowing this is what awaits us? I would do my clients who fear such things a disservice by trying to get them to think positively about it. I can't say there is much that is positive about Alzheimer's, heart disease, and nursing homes.

When clients become anxious about aging and death to the point of it becoming a disruption in their lives, I suggest that they should not become overly focused on this prior to the need to do so. Death will come when it comes, and since there isn't anything we can do to avoid it, trying to understand it in its every detail just doesn't do any good, and it does do a lot of harm. Proper planning for our last years is a good idea, but it is just planning for possibilities, because no matter how hard we might try, we can never know when or how each step toward aging and death will come. We only know it will come.

The best way to cope with the anxiety many of us face about aging and dying is to embrace what is coming as inevitable, let it be for the time it will come, and focus instead on what is happening in our lives now, and before the final years that will eventually come. One of the reasons we give ourselves permission to care less about what others expect from us is that we recognize with increasing importance that our time in this life is limited. When we age into and then past our middle lives, we learn from others who have or are about leave this life not to waste it, not to worry about things that we cannot control, and need not be overly concerned with—like the judgments and expectations of others about what we should do with our lives. The time of our lives hopefully becomes ever more precious the more we consider its finiteness.

At every stage in your life, you can measure a likely amount of time you have left before you are gone. With this guess (and it is only a guess after all), ask yourself what you want to do, what you want to accomplish, what you want to be able to say you did, before this time comes. If you ask yourself, "what's left in my life," and you are 45 or 55, it might be a new career or a job you've never done. If you are 65, it might be to live somewhere you have always wanted to live. If you are 75, it might be to visit somewhere or someone you want to see. If you are 85, it might be to read a book you've never read or haven't read in a long time. There is no time in your life when you can't think of something you want to do and still can do. So do it. This is autonomy, exercise it, and as you get older, I hope you give yourself permission to care less and less how others see you. Choose what you want to do in your life while also caring more and more about what you want to do, what you want to be.

IDENTITY

I use the term "identity" to mean the idea of who we are, who you yourself think you are, who you think I think you are, the kind of person you *are*. Our identities are mostly solidified around the age of 25. When I describe my thoughts on this in therapy with a client, I will sometimes make my hands into the form of a ball, and then bring them together around my head, while making a shrink-wrap sound (sucking in), implying a kind of "locked-in" event that happens in our mid-twenties. Even if this turns out to be true on a neurological level (I am not saying it is true, it's just my observation), it doesn't mean our identities are completely fixed—because at the age of 25, we still have 50 to 80 years to learn from our decisions, relationships, and circumstances how our now-formed identities influence the way we feel about our lives. This is a constant, always-evolving process. It is what makes life at various times interesting, troubling, satisfying, complicated, and rich.

When I meet with a teenager, I often ask them what they think is their main task in life, at this point in their life. They usually tell me something about *what* they think there parents want them to be *doing* (getting good grades in school). I agree with them that doing well in school is a fundamental expectation and something they need to attend to in order to avoid trouble now (drugs, pregnancy, law) and in the future (school, college, career). I also tell them that I do not think this is their primary function in life as a teenager. Rather than what they are doing, I suggest their main task is really trying to figure out *who they are and how to be in their lives.*

Think back to high school. What sticks out now? It isn't the grades you got, although you may remember them. It isn't how late you stayed out most of the time, although there might be a few all-

155

nighters you shouldn't have pulled but did. What likely sticks out is the kind of friends you had, the kind of friends you didn't have, how you looked, dressed, thought about yourself, defined yourself, by the clothes you wore and didn't wear (prep, punk, or vintage), the activities you chose to participate in (sports, debate, choir, band, or nothing except parties). Maybe these things mattered to you, or maybe they didn't. Either way, they began to define you for the rest of your life in ways that stayed with you for the most part, but with some changes still coming after high school.

We cannot separate completely the decisions we make about what to do in our lives from who we are as people. They are certainly intertwined—meaning they both influence each other. Our decision whether to follow high school with a four-year college, a trade school, the military, or straight to work might have been part necessity, but it was also probably partly the result of the kind of person we were already becoming at that time. Those decisions then further solidified how we see ourselves in the world. They also reinforce how others see us. If you were studious in high school, obtained stellar grades, and then end up doing very well at a prestigious university, go on to get a doctoral degree, all along the way, others will treat you as if you care a lot about academics—because they will be right about a big part of who you are and how you see yourself in the world. If, on the other hand, you are good with your hands, you don't care much for the classroom, and you are now occupied in a trade that you enjoy and it satisfies your career needs and desires, others will use these decisions and activities to define who they think you are just as you do yourself.

In both of the examples I just used, the college professor and the machinist chose professions that lined up well with the kind of person they were becoming as they entered adulthood. What happens when this is not the case? Why does identity matter? How does it come up in therapy? Usually, it comes up when a client thinks there is something fundamentally wrong with the way their life is going and they can't seem to figure out what they need to change in order to feel like they are headed in the right direction. The client might not describe it this way at first. They might be coming to me at the suggestion of a spouse, a parent, or their doctor, and the problem has been called depression or anxiety and their medication isn't solving the problem.

Suppose, Susan, the kid in high school with stellar grades and a promising future in the academic world, instead of going off to college, went to work at a local factory because nothing in her life up to that point helped her see how to manage the finances and long-term goal setting required to move toward a graduate degree. Now, Susan is 28, and is beginning to have serious misgivings about her choices. She feels stuck. Susan is stuck, and needs help evaluating her direction, to help it better match who she is.

We could just as well go the other way. Take the student above who is great with his hands; Joe does beautiful work in his shop classes, but struggles with more academic courses. He goes off to a four-year college to get an engineering degree. He manages to graduate, but with great difficulty. Now Joe finds himself still struggling with an office job at an engineering firm. He can do the work, but he doesn't excel, in part because his aptitudes lie elsewhere, and so do his interests. Yet Joe's parents and family cannot tolerate his desire to walk away from this career so he can do carpentry work. Same issue, different circumstances: identity (who we are and how we define ourselves) runs into conflict with the way we are living our lives. In each case, the person slowly realized they had become a misfit in their own lives. They come to therapy to find out a different way of living their lives, making different choices, that better match how they feel about the kind of person they are, their priorities, values, interests and aptitudes.

Sometimes it isn't this grand a problem. Sometimes identity comes up in the context of a specific situation in which a client thinks they should be doing things one way, but they don't feel right about it, and are pulled toward doing something else, and don't understand why they are conflicted. Sarah is in a long-term relationship. She knows the next step she should take is to marry her long-term partner, which is what her partner wants her to do. It just "makes sense." Yet, it doesn't feel right. Sarah is torn. Through therapy she discovers that she and her partner have very different values about class, lifestyle, goals. Sarah's partner Jill is ready to settle down. Sarah isn't. Jill has a good, stable career, here, and wants a house in a safe neighborhood. Sarah isn't ready to settle down, might want to move to a different city even, and not stay there either. She is a bit of a gypsy, a wanderer, and likes this about herself. In therapy, Sarah gives herself permission to explore these sides of herself that she has buried in order to avoid the risks of uncertainty and loneliness. She can either figure out a way to work out these differences with Jill, or if not, decide to leave the relationship. Sarah might decide to bring Jill into therapy to explore ways to have both stability (which is what Jill wants anyway) and stimulus (which is part of what Sarah craves but is afraid she will lose if she marries Jill). Whatever she decides, Sarah will be in a better position to avoid entering into a marriage that doesn't feel right to her. By working through these issues, Sarah is far more likely to have a satisfying marriage with Jill if that is what she decides to do.

All three examples might be difficult for the client to resolve, but they are simplified for the purposes of illustrating the concept of identity. We are not one or even two-dimensional. Our identities are complex; sometimes with opposing or inconsistent layers or parts. The engineer who wants to be a carpenter might also value material wealth and being a good provider for his family, which is also consistent with his spouse's values, so walking away from a lucrative position as an engineer conflicts with his part of Joe's identity and the commitments he and his spouse made when they began to co-create a future. The gypsy might both relish and fear instability. As a visual artist, Sarah seeks new stimulus for her work, and becomes bored by routine. She was also raised as a military kid, moving all around the country during her childhood. Now, she is both accustomed to it, and very anxious about it. Which is more important to her: stability or stimulus? Sarah doesn't know. That's okay. She needs to consider ways to meet both needs, and not try to merely choose one completely over the other. There may be ways she can do this, but she hasn't considered it because she isn't yet fully aware that these conflicting patterns exist within the person she is. Understanding this will help her avoid future either/or situations.

To some extent, therapy always involves an exploration of the client's identity. It must. How else can I help a person address any kind of struggle in their lives without both of us understanding at a basic level the kind of person they are and how they see themselves as a person? This will and should influence my approach as a therapist and their goals as a client. Along the way, by helping them explore their identity, they will also be more able to act as their own therapist after they are done with therapy and for the rest of their lives be in a better position to ask and answer this question: what can I do to continue to make sure my life's circumstance and direction match the person I think I am?

PERSONALITY

In my chapter on Identity, I said I use the term "identity" to mean: "the idea of who we are, who you yourself think you are, who you think I think you are, the kind of person you *are*." Let's make a distinction between "identity" and "personality." I use the term "personality" to mean: "distinct patterns in the way a person is in relation to their circumstances, which always includes interactional patterns with others, but can also include the way they respond to the external world and how they see themselves in the world and in their relationships." So, identity is more about how you feel about the person you are, and personality is more about how you tend to deal with whatever comes your way. Exploring identity and personality leads to the deepest level of self-awareness that we can achieve in therapy. The distinction between these two terms can be useful for helping clients understand the motivation for their choices (based on their identity) as distinct from the patterns in their relationships at work, at home, with their families, their careers, their place in society (based on their personality). Sometimes our motivations (what we want) are consistent with our patterns (how we try to get what we want) so we are more likely to act in a way that will get us what we want. Sometimes the way we respond to our situations is not consistent with who we are at some fundamental level. This is where therapy comes in—it helps us learn how our personality is not always consistent with our identity. We can then learn how to change our patterns of responses so we are more likely to live a life and have the things our identities tell us we want.

These definitions are mine. I use them as I see fit to help me understand clients, to help me decide how I can best help a client, and to help clients understand and help themselves. I am sure other therapists and many clients would have some basis for disagreeing with such sweeping definitions. That's fine with me. I am mostly interested in the utilitarian aspect of the terms, rather than the philosophical implications (at least in the context of actually doing therapy). There is some support for my way of seeing personality in the context of the mental health profession, although I am not sure I like the company. The Diagnostic and Statistical Manual of Mental Disorders (DSM) is the primary book therapists use to describe what is "wrong" with their clients (can you tell I have a certain disdain for the book and its uses?). I have to use it for billing purposes— insurance companies require it and I use it to communicate with other mental health professionals because it has become, for better or worse, the common language in mental health (see the chapter, "Mental health, Part 1" for more information on the DSM and how I feel about it). Anyway, the DSM has a special section for "Personality Disorders." What a lovely name! These personality disorders include things like Borderline Personality Disorder (I loved you yesterday and now I hate you), Narcissistic Personality Disorder (everything revolves around me), Schizoid Personality Disorder (I am fine all by myself), and Anti-social Personality Disorder (I have no remorse for anything I do, no matter how much it might hurt anyone else). Keep in mind, I am being very simplistic and somewhat tongue-in-cheek with these descriptions. Still, they are not wholly inaccurate, even if they are incomplete. The point is, each of these "personality disorders" reflect how a person behaves in relationships with others. For instance, the DSM-IV-TR (the current, but soon-to-be-replaced version) says this about Borderline Personality Disorder: "The essential feature of Borderline Personality Disorder is a pervasive pattern of instability of interpersonal relationships, self-image, and affects, and marked impulsivity that begins by early adulthood and is present in a variety of contexts."

Although you can see that my concept of "personality" is somewhat consistent with the way the DSM defines personality, I tend to stay pretty far away from using any of these labels to diagnose my clients. In my ten years of practicing therapy, I have only diagnosed two clients with an actual personality disorder. On several occasions, a client has previously been diagnosed with a personality disorder and I did not confirm that diagnosis. I did not find it useful or accurate and it was a harmful way for the client to define themselves—in part because it is such a permanent diagnosis (as it is intended to be when it is accurately applied). So, although I think there can be some merit in the diagnosis of a personality disorder, I also think it is extremely rare, and far more rare than the frequency of diagnosis might make it appear to be. I have no "scientific evidence" of this, just my observations after doing therapy for over ten years in a multitude of contexts. I often talk to clients about their personality "features" rather than "disorders." I do this because I think personality traits and features can be a powerful way to learn about tools the client already has within them to resolve issues in their lives.

Gary's personality tends to drive him to succeed, to push out of the way any obstacles and barriers to his goals. This trait has served him very well, to a point. Gary is successful in his career, admired by his colleagues, his family, and a large network of friends. Gary is also in the process of ending his second marriage. He is 32. Gary wants to learn in therapy how he does so well in some areas of his life but has such difficulty sustaining primary relationships. His identity tells him he likes being married; he likes "being a husband" and "having a wife." Yet his personality seems at odds with the needs of daily-negotiated conflict resolution that is a requirement in any long-term primary relationship. The very thing that makes him successful in other areas of his life (work, career, even friendships with other competitive-type folks), makes it difficult for him to compromise, to leave competition outside the door to his home. A fundamental aspect of his personality is at odds with a fundamental aspect of his identity. This is why the distinction and the combination of the terms "identity" and "personality" can be helpful in therapy—it can help Gary measure the importance of each and the extent to which he can alter his way of being with others to align it with the values that are part of who he is.

Another way personality traits come up in therapy is the way they become a problem when they had at some other time been very helpful. Marge is 52. She lives alone. She was married for 14 years, but her husband left her because he said, "You are so distant, I don't even know who you are." That was three years ago. It occurs to Marge that he was at least partially right—she is distant with others. Marge has few friends. Her brother lives in a different city; she visits him once or twice a year, but she does not suggest he come to visit her. Marge had a close relationship with her mother, who died six years ago. Marge is lonely. She doesn't want to spend the rest of her life distant from others. In therapy for the first time, Marge begins to piece together why distance in relationships became a pattern in her life: her father sexually abused her from the time she was nine until he left the home when she was 11. She never told anyone about it until she was 34, when she told her mother. Only then did she discover that her mother kicked her father out after thinking he was doing this, and her mother felt terrible about it her whole life, but had concluded it was best not to discuss it with Marge because she thought bringing it out in the open might make things worse for Marge. Marge felt the need to distance herself from her father to protect herself, and she had to keep it a secret, or so she thought, which added to her feelings of distance from those she wanted to be able to love openly the most. Distance was an appropriate and necessary coping skill to the 11–year old Marge, but is now a significant problem for the 52–year old Marge.

Being distant is just one of Marge's personality traits. She is also kind, considerate, and when you get to know her, she's very funny. She has a deep desire to be connected to others, but needs new relationship tools to find ways to do this. In therapy, she creates goals for herself to be more honest with others about her emotional needs. She tells a good friend about her work in therapy, and this friend comes to therapy with her to support her work. On a trip to see her brother over the holidays, Marge tells him about her therapy work, her sexual abuse, the secrets, the conversations she had with her mother. In doing so, Marge learns that her brother had been in therapy before, had tried to tell Marge about it, but she had seemed uninterested at the time. She remembered the conversation differently, but understood why he felt that way about it. Marge thinks she might be ready to date again, and has set up a profile on an online website, although she hasn't actually started communicating with anyone. First, Marge wants to be sure she knows how to recognize whether she can trust her instincts about whether a man is actually interested in her feelings and can trust in her ability to reach out to him when the time comes. Through therapy and her own self-exploration Marge has learned a great deal about the way she pushed her ex-husband away and doesn't want to repeat those patterns.

Personality is an important concept for us all. It can help us understand patterns of interaction with others that are both beneficial at times and problematic at times. Learning how to avoid traits that are harmful and emphasize those traits that are beneficial is an integral part of therapy and personal growth. When we think about both our personality (how we relate to others and the world) and our identities (how we see ourselves in the world) we can encourage ways to make them more consistent so the relationships we have with others is a better fit for who we really are. This might just be the most important roadmap for satisfaction in our lives and with ourselves!

PART FOUR:

PERSONAL GROWTH

In the first part of this book, when I discussed my ideas about what is "mental health," I wanted to make sure I conveyed my very strong belief that my task as a therapist is not merely to help people rid themselves of the negative symptoms of "mental illness." I am not at all convinced that eliminating certain symptoms of mental illness leads to any kind of sustainable mental health. There is more to mental health than mere lack of notable symptoms of mental illness. Besides, if at the end of therapy, I have only helped someone to remove symptoms of mental illness, I doubt those symptoms would not return in some form.

Therapy is about solving problems. The current medical model of therapy calls for therapy to solve the problems of mental illness. Whatever the problem, the process of therapy always involves a deeper understanding of the client. The therapist gains a deeper understanding of their client to help the client gain a deeper understanding of themselves. This is how therapy helps the client engage in a process of self-discovery. Self-discovery, as we saw from Part Three of the book, has a value all its own. It is "an end in itself" and worthy of the trek. Self-discovery is also a "means to an end" because it can lead to personal growth. Keep in mind that self-discovery, by itself, is no guarantee of personal growth. As explained in the chapter, "Acknowledging the problem is not enough," people can learn a great deal about their issues, and yet not make meaningful changes, if they are not willing to take the next step—find solutions and implement them. Self-discovery leads to personal growth when we take what we have learned about ourselves and proactively make the kinds of changes that will lead to more satisfying, meaningful, and happy lives. A more detailed description of moving from self-discovery to personal growth is explained in the chapter, "Solutions, not problems" in this part of the book. The value of making changes (personal growth) based on our self-discovery is highlighted at the end of this part of the book when I discuss the relationship between meaning, purpose and happiness.

When I work with clients to write goals for what they want to accomplish in therapy, I have a preference to write them from the client's perspective as having gained some new capacity to address the mental illness issues that brought them to therapy. A typical goal for depression would not merely say, "George will have had 60 days without significant feelings of worthlessness." Instead, I'd want to say something like this: "George will be able to report to me that he has gained new understanding, insights, and tools to address and avoid feelings of low self-worth on his own." If George can say these words to himself and me after working with me in therapy, only then will I feel confident that he has done what he needs to do in therapy to rid himself of the problem of low self-worth because he will also know what to do if it comes back.

The path toward mental health doesn't reach a plateau, or a target, at which point you say, "I have grown enough as a person, no more need to explore who I am, what I feel, where my feelings come from, how I can best express them to get my needs met in a respectful and effective way. Now that therapy is done, and I've addressed the issues that brought me here, I never need to consider these things again." No one says this. If they did, they would find out pretty quick that old problems would come back, they'd regress, much of the therapy and self-improvement work they had done would be for naught. Self-improvement doesn't ever end, until we die. This part of the book is more focused on the kinds of things clients can continue to do for themselves, not just during therapy, but also after they have completed therapy, so they can continue their own self-exploration, self-acceptance, self-love, all to increase meaning and satisfaction in their lives.

SELFISHNESS AND LOVE

As I've mentioned elsewhere, I used to teach classes about healthy relationships to prisoners. The topic of selfishness came up when a class member asked me how to integrate what I was teaching into his own life after his release from prison. This prisoner had killed someone with a gun at point-blank range. He didn't want to "blaze a weapon" ever again. I told him I didn't know how to answer his question. I asked the class to help us figure it out. The answer we came up with: he needed to be *more selfish*. I remember thinking, "This feels right, but can this be right?" I now incorporate that answer into my daily life and my work as a therapist.

I searched the Internet for the definition of "selfish." Here are the two primary definitions I found:

1. Caring supremely or unduly for one's self in disregard, or at the expense, of others; and
2. Believing or teaching that the chief motives of human action are derived from love of self.

The first definition is the one we most often think about when we think of the word "selfish;" that selfishness is a bad thing, because it means we *only* care about ourselves, and do not care how we affect others. This definition is not only incorrect, it is harmful. Why? For one thing, selfishness is unavoidable. Even if we'd like to think we are not selfish, we are. Everything we do is based on selfishness. Ask yourself this question: is there anything we do that is not in some way based on what we want for ourselves, even if it also means sacrificing ourselves? No. There is no point in denying our selfishness, or pretending that we are not selfish. In fact, pretending we are not selfish, trying to see ourselves as something other than selfish, can confuse us, and lead to bad decisions—because it prevents us from acting in a real way, it prevents us from seeing ourselves as we really are, it prevents us from asking ourselves what we really want and need for ourselves and from others, it keeps us in denial about why our lives and our relationships have problems. Denying selfishness removes the possibility of taking honest responsibility for our decisions, and why we make them.

If we embrace selfishness, not based on the first definition I found, but on the second one—that what we do starts with love of ourselves—if we act in accordance with "love of our self," then we can finally begin to internalize what we learn, to own who we are, and to make our life our own. We can then take responsibility for what we want and need, and make better choices for ourselves, which will in turn be better for our partners, children, family and everyone we love. We can shed the pretense that what we do is not for ourselves, but is for others. We can accept that love of self is where everything begins.

There is a second part to selfishness, which is no less important. It isn't enough to merely see that everything we do is motivated by love of ourselves. We have to ask ourselves what do we really want for ourselves, what do we really need? I believe that what we all want for ourselves is *love and respect for and from the people in our lives*. We want to feel like we belong somewhere—we belong with the people we love; our family, our communities, our friends, even the stranger on the street. Is that a bad thing? No. It is a beautiful thing. And it is also selfish. And that makes selfishness not only reality, but good.

Sometimes we make mistakes about how to give and get the love and respect of others. We ask what others seem to want from us, and then pursue that, things like big houses, large incomes, social status or sacrificing ourselves for others without knowing why. Instead of asking what others might want from us, we need to be more selfish, we need to ask what we want for ourselves, and realize that money, big houses, and social status will not get us real love and respect, just false respect, and maybe no love at all. Learn what you want and need and then learn how to ask for it. Then, you can offer love and acceptance to others. We must first have hope, compassion and love for ourselves, to truly offer them to others.

My therapy work is not "faith-based," although many of my clients' faith is a powerful part of their internal strength. I respect all faiths. I also respect those that have no religious beliefs at all. Still, we can all learn from religious teachings. So, I want to offer a quote that sums up everything I am saying here about selfishness. "Love your neighbor as you *love yourself.*" Jesus said that 2,000 years ago. He understood that, in order to truly love others, you have to start with love of yourself. That is selfishness, and it is good, and real. Starting with love of yourself will lead to important changes in the lives of all of the people you love, including most importantly, and I really do mean most importantly, you.

GRATITUDE

Therapy is about solving problems, people's problems, serious and sometimes very deep problems. Naturally then, a therapist's book (like this book) is going to discuss problems, and hopefully also something about ways to solve those problems. Looking through the topics of my own chapters in this book, they are almost entirely focused on problems—on the negative side of human existence. This is as it should be. Life, though, outside the context of therapeutic issues, is not inherently negative. People encounter histories, attitudes, and prolonged emotional states which are certainly and deservedly upsetting. Sprinkled within nearly all these situations, though, are experiences and moments of brightness, goodness, small beauties to consider, like a sprinkling of cinnamon to offset the bitterness of strong coffee!

I thought of the topic of gratitude this morning while watching a raven from my kitchen window on this cool, dark, misty fall day. At first I noticed his gorgeous black sheen, the way his neck shines purple-blue even on a cloudy day, how he so gracefully swings his head around to watch for... I don't know what ravens watch for, predators maybe? Anyway, I was caught up in the moment of appreciating him. Then I thought about what he was doing there, right there in that particular spot. He was pecking in among the straw I'd laid down a few days ago where I had seeded bare spots in my lawn. Crap! This bird was eating up my grass seed!

Just before gazing out at the raven, I had been outside on the other side of my house repairing a broken Christmas light that had burned out (turned out it was just loose). As I walked back to the house, I noticed that one of the birdfeeders was nearly empty—mental note to self, fill birdfeeder later today. Back to the raven. I realized how silly it was for me to be upset with the raven. What he was doing was no different than the little blue birds that had emptied my birdfeeder. He was eating what I had set out. Yes, I would need to reseed there in the spring, but so what, really. I then made the choice to reconsider his behavior from a different light, to alter my emotional reaction to the sight of him. I decided to be grateful that he decided to eat my seeds at a time and in a place where I could watch him so close to the window, where I could enjoy his beauty and grace. I smiled, holding a warm cup of coffee, noticing the moment in the light of gratitude again for his beautiful coat of feathers, his grace, his audacity.

Gratitude starts with noticing. You cannot feel gratitude unless you consciously decide to notice something happening around you or in your life that makes you glad. I could just as easily have called this chapter "noticing." We so often get caught up in all the worries of the day, of our lives, distracted by the next task, the next obligation, our previous and future failures, that we do not pay attention to what is happening right now in front of us, within us, around us. In order to influence your overall experience in life with gratitude, you must force yourself at first to consider the things in your life for which you are grateful. In time, and after becoming accustomed to forcing yourself to see the good stuff, you will become more able to naturally, without force, take opportunities to be grateful for things that present themselves to you; you will begin to notice the present moment more and more, which is a good thing, because it provides relief from all that worrying and anxiety about the past and the future. I am not suggesting you ignore your past or your future. I am suggesting you often, just for a moment, take a break from it with gratitude.

Throughout most days there are plenty of things we could notice and appreciate if we took the time, if we stopped for a moment to just realize it. Try feeling glad to see the way rain or snow or leaves hit the ground, bounce off a window, or make a tinkling sound, a pleasing pattern when they hit anything around you. Notice when a squirrel stops to look around to make sure it is safe, and then continues on its way, doing whatever it was doing before it stops. Notice the soothing red, cream, blue, white, or brown glowing through a lampshade or curtain in your living room, bedroom, or office. Be glad you experienced it, no matter how small. Sometimes noticing the smallest thing and appreciating it for the smallness of it has a kind of special joy to it.

We don't need to notice anything in particular happening outside ourselves to feel gratitude. We can think of any number of things within us to appreciate, if we choose to think about these things, realize them, pay attention to them, and decide to feel grateful for them. Within us are thousands of memories that come with thousands more feelings, attitudes, interactions, moments, experiences, some of which may have brought us joy at the time, or even if they were very difficult experiences at the time, we can feel grateful now because we have survived them. Think of the times you've felt miserably cold, wet, when it was dark outside, you just wanted to get home, change into your pajamas with a warm dinner, a cup of hot tea, or soak in a hot tub, and you thought you'd never get home soon enough. Then, there you were, home, warm, the cold outside, a quickly dissipating memory. Satisfaction! We all have these kinds of memories. Once in a while, no matter what else might be going on, consider these times, or any others like them when for even just a moment, you could have said out loud, "ahhhhh!" as you basked in the experience of satisfaction, comfort, safety, well-being.

Gratitude doesn't come from experiencing great things. Gratitude comes from intentionally, consciously, noticing, considering, and appreciating the experience of a great thing or a small thing that is great. You know and I know we can experience a really good thing, and barely appreciate it, before rushing on to whatever we need to do next. Sometimes, noticing just amounts to giving yourself credit, or giving your life credit, where credit is due, a way of patting yourself and your circumstance on the back and telling yourself, "Nice, I like the fact that I have it in me to appreciate what is happening around me, even the littlest things."

Gratitude builds up our capacity to consider both the good and the bad in our lives. It is more than a simple distraction from the negative aspects of our lives. Think of it like a muscle we need to use to appreciate the good things in life, and if we don't force ourselves to use it, like a muscle, it will atrophy. Go ahead, use gratitude, often, so you are not constantly preoccupied by what is wrong in your life, what kind of problems you have that need to be solved, but so you can. Use gratitude by deciding to notice what can be appreciated. The more you tell yourself, "Notice!" the more you will notice things without having to tell yourself to do so. The more you notice even the smallest things, the more grateful you will feel about your whole life, not just the momentary experiences.

CURIOSITY

The chapter about gratitude led me to write this chapter about curiosity. They are similar in a lot of ways. Both gratitude and curiosity are important parts of mental health, and are each vital to progress and growth in therapy and in life. Curiosity and gratitude both compel us to notice things we otherwise might not notice.

Curiosity though, unlike gratitude, does not require us to be glad about whatever we are paying attention to. In fact, often our curiosity can lead us to very troubling things. If we hear a strange noise outside, and we let our curiosity pull us toward opening the door, we may find a stray cat, lonely, sick, hungry, in need of our immediate attention. If we ignore that sound, maybe the cat dies without our aid. If we have a strange or troubling or depressing thought, curiosity about it might make us feel more troubled or sad, but it might also help us figure out what we need to avoid associated feelings later. Curiosity is still helpful even when troubling because we sometimes need to pursue darker avenues to find places to heal, feel better, understand, and overcome that which troubles us.

Curiosity is fundamental to our mental health because it tells us to question important parts of our lives that we usually need to address, but might ignore if we lacked curiosity. When curiosity recently led a client to attend an upcoming workshop she hadn't originally planned to attend, she discovered the workshop opened the door to new career opportunities.

Before you put a book down and walk out of the bookstore, consider why you picked the book up. Pay attention to the reasons; follow your curiosity. Consider the possibility that your curiosity is telling you something you find interesting, but don't know why. Maybe the book is telling you something you want to know about your life in a different way, about relationships you want to improve but don't know how, about a friend you don't understand but wish you did. Allow your curiosity to pull you toward making decisions that you might first want to reject. Buy the book. Read it. Who knows where that curiosity will lead you.

Follow your curiosity. It might be based on something you know or suspect at some level but you don't quite realize at a conscious level. In other words, there are reasons we are curious, even if we don't actually know those reasons. You rarely have much to lose by following your curiosity within reason—meaning you don't always want to act on where it might lead you, but seeing where it leads could be helpful even if you decide not to act on it.

You might also have much to lose if you ignore your curiosity. This is especially true when it concerns curiosity about yourself, your inner life, your identity, who you are, who you want to be, where you've been, and where you want to go. Be alert to these questions. Stay alert! Stay curious!

Curiosity about ourselves and the relationships in our lives is probably the single greatest incentive to finding out what makes us interesting. Being interested in yourself makes you more interesting to others, makes you more interested in what you are doing in your life. Being interested in others makes them feel (for good reason) truly appreciated by you. If others see you are curious about yourself, they might find themselves more interested in you. If they see you more interested in them, they might find they become more interested in themselves too, at least where it concerns you. And, really, what could be more interesting than all the stuff happening inside you all the time? I really mean that!

Being curious makes us less afraid to be complicated, to be multilayered, to seeing things from multiple perspectives all at the same time. If we pay attention to the curiosity we feel about ourselves and the direction of our lives, we are far more likely to take paths we will find later on we feel good about.

Think about the alternative to curiosity, which is apathy. If curiosity is "a desire to know," apathy is the lack of that desire. Apathy means, "I don't care." Which sounds more mentally healthy? Of course, it's curiosity. Apathy tends to be based on a belief that curiosity is pointless because it can only lead to a negative or useless outcome. Why should I care about my career when it is obvious I will be stuck in this crappy job until I retire, and then I will be forced to live on the meager resources of retirement. Curiosity considers alternatives and possibilities that apathy shuts out before they are even considered. Apathy answers questions with "I don't care" based on the attitude "It doesn't matter anyway." Curiosity answers questions with "I'd like to know" based on the attitude, "It can't hurt to ask, and maybe it does matter."

In the chapter about gratitude, I noted that frequently feeling grateful might not come naturally at first, requiring you to force yourself to pay attention to it. The same is true with curiosity. You might need to *decide* to follow your curiosity. You might have become oblivious to your own curiosity because you've become so used to ignoring it. That's why writing about gratitude made me think of other beneficial mental states, like curiosity, that often initially require intentional choice. As is the case with gratitude, if you force yourself to pay attention to curiosity for a while, you will find yourself naturally paying more and more attention to it as time goes on. Maybe we have a kind of mental muscle for gratitude, and another one for curiosity. We also can train ourselves to notice the benefits of each. If you let your curiosity take you places you wouldn't otherwise explore about yourself or your life and that exploration ends up helping you create new opportunities for yourself, or resolving old disputes or issues, you will appreciate and trust your curiosity more.

I want you to consider this question about curiosity, "What would it be like to not be afraid to ask yourself any question about yourself, your life, or life in general?" Most of us may find such a state hard to even comprehend, even impossible to achieve or come close to achieving. Or you think, who would want that? Sounds terrible. Maybe you read that question and think, "I am already there, big deal." Just think about it. Are you there? Really? Are you really willing to follow curiosity about yourself, your attributes, your history, your future, your issues, your relationships, the span of your entire life and yourself, without fear? What if you could? What if this is the course of curiosity, true curiosity when pursued regularly in your daily life? What if over time you lose fear, eliminate it bit by bit, nothing to hide from, run from, become numb to, ignore? Is it possible? Well, I've stated it as an absolute, and there is probably nothing absolute about being human. But isn't it worth pursuing, to whatever extent it is possible? This is curiosity. Consider it, pay attention to it, to what it tells you. Take it as you can, be reasonable with it, but don't let fear of yourself override curiosity about yourself. Eventually, curiosity will rule fear, and fear will no longer lead you to ignore curiosity, or become apathetic. Stay alert, stay curious, and change will come more than you know.

FLEXIBILITY, PART 1:
"FLEXIBILITY IS THE
HALLMARK OF MENTAL HEALTH"

What would it be like to have many more choices about how to respond to people in your life–your husband, wife, daughter, boss, and the grocery store cashier? What if you could predict how you will feel in different situations and have a good idea of how you want to deal with those feelings ahead of time? Wouldn't you be less likely to regret impulse decisions later, more likely to feel better about your ability to deal with those kinds of situations the next time? This is you. This is who you are right now, but with the added ingredient of flexibility in your everyday life.

Flexibility is not just about bending to the needs of others. I am talking about flexibility based on choices you make, not choices others want to make for you. I am talking about choices you already have the ability to make, once you give yourself permission to try new approaches and start learning more about what feels best for you.

Therapy is about change—about wanting someone else to help us come up with ideas about how to get unstuck. We come to therapy to learn new ways of handling issues, relationships, situations and our moods and feelings. Flexibility is what we seek. We get into ruts and habits that keep us doing the same stuff over and over again until we feel stuck enough to do something about it. Flexibility gives us the way out, new ways of seeing things, different ways of dealing with ourselves and others. With some trial and error, flexibility gives us the chance to explore what works best for us to have what we want.

This series of chapters about flexibility is a culmination of thoughts I've had over the past year about an issue I think about every day I go to work. What is "mental health?"

In the chapter "What is Mental Health Part 1," I encouraged clients looking for a therapist to ask that therapist, "How do you define mental health?" I suggested then that many therapists might be great at defining "mental Illness," but haven't given much thought to what constitutes "mental health." I also said that getting rid of the signs and symptoms of mental illness is only part of becoming mentally healthy.

In the chapter, "What is Mental Health Part 2" I wrote, "mental health is a state in which a person is able and willing to address every aspect of their inner life, regardless of whether they experience difficult feelings, including fear, while addressing those aspects of their inner life." This answer felt mostly right, but incomplete. It leaves several implied questions. How does it benefit us to be able to "address every aspect of our inner life?" If that is an ultimate goal of doing therapy in some sense, why does it matter, how will it change things for us? I ask myself these questions all the time. I'll try to give answers I've been considering lately.

I can think of three possible reasons why it is better to be able to address all aspects of your inner life. First, addressing your inner life as much as possible will help you remove over time many of your most difficult feelings by giving you the chance to understand and then actually resolve previously unresolved emotional issues. You will feel better being you, living your life, being with your feelings. This is actually a significant part of the initial stage of making change in therapy. Second, addressing your inner life will help you stop doing things you might have been doing to avoid difficult feelings, like drinking, drugs, gambling, creating instability and distraction, becoming overly focused on the needs of others, of work, of things outside yourself. Third, by listening to your feelings, both those that feel good and those that do not, you can learn from them, and in doing so, will have the capacity to make decisions that are more likely to feel good to you after you've made them. You can think before you act, rather than acting, then realizing you've said or done something you regret. This process, including some trial and error, becomes part of the final stage of making change in therapy. Once clients can see for themselves their capacity to do this in their lives without further assistance, they are ready to be done in therapy.

This is flexibility. People who exercise flexibility, who can react to difficult situations in many different possible ways, whichever seems to suit their needs the most, are more likely to make better decisions for themselves. Over time, it shows up in many ways. Most notably, it shows up in how good they feel about themselves and their lives. Flexibility is a strong sign of increased mental health because flexibility requires that we pay attention to our inner lives to achieve and exercise it. Flexibility is also one of the greatest benefits of mental health as I define it because it creates enormous capacity for meaningful change.

In the next chapter "Flexibility, Part 2: The big decisions," I explain how increased self-awareness about your feelings will allow you to use flexibility to make better choices about the "big decisions" in your life.

FLEXIBILITY, PART 2:
THE BIG DECISIONS

In this chapter, I will explain my thoughts about how increasing our awareness of our inner lives and using that awareness to be more flexible in the way we do things will greatly increase how good we feel about the direction our lives have taken. This is because emotional and mental flexibility require us to know our values, or what is important to us at a deep level, so when we make decisions based on this kind of self-knowledge, we are much less likely later to realize that we made a decision that goes against fundamental aspects of who we are and what we really want, in the short term and in the long run.

At the core of being stuck for most people is some kind of fear. Being stuck in fear can simply be the result of being afraid of change, which is a kind of fear of the unknown, fear of things being different than they are now. Many of us have made some kind of unconscious decision (meaning we might not even know we've made the decision, but it is in the back of our minds anyway) that being stuck in our lives, no matter how bad it might feel sometimes, is not as bad as what we think might happen if we try to bring about real change. For others, a traumatic event, like the death of a family member or friend, or a bitter end to a previous relationship, makes them wary of taking risks of that kind again (getting close to someone who might die or leave them).

Yet, we do not want to live in fear. We do not want fear to control us, to limit our lives, our choices, the way we feel about ourselves, our relationships, all of our situations. This alone is a good reason to be able to address our inner life. As hard as this is to admit sometimes, fear is a driving force behind so much of our experiences in life and the decisions we make. The more we know about the sources and the impact of our fears, the more we can avoid allowing those fears to control us.

Our "inner life" has a great variety and depth to it. It evolves as we age and learn and build new memories and skills. Fear is always there, though. Fear of change itself is a common element to clients who are stuck in a bad place in their lives. If we are not willing to address our fear, then it is not likely to go away, or diminish. If we are willing to address our fears, we can break them down, question them, see them from different perspectives, and often realize that we have far less to fear than we thought we did. I see this all the time in my own life and when I am doing therapy with clients. Fear of conflict, change, abandonment, failure, disapproval, loneliness, and death are all legitimate fears at some point. Unfortunately, these legitimate fears often take on a kind of life of their own when they are allowed to grow within us, unchecked by a willingness to question these fears, to put them in their place, to overcome them by taking action for our benefit in spite of them.

Think of the times you yourself have stayed in a bad situation far longer than you should have, but you didn't realize this until after you left that situation. Maybe it was a job, or relationship, or housing arrangement. You stayed, despite your dissatisfaction, based on fears that making the decision for change would make things worse—and those fears felt so powerful at the time you didn't think you could do anything about it. Eventually, you felt you had little choice and took the necessary risk of bringing about change because you simply couldn't tolerate things staying the same. Maybe an alternative presented itself that was just too good to pass up, and you jumped at it. Either way, you finally made the decision to act despite your fears telling you not to do so. Looking back, you could see that much of your fear was unwarranted, irrational, or just blown out of proportion to likely outcomes. You see then that you wasted time worrying so much and being stuck so long in a bad situation.

Fear can be a good thing, though. Fear can wisely slow us down when we need to think carefully about what might otherwise be impulsive decisions. The problem, then, is not the fear. It is our reaction to the fear—we give it far more power or meaning than it needs to have, even when it is a fear that has wisdom behind it. When we are in a bad job, where the pay isn't what it should be or could be, our boss is at times mean and unpredictable, we are not appreciated, it is going nowhere, we need fear of unemployment to check our hand during an argument, to avoid announcing "I quit" and the immediate feeling of satisfaction that will surely come with it, only to find an hour later that we have no way to pay our bills, and not a lot of extra money to stretch things out until we find something better. So, yes we should fear unemployment. But we should not stay in a job in which our self-respect is shredded because we don't want to tackle the fear of not finding a better job. We should look at the fear, listen to what it tells us, and then take action to address the bad situation while taking into account what we've learned from the fear. Don't quit on the spot. Remember the berating boss when you get home to motivate you to fire up the computer, build that resume, and pound the pavement (email) sending out job applications, so when you do announce "I quit" the next time you feel berated, you have already found another job and your fear of quitting is sensibly gone.

Likewise, it makes sense to fear loneliness and grief when thinking about ending a relationship. The momentary and seemingly insurmountable issue that makes us think we should "end this" might seem relatively trivial in a week or two when cooler heads prevail and we are able to think about the deep love we have for this person, and how much they have meant to us over the many years we have been with them. Fear of losing the person we love doesn't need to mean putting up with years of fighting over the same issues, though. We can listen to the fear, while also demanding the respect, attention, the voice we deserve to have in any relationship. We can ask for our needs to be met, while trying to avoid the end of relationship with someone we don't want to lose. This is flexibility in the face of fear. We can listen to our fear; use what it tells us, to take action. The alternative is a nagging paralysis that stretches on because we don't want to pay attention to deep-seated fears that we don't want to address head on.

Although fear can be a useful tool to remind us to think long and hard about big decisions with big consequences, we should not allow that fear to keep us in a relationship or job in which we are treated badly with little hope of change. It's a balance. Until we are ready to really examine whether the fear we feel is warranted and appropriate, we are likely to avoid taking action, or if we do, we are likely to take action we will later regret. We need to understand our fear, listen to it, and not run from it, to make the best decisions both in the short and the long term. We cannot do this unless we are comfortable addressing our inner lives, including what might be our most difficult feelings of fear.

I have so far tried to show, using fear as an example, that understanding, exploring, identifying and then listening to our feelings will help us make better decisions (in addition to allowing us to be less uncomfortable with ourselves). I didn't need to use fear, although it adds punch because it is usually the most difficult of all feelings to face head on. I could still have used any number of other difficult feelings to demonstrate the same thoughts. Feelings of inadequacy work as well as fear. A corporate director who spends 60 plus hours at work and works on the weekends at home might miss most of his children's upbringing, not because he loves his job, but because he cannot bear the imagined or real disapproval of his parents, wife, older brother, or children if he doesn't "make the grade" (however "the grade" gets defined in his mind).

Shame is another example of a feeling people often take great pains to avoid, which keeps them from making good decisions for themselves. A woman refuses to reach out to her family for financial support because she feels ashamed that she has been laid off and is a single mother, despite knowing her parents have plenty of money and would be more than willing to help. She doesn't want to look at the primary source of her shame, which is a series of poor decisions in her life over the past several years, including becoming involved with the father of her children despite his drinking habit, dropping out of college, cutting ties with her family. So, her shame compels her to continue to make poor decisions, forcing her and her children to struggle without adequate resources to make real change for the better. If she were willing to look at her shame, see it for what it is, and also for what it is not (all about her), she would see that some of this shame is based on her mother's scorn over the years, and giving her father's ideas of who she "should be" more value than it deserves. If she could value the shame she feels based on her poor decisions, but reject the shame she feels due to her parents' opinions, she might be able to get the help she needs, go back to school, get a better career and then need no more dependence on an alcoholic boyfriend, or a parent whose scorn no longer has the meaning it once had. This would be flexibility in the face of shame.

Flexibility is not possible in our lives unless we are willing to look right at our feelings, all of them, the good and bad, the easy and the difficult, and consider with each the likelihood that they are telling us something valuable, but they are not telling us the whole picture. Flexibility requires that we realize that we always have many feelings all at the same time, and each of those feelings gives a different piece of the complete puzzle. If we can pay attention to them all, we can decide which ones should influence us the most, and make decisions consistent with what we know about the kind of person we are, and the kind of life we want to have. And then we can have that life because we've made decisions based on our deep and real feelings, not just on what we happen to be able to face. This is flexibility in the face of our own complexity. This is the benefit of mental health, which is so much more than merely removing signs of mental illness. Attaining flexibility has no fixed point. It is a process, a life-long process, in which we increase as the years go by our capacity to see the feelings that are there and act on them by our increasingly conscious choice.

In the next chapter on the topic of flexibility, I will show how we can use our understanding and comfort with our inner lives to change patterns of interactions with others, so our feelings give us insight into the momentary decisions we make again and again that form these patterns. If this chapter was about the "big decisions" in our lives, the next chapter is about how flexibility, which is the result of self-awareness, will aid us in making all those "little decisions" we make over and over every day.

FLEXIBILITY, PART 3:
DECISIONS IN THE MOMENT

Relationships, jobs, career, school, housing, marriage; these are all "big picture" kinds of decisions. They require serious and sometimes lengthy consideration in order to make the best decision possible. Flexibility as the result of having a good handle on our inner feelings is certainly an important part of these kinds of decisions. In this chapter on Flexibility, I am more interested in exploring how deep understanding and sustained comfort with our feelings affects our capacity to be flexible when we must make decisions in the moment, many times a day, every day, in many different contexts.

Over time, these "small picture" momentary decisions become embedded in our relationships, our personality, the way others see us, expect us to behave, and how we see ourselves. Flexibility in these situations allows us to adapt, alter, change, modify, and most importantly, decide in advance how to respond to different situations differently. We do this more than we think we do. A hothead boss or colleague at work goes off on something we think is pretty ridiculous, or someone gets drunk and acts the fool at a holiday party, yet we say nothing. When our job is on the line, we keep our cool, even if we are seething underneath, waiting with measured reaction for the right time to respond in the right way, when it will not cause us serious financial consequences. We act by not acting. This is flexibility in the face of situational realities (we need the job more than we need to tell our colleague he's acting like an idiot). Our silence demonstrates flexibility because this might not be how we would normally act if a family member or a friend at a holiday party did the same thing. We react differently to similar behavior because the circumstances, the stakes, the nature of the relationships are different.

Rigidity is the opposite of flexibility. Someone who is rigid reacts pretty much the same way all the time. Their expectations of "how things should be" do not differ between home, school, the mall, or work. Rigid behaviors do not change, even when they should change. A person who acts by shutting down and trying to change the subject whenever there is something difficult happening, regardless if it is with his wife, boss, friend, or son has very few options for dealing with adversity. Rigidity is like a toolbox with one shelf and very few tools. Flexibility is a toolbox with many shelves, all of them full of different kinds of tools to handle many kinds of different problems.

In therapy, I often tell clients their problematic responses now might be the result of tools learned very well in circumstances (like our childhood or a previous long-term relationship) where they were highly effective coping skills. Without understanding this, or the feelings that trigger this response, they are more likely to use that tool again in a situation in which it is no longer helpful, and is in fact counterproductive to meeting their current needs. A great example, and one I've used elsewhere in this book because it comes up so often, is a kid who grows up with an alcoholic or otherwise erratic, unpredictable, or abusive parent. As a child, she learns to watch everything very closely, to read the signs of a brewing storm (mom and dad are not speaking, or dinner is late, or dad hasn't come home at his usual time), to be prepared for the worst (how hard will it be to hustle little brother and sister to their rooms if dad comes home right now). She hangs onto these behaviors into adulthood. She remains "hypervigilant" in her adult relationships, watching closely for signs of trouble. She sees trouble when it isn't there. She creates self-fulfilling prophecies, thereby causing what might have been good healthy relationships to deteriorate into jealousy and defensiveness and demise. Or when there is a real conflict brewing, she "catastrophizes" it by imagining outcomes that are far more negative than is anything likely to happen (he is going to break up with me). Because she gets ready for the worst, she becomes very reactive, defensive, and hostile; to protect herself from the feelings she is sure she is about to feel (when he breaks up with her).

Confronting these issues in therapy, learning about where they come from, why they were there in the first place, validating them for the successful strategy they once formed, while also recognizing their destructive force now, this is a kind of flexibility. It can help that kid learn to use her skills of observation when it is beneficial (e.g. when she later becomes a corporate manager and uses them to facilitate constructive staff meetings by reading the complexity of all the needs and nonverbal cues of her employees). Flexibility also allows her to notice when she is doing it at home, when her boyfriend is arguing with her and she begins to look for the door, fearing things will get out of hand, when she shuts down, fearing he will become irrational, dangerous, but he is in fact just venting about his boss, wanting her support, and he isn't mad at her at all. She can say these things to herself, listen to herself, remind herself that this is a different situation and needs a different response. She can soothe herself, see the fear for what it is, that it is not really related to him, to now, to her, to this place. She can be flexible, not feel the need to argue, or flee, to set the stage for a showdown. She can calm herself, so he can calm down, mostly on his own, without her help, guidance or vigilance. She can hang her hyper-vigilance at the door, and realize her boyfriend is not her father or the last two boyfriends she had, she is safe, and maybe even tell him about her fears, but without making those fears his responsibility, while also asking for his support. Hopefully, in doing so, she will be able to test the waters to determine if she has found for herself a relationship in which she can not only address her own inner life, but can feel safe in expressing it to those who are close to her. In this way, she is exercising flexibility within herself that allows her to be flexible in how she expresses her needs in the moment and find a relationship in which this can actually work to her advantage.

Let's take a moment to review the previous example. "Flexibility in the moment" has two parts. One internal. One external. The internal part goes like this: How do I feel? Where does this feeling come from? How much of it is due to this situation, this person, this thing they did? How much of it is really not related to this person or situation? How much of this is really about me, my issues, or my history? Are my feelings right now based on old negative messages I heard, or told myself for years? Are my fears valid, right here, right now, or can I put them away (at least for now until I have a better opportunity to understand them) and focus only on the fears I am having about what is really happening here in this exact situation? Is this something I've noticed I seem to feel a lot, not just with this person? If you've previously done your work at understanding your inner life pretty well, answers to these kinds of questions will come a lot easier. Doing the work requires you to have explored much of this kind of thinking, feeling, reacting when you are not in the situation, but when you are thinking about it and exploring it in your journal, or with a good friend, or a therapist.

The external part goes like this. Once you have considered where your feelings come from, and you've separated out the feelings that are not really about this situation, this person, what they said, or what they want from you, you will have a much better chance at deciding for yourself how you want to respond based on what you want or need, right now, rather than what a whole lot of history tells you what you should want. After you've gone through the internal process explained above, you will make it external by expressing what you want to express, right now, to respond to what is happening, right now. You will have the chance to decide, actually decide, how you want to be seen, heard, understood, by this person in front of you, rather than allowing your feelings to dictate and decide for you how you will be seen. You can quickly do this internal-external process every time there is an interaction, every time he says something, and then you need to do something. At first this will take time, and it is okay to ask for time. Eventually it will become easier. At some point it becomes like second nature.

In making conscious decisions about how to interact with others based on the actual needs of the current situation, you will be able to exercise greater levels of adaptability, flexibility, and you will be far less likely to allow yourself to fall into entrenched patterns of interaction that do not work well except in very limited circumstances. You will be able to create new patterns of interaction based on the kind of relationships you want in your life now, so you don't become trapped in relationships that look like the kind you might have watched adults have when you were still a child.

Ultimately, the greatest benefit of flexibility is that you get to decide and own all of your responses. You are responsible for all of your actions, no matter what someone else does. This doesn't mean that anger, tears, or yelling are never justified. They can be, depending on the circumstance. Flexibility does mean, though, that when you do become angry, cry, or yell, you are much less likely to regret it later, or doubt yourself, because you made the decision to become angry, to let yourself cry, to yell, because you decided that is what was appropriate right then, in that circumstance, with that person. And over time, you've learned that you are not likely to do that kind of thing unless there's a pretty good reason. At this point, our outward expression (what others see) will have become an accurate reflection of an internal process of discovering what we want, what we need, and who we are right now. Flexibility is a goal, but is also a continuing process we can use for the rest of our lives. This is why flexibility is the hallmark of mental health—it requires us to get to know ourselves now so we can make better decisions in our interactions every day, every minute, in everything we do; and each time we do, we change, grow, improve, evolve, we move closer to being the person we want to be.

"SOLUTIONS, NOT PROBLEMS"

Have you ever been in a meeting that starts to really bug you because it seems to go nowhere, yet others in the room still have lots of energy invested in the discussion? Have you ever had someone call you complaining and you think (but do not say) "Why did you call me? What do you want from me? Where is this conversation going?"

This might sound pretty impatient, especially coming from a therapist. Don't worry if you are one of my clients or are thinking about becoming one of my clients. I do not feel this way in a therapy session. In a therapy session, I am there for the client, they are not there for me. But I have felt it in plenty of meetings, and in conversations with friends and co-workers. What's the difference? Simple. My clients in therapy sessions are there to solve problems, and they want my help, which I am happy to offer. That's why they've come to therapy with me. And they know, or if they don't, they learn pretty quickly, that I am not at all interested in sitting with them week after week listening to their problems just to listen to their problems. *I am there to hear their problems* and I definitely want them to feel understood and appreciated, but that isn't all, and it shouldn't be all. The last thing I want to do is to encourage my clients to remain stuck in their problems.

Probably the number one complaint I hear from clients that have not received what they needed from previous therapy experiences is that they never found their way out of the problems they brought to therapy. If a client told me that I had not helped them find a solution to their problems, I would conclude that I had failed them. And I don't like feeling like a failure. Who does? Success in therapy only happens when I can help clients find solutions to their problems so they can get rid of their problems. How? By focusing on problems for one and only one purpose: to find a solution and then use that solution to solve the problem.

Some of my clients know that before becoming a therapist, I had been a trial lawyer for 13 years (technically, I am still a lawyer now, but I no longer practice law). I often rely on my experiences as both a lawyer and a therapist to help clients heal and resolve their issues. One of my first experiences as a lawyer was a great learning experience for me. I had come across a thorny and complicated legal issue with one of my larger cases. I brought it to the law firm partner whose case it was. We didn't know each other well (yet), so I wasn't sure what to expect. He had started the meeting with a friendly and inviting tone. While telling him about the problem, he listened silently, without asking a single question. This made me a little nervous, but I finished my presentation and sat back to hear his solution. He didn't give me a solution. He gave me something better. A lesson for life. He became stern and irritated, maybe even angry. He told me, "Don't ever come to me again with a problem, without first coming up with at least one possible solution. I don't even care if the solution you have is something I don't like—at least I know you've tried. When you hand me a problem without so much as even a single proposed solution, it looks like you are just handing your problem over to me!" I remember feeling one foot tall. After scolding me, he told me to come back when I had come up with at least one solution. A day or two later I came back with several possible solutions, we resolved the issues, and eventually won the case (in case you were curious).

Like I said, this became a life lesson for me. As a parent of a small boy at the time, I began to use the same philosophy (although with a much more caring demeanor) with my son, proposing that he focus on "solutions, not problems." This taught him to try to solve problems on his own, and hopefully helped him also learn to become independent for adulthood responsibilities.

Later, when I managed several attorneys as the head of a litigation department at a law firm and then when I was a Director at a nonprofit organization, I used the same philosophy with my staff. Although it was an adjustment for some, most of my staff eventually began to really appreciate this approach because it encouraged them to believe, rightfully so, that they almost always had the solution right in their hands (and heads), but just needed someone to give them the space and encouragement to find it and a way to express it. I remember sitting in long meetings, where a manager had raised some issue that needed to be resolved for a program to meet the needs of its staff or clients. Staff would sometimes become so focused on detailing all the particulars of the issue they would forget that the whole point of raising the issue was to try to work together to find a solution. Meetings that ended this way would often leave everyone in attendance frustrated and discouraged as they left. Only when the focus shifted to solutions, by disallowing further discussion of the problem itself, was there a realistic possibility of building a collaborative approach to solving the problem.

How does this apply to therapy then? In every single session, with every single client, I ask myself, do I have enough information from my client to suggest shifting to a focus on solutions? Are we getting stuck in the problem? Sometimes the answer is that we need more time focusing on the problem. Sometimes, even when we decide its time to think about solutions, we have to go back to the problem for a while. That's just fine. We can do that and still be productive. The point is this, if our whole point in talking about the problem is to find a solution, then we cannot be wasting our time. We will eventually be successful together.

Does this mean that talking about issues itself is not helpful? No, it doesn't. The expression of feelings, the re-telling of the story so that it makes more sense, finding lost memories, re-directing shame outward, or guilt inward, shoving off of useless and painful self-blame, and yes even taking of responsibilities for our own behavior, all of this is a helpful part of talking about our issues. If directed properly, kindly, without judgment, and with care, concern, and attention, the telling itself becomes part of the solution. And as long as resolving the issue is the primary point of the discussion, no matter how the solution comes, we will have success in our therapy work. I want for all of my clients to use this approach, solutions not problems, continuously and always after they are done in therapy.

THE FOREST AND THE TREES

At a holiday party a few years ago, everyone was asked to dress as an archetype (Wikipedia has a good entry on "archetype:" http://en.wikipedia.org/wiki/Archetype). I came as a modern twist on the archetype of "The Wanderer," best personified by the character Odysseus in the Homeric epic, *The Odyssey*. My modern twist proposed that today, we would not see Odysseus as a lost king without a kingdom (in the original story from about 3,000 years ago, Odysseus got lost on his way home from the Trojan War and his army was essentially killed off on the way). Today, Odysseus, the Wanderer, might best be personified as a hobo, someone riding the rails, lurking on the edge of communities always on the outside looking in.

Part of our job to get ready for the party was also to come up with a short statement that captured the idea of the archetype. This is what I wrote: "*I get lost in the forest, when I am surrounded by all the trees. I move around; move away from the trees, so I can see the whole forest, and see myself too.*"

The wanderer lives this way—lives outside the forest, never really entering to be with the trees (us). Why? Maybe because he or she cannot find a way to stay connected to the community, to a steady life, to a fixed location. Maybe because he is schizophrenic. Maybe because he is resigned to a place of not belonging. In the mental health community, this might be called dissociative. The condition of "dissociative identity disorder" can be a devastating handicap. It sometimes arises as the result of deep, long-lasting, inescapable trauma, especially childhood trauma. In a less pronounced way, living outside the forest can also be a sign of attachment issues, which can result in a perpetual state of detachment. This might be the result of abandonment or severe neglect at a very young age. In these cases, a person may not be able to experience living in the forest. Or, they may simply find it unbearable to live in the forest, so they live alone, detached, isolated, and in that way, as comfortable as they can manage to be.

I know from personal experience the distinction between using this capacity to dissociate (leave the forest) as a tool versus letting it control you, keep you separate, isolated, lonely, detached and disconnected. As a child suffering near-daily beatings for years on end, I had to find a way to survive. I hid. I couldn't hide in a room. My father would find me. I couldn't hide behind anyone. No one was big enough for many years to stand up to him. So, how did I hide? I hid within myself. I removed my sense of "being" from the experience of being beat. I became so good at it, I made the decision to no longer let my father make me cry. So, I didn't cry. No matter what he did to me. I cried later, after crawling off to my bed. In this way, surprisingly, I managed to keep my dignity, my sense of self, of wholeness, without allowing these experiences to crush me or fragment my personality.

Dissociation from my father beating me was a very effective tool to survive with my sanity. Later in life, though, I continued to rely on dissociation to my detriment—when it wasn't necessary, and became harmful to me and my relationships. I also see this problem in many of my clients who have suffered from their own kinds of trauma. Women who had to dissociate from the experience of rape as children continue to dissociate during sex with the adult partners they love knowing that continued dissociation from them is destroying their relationship. They don't know how to stay in the forest and enjoy the intimacy of their relationships. Intimacy sends them running out of the forest, every time.

In my therapy work, I try to glide back and forth into and out of the forest with clients; and in the process, help them do the same thing in their lives. I try to imagine as best as possible what it would be like to experience what they experience, how it would be to have a certain memory, or dream, or be a participant in a fight with their spouse. I then ask them to step back with me and take a look at how their experience is affected by time, age, circumstance, history, and the constantly evolving nature of their relationships with friends, family and other contacts. We move back and forth together.

I advocate leaving the forest whenever possible, if even just for a moment, as long as it doesn't simply become an escape hatch from difficult situations or experiences. It is a tool, but it is not a place to be. We must live in the forest, where we remain connected to others. It is our natural state to be connected. We leave the forest for only just a little while and then must come back into it, to be mentally healthy, whole, and happy. The main benefit of removing ourselves from a situation is that we can then "see ourselves in it," in the situation. This allows us to see how we act with others and how they act with us. We can more easily take responsibility for our actions and decisions. We can more easily hold others responsible for their actions and decisions. We can see ourselves as separate from others so we can maintain good boundaries, not allowing ourselves to simply react, but be more proactive.

Some clients have trouble ever leaving the forest, responding to one thing at a time, lost in the maze of their lives because they cannot plan beyond the current set of seemingly overwhelming issues. Some clients leave the forest as an escape, by using alcohol or drugs, or something else that will numb them. This doesn't actually help them leave the forest even though it might feel that way. It is more like going to sleep in the forest. You wake up just as lost as when you started drinking or getting high. Some clients cannot seem to find a place to be in the forest—they can't "get in." These clients are often surprised when I tell them that in one sense, their capacity to be dissociated can be a real tool for healing and improving their lives. They are essentially "too good" at leaving the forest, and leave it when they might be better off staying. But, at least they know how to leave the forest, which means they can more easily see themselves as they are when they are in the forest. They can step back from their relationships and situations more easily, if also too easily.

Perhaps I do what I do as a therapist because I started out living most of my childhood outside the forest, and have had to learn how to live in the forest. So, I am a kind of wanderer now with my clients —wandering in and out of their lives, as I have done with my own life, helping them along the way to learn either how to leave the forest if that's what's needed for that client, or helping them find a place within the forest to live if that is what that client needs.

As is the case with many mental health issues, balance is essential to be able to leave the forest by removing ourselves mentally from a situation when necessary while living in the forest and staying connected most of the time. This is a balance between two different ways of being, of seeing, of responding in the moment to the always changing, ever unpredictable, and yet hopefully also engaging relationships we maintain in our lives.

THE DEA AND CIA:
MAKING A LIFE PLAN
STARTING WITH YOURSELF

If you make a plan about where you want your life to go and then you make all your decisions based on following that plan, your life will take the direction you want it to take and in the process you will become a better person for it. I know this sounds simple. And it is not a very complicated idea. But that doesn't mean it's easy.

DEA, Decide Every Action. Before you do anything in your life, ask yourself this: does what I am thinking about doing right at this moment fit into my life plan? Obviously, to do this, you need a life plan. A life plan can include employment goals, educational goals, family goals, or goals for your personal growth. Have goals. Know you can reach them, and know that in order to reach them, you have to make good decisions, how to not continue to make bad decisions, decisions which help you along the way toward your goals. How do you do that?

CIA, Consequences, Intent, Act. When you are trying to decide whether to do something in your life, anything, if you think about these three things, C.I.A., you *will* make better decisions for yourself. If you have a life plan, a set of goals for yourself, then when it comes to your daily life, you can ask yourself the following three questions to decide whether what you want to do is what you should do.

- **Question 1**: Does this thing I want to do have *consequences* that will take me away from the direction of my goals, or get me further toward my goals?

- **Question 2**: Is this thing I want to do something I really want to do, am I thinking about it really, what is my reason for wanting to do it, what is my *intent*?

201

- **Question 3**: Does the *act* itself, the thing I want to do right now, does it feel like the wrong thing to do? If it does, don't do it.

Example from your life (maybe): You're at home. Your life plan is to go back to school, get a college degree, a good office job. On your way to the convenience store for milk and bread, you run into a couple of old friends. Good guys, but you used to drink or do drugs with them. They want you to hang out. You have to decide: stick around, hang out, maybe get high. No big deal. Decide. Consequence: cops pull up, tag you for use, or worse. Get high, or drink, then the downward spiral, life plan a distant memory, again. Intent: you didn't intend this at all. You were here to get milk and bread, that's all. Act: if you stick around, you're back to old patterns. Doesn't feel right. You say thanks, tell them you need to go, get your milk and bread, head back to your place. Stay on course.

Sounds easy. It's not. I am not pretending it is. You will make mistakes along the way. We all do. I certainly have. If you follow these simple ideas—DEA and CIA, Decide Every Act, and Consequences, Intent, Act—your life will take the direction you want it to, not the direction others make for you (like old friends down at the convenience store). If you make a mistake, if you did hang out with those guys at the convenience store, got drunk or high. Later, think about it. Think about the consequences, the intent, the act, why and how you decided to stick around. Don't make that mistake again. Learn from your mistakes, review your decisions after you've made them, and maybe next time, you'll find a different store to get milk. Maybe you'll decide its time to move somewhere else, where it will be easier to avoid old friends with bad habits, so you can follow your life plan more easily.

THINKING IN THIRDS

A common problem that leads people to therapy is a recurring pattern of self-destructive behaviors in response to complex situations. The issue and the nature of the relationship can vary widely, even though the pattern itself is similar. The problem might be a marriage that seems to be falling apart, or losing a job, or not knowing how to help your spouse who is struggling with a drinking problem. So, what's the common pattern: "false dichotomies." What do I mean by that? I mean the incorrect or false belief that there are two and only two solutions to a problem. The belief is false when there are actually more than two solutions to a problem or more than two ways of seeing a situation. And there almost always more than two possible solutions to a problem, so the dichotomy approach is almost never a good approach. Therapists will sometimes call this pattern "splitting." It's "either/or" but not "both." This is actually not what I mean, or at least it's not all that I mean. Let me explain.

"Splitting" happens when someone believes they have to make a choice between two extremes. A good example, and one which is currently used in the common language of therapy, is the "fight or flight response." This is also called the "wounded animal" response, and seems to be tied to the limbic system in our brain. I've also heard this response referred to as our "reptilian response," because it is viewed as simplistic and primitive, occurring at the base of our brain, rather than at the top. Sometimes, this knee-jerk or immediate response is the best quick solution to a particular situation. Sometimes, an extreme situation calls for an extreme response. The "fight or flight" response becomes a problem when the situation doesn't call for it, which is often the case. When we respond with fight or flight, we often make the situation worse—we escalate it when we choose fight, or we fail to resolve it when we choose flight. Resolution of the immediate problem might call for a third solution, something other than either fight or flight, do or don't, right or wrong, etc. This is what I mean by "thinking in thirds."

Before explaining, "thinking in thirds," I want to spend a minute distinguishing between "splitting" and "false dichotomies." Splitting can be a kind of false dichotomy, but not all false dichotomies amount to splitting. The reason? Sometimes a solution is neither one thing, the other, or both. Sometimes a solution calls for something completely different than either of the two proposed for splitting. In the fight or flight response, which is a kind of a splitting, a "both" or "and" solution would be to not leave and not fight. That can be a good solution, but might not be. Thinking in thirds allows for the possibility of not restricting yourself to some combination of the two choices in splitting.

When I am in a therapy session with a client who seems to be dealing with a situation by creating a false dichotomy, I will often draw a simple table on my whiteboard. I will draw two columns with their two proposed ways of seeing the problem or the two proposed solutions. We will look at the pros and cons of each column. Then, I will draw a third column on the whiteboard with nothing in it but a question mark.

Solution 1		Solution 2		?	
(either) (black)		(or) (white)		Solutions 3, 4, 5,... (and/other) (gray/blue)	
Pros	Cons	Pros	Cons	Pros	Cons

Like I said, the third solution might be some combination of solution 1 or 2, or it might be something completely unrelated, but not considered before. My reason for drawing this table can be a "solution-focused" approach, in which I am just trying to help a client sort out the best way to solve a problem. Mostly, though, I view it as an "experiential" exercise in which I am really trying to help the client see their limited response to the situation in a completely new way, which can open up all kinds of solutions or responses never previously considered.

Let me offer an example that's come up a number of times in slightly different ways. I am meeting with the spouse of someone with an alcohol or drug addiction that has come to the point of necessitating a choice between continuing to care for him or her or asking them to leave. See the either/or here? Stay or leave. Care for spouse to my own detriment or abandon them to the street. Extreme solution vs. extreme solution. Now they stay or they leave and never come back. This is not a problem simply because it ignores other possibilities. It is often mostly a problem because it forces you to choose a bad solution to avoid an even worse solution. A client may come to see me after enabling a mostly out of control spouse for years on end, thinking that their only other choice is to abandon them to the streets. What choice is that? They can't do that to their spouse, the parent of their children, can they? Think in thirds!

If that client can bring themselves to see another option, a third option, it doesn't have to be so dire one way or another. The problem may be extreme—he is killing himself with alcohol by destroying his liver, but that doesn't mean there are only two choices left. Think of the parable of the Prodigal Son. The father could not allow the son to behave irresponsibly at their home, and involve the entire family in his misguided behavior. So, the son left. Father had two choices right? Son can stay, or be gone? No. Think in thirds. What's the third solution? The father allowed the son to chart his own course and leave, but he didn't have to be gone forever, his son was welcome to come back if ever the son decided to change his behavior. So, the client whose spouse is drinking himself to death can tell her spouse, "You cannot stay here and do this anymore, you need to leave, but if you go to treatment, if you get sober, you may be able to come back." I would not recommend that my client wait forever, but if the client was still able to see a possible future with the spouse when sober, then this third alternative is readily available. This doesn't mean it's easy, especially if you believe the spouse is not likely to make the choice to be sober. But that's their choice, not yours, and it frees the client from the awful, but false, dichotomy of choosing between the two extremes of enabling vs. abandonment.

Thinking in thirds can be used as a way of seeing many different kinds of problems in an entirely new way. I suppose it's a more specific way of "thinking outside the box." It is more particular because it is a way of thinking about the particular problem we often create by thinking in twos. Once you leave that box, you can then come up with a third, a fourth, a fifth solution, and so on. Once you leave the trap of false dichotomizing a situation, new ways of seeing that situation really open up.

TRANSPARENCY

I love words. In the context of therapy, I especially love words that capture ways of being. Transparency is a great word because it so aptly describes a way to be with others that tells others what is happening within you as part of whatever else you are communicating to them. Transparency seems so beneficial; it's hard to imagine when it is not a good idea to be transparent (there are a few times actually).

Think of the word "transparent" and what it literally means (outside of using it as a way to describe being clear to others). The word-processing program I am using defines "transparent" as "see-through" or "crystal clear." A window is "transparent" because you can "see through" it. The opposite of transparent is "opaque" (not "see through"). If a window is transparent, a block of wood is opaque.

Why would we want to be transparent with others, to let others "see through" (into) us? The quickest answer is that if you can be transparent you are far more likely to have your stated needs and wants understood in a way that will result in a greater chance of getting those needs or wants met. The more transparent you can be, the more likely there will be no misunderstandings between you and whomever you are communicating with. This is at least true in personal relationships. A side effect of transparency (within limits) is that it also encourages you to stay on top of being responsible for what you want, to ensure you are not playing games with others or yourself. Also, if you state your needs with transparency, and your needs are not met or recognized, you can be more confident that the other person didn't decide not to meet your needs due to some misunderstanding. They more likely understood you perfectly clearly, but decided for their own reasons your needs were not something they could or wanted to meet.

If it is such a good idea to be "transparent" with others, then why is it something we have to try to do, why doesn't it just happen all the time? Balance, as usual. The world is not black and white. The world has much grey in it, and many shades of grey. There is not just "transparent" and "opaque." There are "filters." We have to use filters to some extent to control the transparency of what we communicate. We do this to avoid giving more information about ourselves than we think we should, to protect ourselves from undue vulnerability, and to protect others from information they don't need, or want, or care about, and might actually not want to know.

My boss (when I had one) didn't (usually) want to know how I was feeling about my personal life. So, when she gave me a deadline for a task, she wanted to know if I could get it done on time, but not how staying late might affect my marriage (semi-transparent). When the grocery store cashier asks, "How's it going?" he only wants to hear "Fine, good, great, etc." (semi-opaque). He is saying "I see you there, am acknowledging you, asking you to recognize this, and let's just leave it at that..." A perfectly fine use of filters is to control transparency to the extent appropriate for that circumstance. When a good friend uses this same filter, you will probably feel hurt, for good reason. A friend should actually care how you are doing, not just be going through the motions like a cashier. Filters are very context specific. Using the right filter in the wrong context can be troublesome. I think we've all been there, maybe on both sides.

This filtering is necessary out in the public sphere, but that seems obvious, so let's get back to how transparency can help us improve our mental health and our personal relationships. A techno-synonym for transparency is "WYSIWYG" (what-you-see-is-what-you-get). I discussed this idea in the chapter "Authenticity." Authenticity is necessary for transparency. You cannot let others "see through" the filters you use to keep yourself hidden from others unless you know those filters, and what lies behind them (your inner self). The process goes like this (in this order):

1. Know yourself (self-aware);
2. Be yourself (authentic);
3. Let others see you (transparent).

Based on this three-step process, being truly transparent cannot happen unless you have a good level of self-awareness and have practice at being the person you have come to know yourself to be when you are around others. Once you have a good handle on these two parts of the process, you'll be ready to be more transparent (and know you are being transparent).

I'm not trying to make it sound simple, because it isn't. I could also add intermediate steps. Part of knowing yourself is getting to the heart of the things about yourself you most fear, including shame, guilt, inadequacies, anxiety, depressive triggers, anger, childhood crap, maybe the whole enchilada of therapy issues you might have within you (we could call this Part "1(a)"). Then there is taking responsibility for what you want as part of knowing what you want, so you can let others know why you believe what you want is valid and important (we could call this part "2(a)"). The process toward "authentic transparency" (being transparent because you decided to as part of who you are) is complicated, long, and sometimes very difficult, but it is achievable.

Moving now from the more abstract and theoretical to real-life, let's get to what transparency actually "looks like" (how's that for a therapy-talk). A client, we'll call him Jack this time, wants to tell Tracy, his wife, he wants to make a career change. Sounds good. The problem is Jack gets really angry and defensive whenever they've tried to discuss it. He doesn't know why. We explore his reactions in detail. As soon as Tracy begins to call Jack's logic into question, he either shuts down and walks away, leaving the discussion for another day, or he fumes, cuts her off, criticizes her points even when some of them are valid. Okay, we explore how Jack feels about their interaction about this issue when they are not discussing this issue. Jack tells me he believes she will never approve his desire to make a career change because he makes good money now and they cannot afford the risk of loss of income, even temporarily. Before Jack even starts a conversation with Tracy, he feels vulnerable, invalidated, even a little guilty for even considering giving up his current good job for the unknown of a career change.

This is Jack not being transparent with Tracy: "Okay, so I just want to say again that I've been thinking it is time for me to make a move to doing something different." Jack is telling Tracy what he wants, she can see from the outside (she is outside of Jack because only Jack is on the "inside" of Jack). Hearing this, Tracy says, with some level of frustration "We've been through this, Jack, why do you keep bringing it up?" Jack walks away, or it continues on the upward spiral it did before.

This is Jack being transparent with Tracy: "So, I want to talk about making a career change again. Before we talk about it though, I want you to know that I am afraid to bring it up because I don't want either of us to get mad. I am also aware that I have responsibilities to you and the kids to help provide a good income for the family and so I feel defensive about even thinking about it, but it is important to me and I want to figure out a way to talk about it that will not result in me being angry or you criticizing me for wanting to do something different in my work-life." This is transparency. This is Jack telling Tracy, not only what he wants (a job change), but what is going on emotionally within him that motivates his communication with her (why he wants what he wants and how he feels about talking to her about it).

Obviously the language Jack uses is contrived, and not likely to be that well-rehearsed in the real world, but that's okay. It doesn't need to be so "marriage-counsel-y" to work. The basic concept is simply to make choices about how much you want to share with someone about what is happening within you, what you are feeling, thinking, experiencing, as the basis of what you want from them. In therapy, I do this all the time, many times a day. I can't stand the thought of "playing games" with therapy clients by telling a client one thing, but internally having in mind something much different. So, I use transparency to tell them why I am asking a question in addition to actually asking the question.

This reminds me of a funny story (funny to me anyway) about the opposite of transparency: (what-you-see-is-*not*-what-you-get). I guess that would be "WYSINWYG." A long time ago, I was applying for a job as a lawyer. The firm liked me, wanted to hire me, and made me a "conditional offer of employment" contingent on meeting with a psychologist they'd hired to screen candidates. Weird, but okay, I'll meet the guy. They sent me a packet of questionnaires to fill out for the meeting. I fill it all out. It's aptitude kind of stuff, with some personality tests thrown in too. At the meeting, the guy asks me a question that is identical to a question I answered on the forms I just gave him. I tell him this. He knows. He asks me to answer the question anyway. I do. He takes notes. Then he does it again. I tell him again. He says the same thing, says, "Please just answer the question." See where this is going? He wants to compare the answers I give "on the spot" to the "canned" answers I gave to the questionnaire to see if I am being consistent (think: honest). I ask him if this is what he is doing. He says no. I ask, then, why is he doing this? He says, "It's just part of the process" (as if that somehow even remotely answers my question). I tell him to stop, I am not willing to answer any more questions already answered on the form. I tell him I am offended and feel like he is playing a game with me, questioning my personal integrity (this is me being transparent). He gets mad. I've given him a chance to tell me why my suspicions of what he is doing are wrong. He doesn't. Oh well. He moves on. All of a sudden, he stops, taps his watch, tells me it's not working, and asks me if I know what time it is (I wasn't wearing a watch, but had one in my briefcase). I don't believe him. I ask him to show me his watch, so I can see for myself if it is working. He becomes defensive, won't do it, and asks if I think he is lying. I do, but giving him the benefit of the doubt, I tell him he can prove very easily he is not lying by showing me his watch. He refuses. Interview over. I'm done with this guy and his process. No transparency. I walk out. I didn't get the job (thank heaven).

This story illustrates the very worst of being "opaque," of trying to "appear" one way (just part of the interview, very professional, etc.) while being another (playing games with me to see if he could "trick" me into answering questions in some way that I didn't intend). You can also see how much I do not like it when someone else does this to me, which is why I try as hard as I can not to do this kind of thing with my clients in therapy, and why I welcome when clients ask me why I am asking them some question—it gives me the chance to be more transparent, by letting them "see through" my question into some part of myself that thought to ask the question. Sometimes, too, when I explain why I am asking a question, a client will report that my question is based on a false assumption, which gives me the opportunity to check myself and ask a different question or explore why I've made a false assumption.

Before I finish this discussion of transparency, I want to briefly address a great question someone recently asked about the relationship between transparency and vulnerability. I think vulnerability amounts to letting yourself be emotionally open and available with someone else. You become vulnerable because you take the risk that the other person will not respond to your openness by being open themselves with you. Transparency, in allowing someone else to "see through" your filters, seems like it must be a part of being vulnerable. In other words, it doesn't seem like you can be vulnerable, without being at least somewhat transparent. However, I don't think being transparent necessarily leads to being more vulnerable in many situations. When Jack told Tracy how he felt about talking about a career change, he may in fact have felt less vulnerable to her criticisms because, by telling her, he was creating emotionally protective space for himself and also giving himself permission to have his feelings. When I told the psychologist I felt offended by his methods, I wasn't more vulnerable. I didn't want to be more vulnerable.

Vulnerability is a good thing, in the right context (when it feels safe enough). Taking the risk of being hurt by making yourself emotionally available with the right person can be a great way to improve relationships and make yourself stronger in many ways. It is also the only way to achieve genuine intimacy with others. Vulnerability as a way to reach intimacy and personal growth is also something I previously discussed in much more detail in "To the weak, I became weak." The point here is that transparency is possible even when you don't want to be vulnerable, but vulnerability always requires some level of genuine transparency.

HAPPINESS IS A SIDE EFFECT OF MEANING

Trying to be happy by searching directly for happiness is like trying to catch water in your hands. That kind of happiness is short-lived, and runs out quickly. We need meaning to sustain happiness. Meaning is the cup that holds happiness, so it can be found again and again, even after it is lost temporarily.

People who search for happiness quickly, directly, sometimes end up using drugs, drinking, gambling, finding happiness in relationships or sex, but the "happy time" always fades, and often leads to a feeling of emptiness later, or worse. A person trying to find happiness might be doing so to avoid unhappiness. Avoiding unhappiness usually involves desperate attempts at avoiding ourselves. This is why those who are trying to avoid unhappiness look for "happiness" in things other than themselves (drugs, alcohol, other people, a new place to live, etc.).

During the goal setting phase of therapy (usually around the third or fourth session), when I once asked a client what she wanted most from therapy, she said, "I want you to help me be more happy." Without meaning to be flippant, I said, "I don't really *do happiness*." I explained some of what I am saying here, that in therapy, people don't "find happiness." Instead, they often find barriers to happiness and remove them (e.g. depression, anxiety, unresolved issues from the past), or they find the reasons happiness has escaped them—which is typically the result of lack of meaning in their lives. I told her I wanted to help her locate her own barriers to happiness, which would probably end up being some ways in which she is prevented from finding or recognizing meaning that already exists in her life, and finding new ways to create meaning in her life. In other words, I suggested she give up trying to "find happiness" and instead try to find meaning, and happiness would come. This is exactly what we did in later sessions.

The things we do that have meaning for us are not always things we enjoy in the moment. We do not enjoy cleaning up after a sick child vomits in the middle of the night, but there is meaning in it, which we recognize later on when they lie back in bed, asleep, feeling a little better, and later when they are in a play at school and feel really good about their performance and we feel good as their parent. We do not enjoy arguing with our partner over finances due to our entangled lives, but we do enjoy coming around the corner together on a walk in the evening when we both spot a cardinal whistling in the tree, and this shared moment means much more than it could have meant if we'd been alone or with someone we barely new, barely shared our lives.

In fact, it is meaning in the things we do which make the things we do not like to do worth doing. Without meaning, those chores that we do not like can fill our consciousness with negativity because there doesn't seem to be a "good reason" for having to do them. This is something often experienced as the emptiness of a life without adequate meaning.

Sustained happiness *is a side effect of meaning*. Happiness is not usually something that can be found or maintained by searching directly for it. Instead, we need to search for meaning, and then happiness will come as the result of personal reward, accomplishment, improved sense of identity and self-worth, enjoyment of our contribution to such things as our children, our creative outlets, our communities, social justice, a created purpose to our lives. Instead of looking for happiness, as the client above had been trying to do, if we look for meaning, we will find happiness along the way, intermittently perhaps, but we will also be able to fill that feeling of emptiness, which is so often the cause of unnecessary unhappiness. Instead of running from unhappiness, we will be walking toward meaning, leaving unhappiness behind, while slowly, and surely, finding happiness again and again.

What is "meaning?" Meaning is what matters to us. Meaning is what we think, decide, or believe is important. Meaning gives reason to what we do and why we do it, why it is important, why it matters what we do. "Meaning" and "purpose" are not necessarily the same thing. I will discuss the differences between meaning and purpose in the next chapter.

MEANING AND PURPOSE WITHOUT LIMITS

In the last chapter, I defined the concept of "meaning" in its simplest form as "what is important to us." Sometimes people define meaning and purpose as the same thing. They can be the same thing, but are not necessarily. It depends on how you look at things. The way some people define purpose can be limiting, and I do not want to define meaning as a limiting thing, so I want to make a distinction between meaning and that idea of purpose.

When people refer to the "purpose" for their life, they might be talking about finding some pre-ordained or pre-existing reason they are alive, or the notion that they are alive for some purpose and they need to find out what that purpose is; they might be saying "there must be some reason I am on this planet...." This is not what I am talking about when I talk about meaning. I make no assumptions either way about some kind of pre-ordained purpose. It's possible that there is some purpose for my life or someone else's life, which was decided before each of us was even born. I can't pretend to know about these kinds of things. But that's not the point of my focus on meaning. If purpose is decided for us, meaning is something completely different. We decide meaning. We find and create meaning in our lives. We decide why things matter to us, and we search for those things we want to matter to us. We even change our minds about meaning.

Something that might have meant a lot to me when I was still a lawyer (winning) doesn't matter so much to me now that I am no longer involved in fighting for other people in litigation. I didn't want the idea of "winning" to matter to me so much anymore. Instead, I wanted to be able to help people more. So, I quit practicing law and went back to school to become a therapist. When we live by a search for meaning, we make individual and collective decisions about our values, what is important to us, and then we try to live by those values. In doing so, we find the rewards of having true personalized meaning in our lives—things worth pursuing and doing, if not in the moment, then at least over time. When we search for meaning in our lives, our lives begin to change, and so do we.

When people search for "their purpose in life," they can end up deciding that some other person or group, a church, a parent, a trusted mentor, can help them determine why they are alive. I am suggesting that instead we need to turn inward, not to someone else. Others can help us find meaning within us, but need not limit the search by a confining definition of purpose. Meaning is something we are free to decide, not something that is already decided for us. We have free will. We decide what matters, and we re-make that decision as often as we like. If we are honest with ourselves about it, we will also address the things we need to change to follow a course that has meaning for us, so we can get closer to our own ideals about how we should live our lives in the most meaningful way we can.

The way people sometimes define "purpose" can be very limiting —some one or some thing other than ourselves limits what makes our lives meaningful. This is why I prefer a pursuit of "meaning," rather than "purpose." With meaning, we are free to decide for ourselves why our lives are worth living, without having to adhere to or find some mysterious notion about why our lives have a point. If you believe you were created for a reason, that you are alive because there is a purpose, a plan, and your life is a part of it, I do not want to contradict you. That might be true for you, and I respect your beliefs.

I am suggesting that if you find meaning in your life, if you decide what is important to you, along the way, you might also find whatever purpose may have been set for you, but you won't be limited by someone else's ideas about what that purpose might be. If you search for meaning, instead of purpose, and you look inward for meaning, you will find your own purpose that is consistent with who you really are, rather than finding purpose based on what someone else thinks you should be. This is personal freedom. This is genuine personal exploration. This is the search for meaning. Meaning might even be said to be the purpose you create for yourself, for your life.

Much of the work I do with clients in therapy has to do with helping them break free of the idea that they have to look outside themselves to find purpose in their lives. By re-focusing their attention to creating meaning from within themselves, they begin to find balance, increased self-worth, the ability to accept themselves as they are rather than what someone else thought they "should" be, they are able to make more concrete goals, and find greater satisfaction in their lives. This is not always an easy task, and is often quite difficult, and yet from everything I have seen in my personal life and in working with clients, the search for meaning is always worth the effort. Give it a try. You might just find that happiness really is a side effect of meaning, but you won't know until you begin the search for meaning.

PART FIVE:

FAMILY AND RELATIONSHIP ISSUES

When I was thinking about what kind of therapist I wanted to be (e.g. psychologist, clinical social worker, professional counselor, or marriage and family therapist), I chose the route of marriage and family therapist because it made sense to me that whatever mental health issues people might be having are either directly related to how well their relationships function in their personal lives, or their mental health issues are either made worse or better depending on the status of their important relationships. Having decided to become a licensed marriage and family therapist, it's not too surprising that many of my clients seek me out to help them with problems in their family and other personal relationships.

I could easily say that every chapter in this book is somehow related to problems we might be having in relationships, or that part of the solution to those problems identified in the chapters reside in reaching out for support or change in our relationships. However, the chapters in this part of the book are intended to specifically address particular kinds of relationship issues clients bring to therapy.

GESTALT PRAYER BY FRITZ PERLS

Before writing this little chapter, I visited with my mother for a few hours, showing her a bit about how to use the Internet beyond email. She recited a line from a poem to offer some insight into a relationship issue we were discussing. She only knew one line, but didn't know the rest of the poem, or who wrote it. So, I showed her how to "Google" it (typing the entire line inside quotes in her Google search box). It turns out, a famous psychotherapist wrote the poem back in the 1960s. It also turns out that the little "prayer" sums up pretty well the basic attitude underlying many of the chapters in this book (see the chapters on "Expectations and Resentment," "Authenticity," "Anxiety," "Boundaries," and "Selfishness and Love.") If you read the poem (below) and you read those chapters, you'll see what I mean.

Here's the Poem:

"I do my thing and you do your thing.
I am not in this world to live up to your expectations,
and you are not in this world to live up to mine.
You are you, and I am I, and if by chance we find each other, it's
beautiful. If not, it can't be helped."

(Fritz Perls, 1969)

BOUNDARIES

I can safely say nearly all of my clients have issues that would be far less important to their daily feelings of well-being if they were able to establish more consistent and healthy boundaries with the people they are close to in their lives. What do I mean by "healthy" boundaries? Boundaries in which you are able to ask for and get what you need, without feeling like you are compromising your independence or asking someone else to compromise their independence.

Boundaries are like walls. Walls are both necessary and can be problematic. We need walls for our personal identities to stay intact. We need walls to filter out how others interact with us and how we decide to interact with them. A person with a healthy personality makes good decisions about when to use walls as needed, and let them down when that is most beneficial.

IT ALL COMES DOWN TO SELF-RESPECT

In the chapter, "Selfishness and Love," I proposed the idea that we are inherently selfish, but in a good way, because we learn how to love others by recognizing what it is like when we love ourselves. I've never really veered from this view. In fact, over the past few years since I wrote that chapter, which actually started as answers given in an interview in a state prison newsletter, my understanding of the importance of being "selfish" (treating ourselves with "self-love") has grown as I have watched therapy clients discover how to apply this frame of reference to exit the problems in their lives.

Now, my default starting position with nearly all therapy issues is to ask, "Is there self-respect in this, or is self-respect absent, diminished, discounted, or hidden from the client's view of things?" Note, this is a starting position, which means that it might not go anywhere, might not be the main problem, might not be the problem at all. However, I believe it is very important to eliminate this as an issue, because it so often is a primary part of a client's problem, almost regardless of the nature, the history, or the cause of the problem. More importantly, it is a part of the problem that so often goes unrecognized, and is very, very difficult to identify and then solve—because it is so deeply embedded in a person's outlook on life and their perception of themselves.

This is all pretty vague, so far, I know. In order to really understand what I am talking about here, you'd need to know how I define "self-respect," and how it relates to therapy and therapy issues clients confront. I'll start by defining self-respect as I am using the term, and along the way try to give some examples of the myriad ways it comes up in therapy.

The issue of self-respect came up directly in a therapy session with a client who'd been trying to figure out the limits of what he should tolerate in a long-term relationship he found dissatisfying, and which seemed to make his therapeutic issues (depression, isolation, low self-worth, etc.) worse. The connection between his relationship issues and his depression seemed plausible. I asked him, "What is self-respect?" Surprised (we hadn't been using that term at all up until I asked the question), he thought about it for a while in silence. Then, he said, "I think self-respect is a very basic, very deep level of acceptance of who you are." I told him, "Nice!" During the ensuing conversation about how his own growing self-respect in his course of therapy might be pushing up against the limits of what he was willing to tolerate in a relationship, he wanted to know how to convey the issue to his partner. I began thinking of the scene in the movie The Ten Commandments when Moses (Charlton Heston) is talking to God, as the burning bush on Mount Ararat, and he asks God (something like), "When I go down to Israel, whom shall I say sent me to do your bidding?" and God said (here's the important part): "Tell them, I AM THAT I AM!" Doesn't this sound like a really great version of a basic and deeply felt acceptance of who we are? In other words, God was saying he didn't need any introduction, any justification, he just is. In some ways, while we are not God, this is no less true of every one of us. In some ways, we just are, and that should be all that need be understood, expected, accepted.

It has a nice ring to it: "I am that I am." You can say it about yourself, anytime, anywhere (okay, maybe not out loud in public, unless you are with friends who know you have read this book). I think it really does apply to all of us. At some level, we shouldn't need to justify being treated with respect, to be heard, to be free from oppression, abuse, or neglect, to be treated with acceptance for some basic level of humanity. The founding words of our nation note this idea. The Declaration of Independence says: "We hold these truths to be self-evident, that all men are created equal, that they are endowed by their Creator with certain unalienable Rights, that among these are Life, Liberty and the pursuit of Happiness." Isn't this just another way of saying we all deserve to be accepted for who we are at some basic level? Should we ever feel we deserve less than this? If we do forget about this basic level of self-respect, or even worse, we intentionally put it aside in order to maintain a relationship, a job, or a way to live our lives (e.g. with addiction, abuse, co-dependency, etc.), isn't it likely we will suffer serious emotional and psychological consequences? Of course it is.

In therapy sessions with clients, I often repeat the refrain, "I don't give advice because I don't have to live with the consequences of being wrong, but you would" (and then contradict myself by listing the specific situations in which I do give advice—when someone is in danger of harm, self-harm or when children are in danger). In my writings, I suppose I can give myself a little more flexibility. So, I will take the rare step of offering this advice here: whatever your life's problems might be, a good starting point might be to ask yourself, are my problems at least partially the result of failing to act with self-respect? Have I put aside self-respect? Have I asserted myself as deserving a very basic level of complete acceptance for who I am? If the answer is no, you have in hand at least a beginning to a solution.

Find your self-respect. Listen to it. Try to act in accordance with it, and hopefully, even if that means you need to reach out to others to help you along the way, you will be on the right track to finding your way out of your troubles.

Depression is often the result of denying your basic sense of power in your life. I covered this feature of depression in the chapter, "Depression and Anxiety, flip sides of the same coin." We often suffer from guilt that has little to do with our sense of right and wrong, and might even contradict it. I covered this in the chapter, "Choose your guilt." We stay in destructive relationships because we do not accept that we deserve better, or we think we have to pay more attention to someone else's needs to justify meeting our own needs. I cover this in my next chapter, "Co-dependency, a way out." These and so many other therapy issues are the result of neglecting self-respect. Find self-respect, and you begin to find ways out of these difficult life situations. Stay in these situations, and your self-respect will become further hidden, ignored, abandoned. This is why, so often, it all comes down to self-respect.

CO-DEPENDENCY: A WAY OUT

Co-dependency has a language all its own. For a couple of decades we've associated the term co-dependent with someone who becomes so involved with another person's problem they cannot seem to be okay unless the other person is okay. This is particularly troublesome in most cases because the other person, who might be an alcoholic, a gambling addict, or who has some other serious issue, is definitely not okay, which by the terms above, means that the co-dependent person is not okay, constantly worried, feeling guilty, preoccupied by the welfare of the other person, paying little attention to their own well-being.

This is pretty similar to how I think about co-dependency, but only at first. The striking thing about this description is that it makes us feel sorry for the co-dependent, and blame the person about whom their co-dependence is related for not getting better, so the co-dependent has to stay co-dependent—if only that drunk would get sober, his wife could stop fretting over him. Again, there's truth in this sentiment. But it doesn't quite hit the mark. That's not the only problem with this description, or the worst part. The biggest problem is that, if this were a complete description of the problem of co-dependency it would mean the co-dependent person is pretty much stuck with a bad situation unless the other person gets better. Of course, this is not true at all. A person stuck in co-dependency is free to leave any time they want to leave. So then, why don't they leave, or at least stop their co-dependent behavior? If we can figure this out, then the co-dependent person might find it easier to leave or stop being co-dependent and negotiate a new kind of relationship. This is what we do in therapy. And this is the topic of this chapter.

The co-dependent person gets something out of being co-dependent: they get control. Specifically, they get to have some control over the "sick" person who is the target of their co-dependence. I am not suggesting the co-dependent person decides to become involved with someone with whom they can be co-dependent or that they make some kind of verbal, conscious deal with the other person. That would be ridiculous. But, just the same, they do seem to be involved in a kind of nonverbal, unspoken, but still very powerful bargain that keeps both people in the relationship, even when it is destructive to both.

Let's take the alcoholic couple as an example, since it is a version of co-dependency we are pretty familiar with, either personally or in the media. Although this is stereotyping, we'll use the example of an alcoholic husband and co-dependent (and not alcoholic) wife. We know, though, that this has many different varieties and versions, but it's just an example for this chapter, so please excuse the over-generalizations. Often, co-dependency is a very gradual, incremental, evolving thing. At first, they might be drinking together, having fun, going to parties, or drinking on the holidays, and weekends. But he drinks more often, and drinks more than she does when they both drink. Over the years, he moves from beer to vodka or whiskey, from light cocktails to stronger drinks. As his ability to meet his needs diminishes, she begins to meet his needs for him. He in turn becomes more dependent on her to meet those needs, especially if this is what is necessary for him to continue his (now addictive) relationship with alcohol. Without meaning to, she becomes more and more involved in "enabling" his continuing downward spiral with alcohol. By the same turn, in meeting more of his needs, she pays less and less attention to her own needs, and if there are children, less attention to their needs as well, just to keep the whole thing going. If the kids are old enough, mom even begins to ask the children to pitch in by helping her take care of their father's needs. Anything that disturbs his relationship with alcohol now becomes an issue that results in conflict—often ugly conflict. In fact, sometimes the conflict can involve abuse, maybe just verbal abuse, or in some cases physical abuse. The conflict can also involve something that feels even worse than abuse to the co-dependent person: the threat of abandonment, of being alone, of losing control over a relationship they have spent months or years of investment of their very selves, their identity, their lives.

At this point, the co-dependent person acts in a way that supports these two mistaken ideas:

1. His needs are more important than they really are;
2. My needs are not as important as they really are.

By overemphasizing his needs, and downplaying her own needs, all just to keep him as functional and "happy" as she thinks she can, she stays trapped in trying to control what she cannot control: his sense of well-being. More importantly, though, she gives up what she can control: her own sense of well-being, by meeting her own needs.

So, where does this get us? If this is a pretty common experience, a pretty common outcome of a co-dependent relationship, whether it is the man or the woman who drinks, or whether it's alcohol, or drugs, or a long-term illness, how can someone who suffers from the affects of co-dependency free themselves from it? The first step is to consider why they allowed themselves to become so dependent on someone else's needs to feel okay in the first place. If they can figure this out, they will often be in a much better position to reclaim what they gave up in order to become so focused on the other person. Almost always, in my experience as a therapist, this has something to do with a great need for approval, either because they suffer from a low self-worth, or there is a version of instability that they fear because it retriggers some kind of deep emotional experience they had earlier in their life.

This might explain why adult children of alcoholics sometimes, despite their best intentions, end up in long term relationships with alcoholics. They aren't merely mimicking their parents' decisions and behaviors. They might need to have such a great need to avoid abandonment or instability in their relationships, they unconsciously choose to be with someone who becomes "sick" so they can take care of them, which gives them control over maintaining the relationship. Put it this way, if you are with someone who is sick, who really needs you in order to function or be okay, then as long as you meet their needs, they are not likely to leave you, are they? Again, this isn't a conscious decision, but it's still a decision. No one is forced to choose to be in a long-term relationship with an alcoholic.

If a person who finds themselves in a co-dependent relationship can figure out the reason they were willing to make the compromise of giving up on their needs to focus on the other person's needs, what they were looking for as their part of the exchange, they will then be able to ask themselves if what they want is really worth the compromise they've made. If it is fear of abandonment, they can then learn to face that fear, with the help of friends, support groups, therapy, family, and other positive influences that will show them they will not be abandoned, but will still be loved by others, even if their relationship with their current partner ends. If it is the need for approval that was denied them as children, or in a previous relationship, they can seek that approval elsewhere, so it becomes less important to get the approval from their sick or needy partner.

While co-dependency can be a very unhealthy way to be in a relationship, it is also important to realize that not all dependency is unhealthy or co-dependency. In fact, all meaningful relationships include various levels of dependency, as they should. Hopefully, though, each person is dependent on the other, maybe not in the same way or for the same things, but with some level of mutuality. In other words, one person does not expect the other to meet all of their needs, or to ignore their own needs. One person does not expect that they will or should need to meet all the needs of the other. A healthy dependent relationship is one in which each person feels the capacity and the desire to meet their own needs, but sometimes with the help of others along the way. In this way, each person is responsible for their own needs, and therefore accountable for how they decide to meet (or not meet) their needs, without blaming others when their needs are not met. Healthy dependency also allows for independence, by encouraging each person to meet their needs in the way that suits them.

Co-dependent relationships often have a great deal of conflict if either person attempts to either meet their own needs, or meet their needs with the help of anyone outside the relationship. Independence does not tend to cause conflict in relationships with healthy dependency because neither person feels they have failed the other if the other person meets their own needs or seeks assistance in meeting their needs elsewhere (with obvious limitations like staying within the sexual boundaries of a committed relationship).

Choosing freedom from co-dependency can take months or years, and usually requires a deeper understanding of the source of the co-dependent person's need to control the other person's ability to leave them, to have the other person be so dependent on them. Once they begin to let go of that need, either because they have a higher self-esteem, greater support and approval elsewhere, or they have thoroughly rejected negative messages about themselves in the past about their capacity to have healthy relationships and stability in their lives, the compromise they make in giving up their own needs to meet the needs of another become far less satisfactory. Eventually, they no longer need to make that compromise at all, and find relationships in which their needs are just as important as the needs of the other people in their lives.

THE PROBLEM OF "SITUATIONAL IDENTITY"

At one point, I was trying to describe to a client an issue faced by many clients over the years, so I made up a new term for it: "situational identity." In a way, the term makes no sense. A person's "identity" can be defined as their "permanent sense of self." If something is "permanent," it must be independent of an isolated and temporary situation. So, situational identity is an oxymoron—it cannot exist because a true identity cannot be situational if it is permanent. Why create a term that by its own definition makes no sense? Because the problem clients bring into therapy that gave rise to this term also makes no logical sense, yet is a very real problem. Situational identity is often the root of the problem when someone is much more afraid of change in their lives than it seems they should be. In therapy, this can often lead to serious issues of anxiety and depression, and it can keep people stuck in their lives for a long time when none of these issues are really necessary, even though they are often very difficult problems for clients to solve without the support of others to help them see what is really going on.

Prior to or during transitions in a person's life, change might be necessary and even very welcome. Take for example a woman who's had her career on hold for several years while she's been raising her children. Let's call her Mary. Now Mary's kids are grown to the point where she can begin to think about going back to work full-time. But, she's really anxious about it, and doesn't know why. The feeling of anxiousness seems to be more than just about what Mary will encounter; whether she will succeed in going back to her career. In fact, Mary feels pretty confident she's got what it takes to be just fine going back to work. So, what's really bugging her? Her fears are more about what she is losing. Facing this change means Mary fears losing a sense of her self, a way of defining herself. Realizing this, Mary also realizes she has become so immersed in the importance of being a "good mother" that when that role becomes a less prominent part of her daily life, she doesn't know who she will be.

Of course, Mary will still be who Mary is at some core level. Mary's fears about how she will define herself arises from not knowing how things will play out for her after she goes back to work and spends less time at home and less time with her kids. This fear is likely also based on her having placed more emphasis on her role as a mother as a defining characteristic of her identity than it can really have. This is the problem of "situational identity" in a nutshell. When we rely on the roles in our lives or the kind of relationships we have with others as a way to define who we are, we become so tied to those roles or relationships that any change, even positive change, can be really frightening because we think we risk not only a change in the relationship but the potential loss of some aspect of ourselves. And then who will we be? Will we still be important? Will we still be able to feel good about ourselves? Will others still like us and want us to be around?

I should point out that I am not referring to "code-shifting" (talking or being one way with a group of friends of a particular ethnicity and talking or acting completely different with others). Sometimes, this can be a useful and beneficial skill for practicing cultural competence, if not taken too far. However, this chapter isn't about that issue. Nor is this chapter intended to address the related issue of authenticity—what it is like to be "real" with others, so our self-image (how we think others perceive us) is consistent with our sense of who we are. I already have two chapters on authenticity. This chapter is about something more exclusively internal, which means the focus is on how we feel about our lives and ourselves rather than how we might look to others on the outside.

The issue of "situational identity" also comes up fairly often when someone is struggling with ending a long-term relationship, even if the client is the one deciding to end the relationship or marriage. Beyond dealing with the grief of losing their partner, which is always an important part of this process, a person might fear that ending the relationship will end some part on their own identity. A client (we will call him Bill) considering this change, might ask himself: without the house, the garden, the wife, the daily interaction with the kids, what's left of me, the person that was Bill? What am I without all of these other things? And then it might seem to Bill there is a big gaping hole, a void, an emptiness, and he can't see what part of himself is left after the marriage is gone.

These are not actually identity questions, although they seem like they are. Are they necessary, well-directed, healthy questions? I would say no, not when they are asked within the framework of thinking that ending the relationship will cause an implosion of Bill's identity. Bill's identity is not really situational, even though it might feel this way to Bill. Bill's identity is not actually dependent on the continuation of the marriage.

Rather than focusing on what part of himself he will lose, a more effective and less painful kind of question for Bill might be: what will stay the same within me if I end the marriage? Or, how will I be the same whether I leave or stay? This is a true identity question. Our identities are not dependent on where we live, whether we are married or not, which job we have, or whether we see our kids every day or half the week. We might even give this particular issue its own name: "relational identity" which is just as nonsensical as situational identity. It is not a good idea for us to let ourselves believe that we are important only because we are important to someone else.

The question of divorce or ending any kind of long-term relationship is not and should not be an easy decision. Too much is at stake for Bill, his wife, his kids, their families and others. It can be even more detrimental to stay in an unhealthy or very unhappy relationship solely because you incorrectly believe that some part of the very essence of who you are will come to an end if you leave. Again, this is simply not true. Once Bill learns this, he will be able to make a good choice about whether to stay in the marriage and try to make it work or leave, knowing that what is essential about who he is will still be there regardless of what he decides.

Why do we allow ourselves to become so invested in a relationship or a way of living our lives that we begin to think of it as an essential part of what defines us a person? This is complicated, and varies quite a bit from person to person and differing situations. A common thread running through these scenarios, though, is that over time we can become convinced that the only way to be sufficiently invested in a relationship (like saving a marriage or raising our kids) is to compromise or give up some part of who we are. When we do this, we trick ourselves into thinking that we cannot be okay unless we are able to maintain the status quo (continue saving a marriage that might need to end or maintaining an equal investment in our children even though they are growing up and need more independence). There is no relationship, no matter how important, that should require us to believe it is necessary to compromise our sense of self, of wholeness, of security about who we are for the sake of the relationship. Any relationship that leads down that path is one that is destructive and taking from us much more than it is giving to us. That does not ever need to be the case in any relationship or role in our life.

Knowing who we are, what we need, what we want, and the ability to express these as clearly as possible as often as possible is an important part of avoiding the false belief in a "situational identity." Choosing how to be involved in our relationships in a way that does not require us to compromise any of these things will help us to avoid allowing any relationships or roles in our lives to lead us to believe that we cannot be whole unless this relationship or role stays exactly like it is. Flexibility is a hallmark of mental health. Realizing that all of us have flexible yet strong identities, no matter how our lives or relationships change over time, will allow us to make the changes we need to make for our own benefit without having to fear that we will lose ourselves in the process.

SUBSTANCE AND PROCESS

Everyone who goes to law school learns very quickly to separate two very distinct areas of law: procedure and substance. In fact, one of the first classes you must take in law school is called, "Civil Procedure" (which teaches you the process of suing people and being sued). If your neighbor's dog tears up your garden, your neighbor owes you money to fix it. That's substance. That's the issue. Taking your neighbor to court is how you make him pay you (assuming a knock on his door or a letter do not do the trick). That's process, the "procedure." That's the way you handle the issue.

Somewhere around 25 percent of my clients at any given time are couples, who come to see me when they are unable to resolve various issues between them which result in either expressed or unexpressed conflicts. We identify the underlying issues that are causing the conflicts and the unsuccessful patterns they have been using to try to resolve the issues. We identify the substance (the issues) and the process (the patterns of interaction and communication) that lead to the conflict. This approach also works for individual clients who are trying to resolve either current or past conflicts with important people in their lives, although the changes may be limited to what my client can do to change their processes because the other person is not in therapy with my client.

My experience with couples confirms that almost every issue is resolvable as long as everyone is safe, but only if both people are willing to change their processes for resolving the issues. I don't mean that in every situation both people are "wrong." Patterns of interaction are always the result of two or more people doing things in response to each other. When these patterns of interaction lead to unresolved conflict, everyone involved in the interaction needs to understand their own contribution to the conflict and why it has not been resolved.

Most of the time, it is not the underlying issues that make it so difficult to resolve the conflict. It is the process or patterns of interaction that prevent people from resolving their issues. In many cases, this is because the interaction patterns are the result of issues that existed for each person before the specific issue came up. Here's an example. Many of my client families experience tension due to economic upheaval. They cannot sell their house, their house is "under water," or one or both of the parents are recently unemployed. The issue is money, at least at the surface. By itself, money is a huge reason for couples to split. But many couples that have very serious money issues do not split, and do not even suffer high levels of conflict. How each person in the couple perceives money, responsibility, their own self-worth, the importance of social status, etc. will greatly affect their responses to a tough economic situation. Suppose the husband grew up with a single mom, fairly poor, on the edge of economic disaster for several years. The wife grew up in a stable middle-class household with a father who always made good money, and a mom who also worked, so she never had any real fear of economic disaster growing up. Now the wife loses her job. The husband becomes extremely anxious about it, and cannot understand why his wife is not more concerned. They fight—he strains to tell her daily to take more action to find a job, she tells him to back off. Conflict. Unresolved.

In the example above, if they each paid attention to, not only the way they are acting, but also their own reasons for the way they are responding to each other, which in this case have little to do with each other, they will begin to understand how they can change. If they look not just at what is happening right now, but how they are influenced by past experiences, before they even knew each other, they could stop blaming the other person. They could begin to work on how to resolve the conflict, which is not just about money, but about serious differences in what it means to have less money, or more money, whose responsibility is it to make sure money is there, how worried they should be. All of these issues are resolvable, but might be very difficult to resolve without a deeper understanding of why they are so emotionally antagonistic about it.

So, there are three steps to understanding how to begin resolving what seemed like unresolvable conflict. First, what is the substance of the immediate conflict (in the example above, it is money)? Second, what are the current processes used to address the conflict (the wife feels "hounded" and de-valued and the husband feels his anxiety is not taken seriously)? Third, what underlying issues for each person are driving their part of the current pattern (their very different childhood experiences about money)? With this information, we can begin to separate out what is being said from why it is being said. The husband and wife can each take a look at what part of the conflict right now is about the current situation, and what part is actually the result of past experiences that have little or nothing to do with the other person or the current situation. The blaming subsides, the emotional energy is redirected. The conflict becomes smaller, and resolvable.

This example is simple on purpose, to illustrate in a short space how conflicts can be resolved by looking at both the substance of the issue and the process of interacting to deal with the issue. When both people are willing and able to look at both substance and process, nearly all conflict is resolvable.

SUCCESSFUL STEP-PARENTING: TWO RULES FOR BLENDED FAMILIES

These days, I see most of my clients one-on-one. I started out in my therapy career seeing mostly families, with many members all together at the same time in the same session. I remember one session at the home of a family in which there were 16 family members present (I used to go to peoples' homes to have therapy sessions). When I worked with Hennepin County Child Protection, we had family meetings that often included 10 or more immediate and extended family members. Now, when I do see families, it is often in the context of couples therapy focusing on how family issues are affecting the couples' relationship.

In this context, a recurring and very thorny issue comes up with "blended families" (in which one or more of the children is not the child of one of the members of the couple). Obviously, this can have many variations. There might be just one child, or a few children, all of whom are the biological child of one of the parents, but not both. There might be one or more children who are the biological children of both members of the couple, while there are also children who are not biologically related to one or both people in the couple. The common element of a "blended family" is that at least one child did not come into the family during the time of the current relationship (strange language, I know, but it is intended to be inclusive of situations in which the child is adopted by both parents or born to one parent and adopted by the other or one of them later forms a relationship with someone else).

See how complicated it can be just describing the variations? Maybe a better way to describe a blended family and still be inclusive is to say that a "blended family" is one in which one of the adults in the family was not part of the family when the child became part of the family. This way of describing possible family arrangements also does a better job of pinpointing the issue for this chapter which is to identify ways in which roles can differ between adults when one of them did not participate in the decision to bring the child into the family, but when both that parent and the child are now part of the family.

The point of this chapter is to offer some thoughts on how blended family couples can begin to make changes to cope with the potentially confusing issues surrounding the relationships each has to the children in the family. Many couples come to see me after having decided by default that the children should all be viewed in exactly the same way, regardless of their biological or family origins. This seems to them to be the most fair way to do things. I guess this makes sense. The problem is it just doesn't work very well most of the time, especially as the children get older and start to ask to whom they must or should ultimately listen to for parenting and life-skills advice and rules. We often hear the step-child teenager lamenting the rules or dictates of their step-parent by saying in a fit of frustration, "You can't tell me what to do, you aren't my [mom or dad]." This can feel hurtful, disrespectful, and disruptive to both parents. It is also at least somewhat true (unless the step-parent has adopted the step-child, but for the child even in this case it might still seem to be true to them).

If parents can accept the truth that a step-parent is in a different position than a biological parent (or in the case of adoption, an "original" parent) in a blended family, an amazing amount of hardship and tension between the parents and the child can virtually disappear. More than ten years ago, a professor told our class in graduate school that he advised step-parents to think of themselves as "parenting consultants" to the biological parent when it came to issues related to their step-children. I have been using this idea ever since, and it seems even more true and sensible now than it did when I first heard it. This removes all kinds of responsibilities for the step-parent, the original parent, and the child(ren) that cause so many of the problems I see when I meet with couples and blended families. When a step-parent takes on the role as an equal parent to their stepchildren, they set themselves up for failure because they have taken on the impossible task of trying to be something they are not. And the children know this is true. This is also completely unnecessary for everyone involved to play their part in a healthy family. Why pretend to be a child's "parent" just like their original parent, when everyone already knows you are not?

If this idea of taking the step-parent out of the role of being a parent equal to the original parent is so great, why don't more people do it? Why does it keep coming up in therapy with couples and families? The answer lies partly in how to replace the role with another role that feels adequate to both parents and the child or children. Fixating on equal roles for both parents is the result of unstated expectations. Many families have told me they just assumed that the step-parent should take on the role of full-fledged parent of children who are not their children because the step-parent would lose respect, authority, family functioning if that role were not given to the step-parent. Sometimes the original parent may feel overwhelmed by having all the responsibility and want to share it with the step-parent, or the step-parent likewise wants to be helpful in every way they can so they assume they need to take on the role as equal parent so they are doing their share. None of this needs to be the case. A step-parent can take a step back, become something different, but not less important than the original parent, without losing anything, and in the process gaining much.

What does it mean to be a "parenting consultant" as a step-parent? It includes supporting the biological parent by offering ideas, suggestions, and help when they have questions about how to meet the child's needs. It means participating in household activities that family members are expected to do. It means supporting the child directly with such things as homework, chores, and also friendship. What might be more important is what it excludes. Chief among these things is the final word on rules and discipline for the child. This might seem like a bitter pill to swallow for the step-parent. If you are a step-parent reading this, you might right now be thinking that this means you have to let the child run the show. Not so. First, you are not "capitulating" authority to the child. You are abdicating your role as an equal primary parent to the other parent, designating them as the only primary parent. You still have a parenting role—it just isn't the primary one. You can have influence on important decisions that affect the child, but not the final word. That role is left solely to the original parent. If you are inclined to stop reading this chapter because it seems I am suggesting something that cannot be workable, I only ask that you read the following paragraph, where I add a second suggested rule: a step-parent is always entitled to no less respect as a person by the other parent and the child, despite their role as a step-parent and in part because of that role.

It turns out that much of the conflict between parents and a child, especially when one of the parents is a step-parent, has less to do with parenting and "discipline," and much more to do with the basic expectations of people who live together and need to function as a family unit. Some of these kinds of conflict include the following difficult questions. Who is responsible for what kinds of household chores needing to be done to keep things running well in the home? When is it time for everyone to quiet down so those that want to sleep can sleep? What kinds of permission need to be requested and given for anyone in the home to use something belonging to someone else or shared (e.g. the car, the stereo or video games, food in the fridge)? How do conversations need to be limited to use respectful language, tone and content? These might seem like parenting issues when kids are involved, but they are also issues you probably had to solve when you had roommates, or when you were dating your partner. These are rules for living together, which affect parents and children differently mostly due to differences in levels of authority and autonomy and differences in capacities for understanding such rules (children are less able to understand rules because they are still developing these skills and brain functions).

Now that we have a slightly new frame of reference for how most conflicts between parents and children arise, let's see what happens when we adopt the two rules of step-parenting. The two rules of step-parenting are:

1. A step-parent's role is limited to a "parenting consultant" to the other parent; and

2. A step-parent is entitled to no less respect as a person by the other parent or the child.

As to the second rule, a step-parent might even be entitled to additional consideration due to their less obligatory relationship to the children of the biological parent (more on this in a moment). Both adults have the same role when deciding what kinds of rules should be created for basic expectations of living together. Both adults can have equal say and influence in terms of priorities. A step-parent is free to complain just as loudly when a child uses something of theirs without their permission, or when a child is not "carrying their weight" when it comes to cleaning up the house, or leaves a mess unattended. In other words, a step-parent is entitled to expect no less than the other parent when it comes to how they will be treated in the home.

A step-parent's response to the child's violation of the rules is where things differ. This is where discipline, consequences, and outcomes are different. The step-parent, as a consultant, is free to suggest ways to respond, but the other parent should have the final say. This will not necessarily resolve the conflict between the parents (they might disagree over whether one or the other's proposed response is sufficiently significant in light of the child's infraction), but it does remove the step-parent from the conflict between the parents and the child, which might be unsolvable if the child is not willing to respect the step-parent's role as an equal primary parent in the home. Giving the original parent the final say in responding to a child's violation of a family rule also recognizes that the original parent is usually in the best or better position to make the final decision. The step-parent can still participate in such decisions, influence them, have a voice in them, and can also establish himself or herself as the other adult living in the home with the child, and demand to be treated with the appropriate respect they deserve as the other adult. By removing from the step-parent the role as primary parent with final say, the step-parent is no longer trying to assert themselves as something they are not (a primary parent), and can thereby avoid the conflicts with the (actual) primary parent and their child that will arise if they do.

Final say is not only appropriate when it comes to violation of rules. It can also be used to avoid unnecessary conflict if the child wants something the adults are not sure they should allow. Suppose a 10-year old boy wants to have a sleepover at a friend's house. It might matter to both adults if the family had plans and this intrudes on those plans. As such, the decision should rest on both parents' needs equally since it affects them equally. If the sleepover doesn't intrude on family plans or otherwise effect the step-parent, then why would the step-parent even want or need to have final say?

Also, this arrangement gives the step-parent some flexibility to address their own needs as different than the needs of the other parent. A step-parent gives to their step-child attention, care, financial support, physical safety, protection, fun, entertainment, and role modeling, even though the child is not "theirs." That's quite a gift. It should be recognized as such. Not that the child or the other parent needs to ingratiate themselves, but there can be some basic recognition that these needs are freely given, even though the step-parent was not part of the original decision to bring the child into the world or the family or both. This also means that the step-parent is not required to give exactly as the child's original parent is willing or wants to give. For example, just because a child's original parent wants to share their personal belongings with a child this doesn't mean that their partner, the step-parent, should have to agree to an equal sharing. Differentiating these roles allows each parent to justify their position based on their actual different positions and roles in the family.

The two rules mentioned in this chapter for blended families allow everyone in the family to see each other for the roles they actually each play, without having to play along with rules that are based on false roles, and expectations that rarely function without significant and unnecessary conflict. As long as the roles are clear to everyone involved, and the rules that flow from the roles applied with some flexibility, reasonableness and care, everyone will have the space to resolve potential conflicts in a way that is respectful and meets their differing needs. These two "rules" are just a starting point for adjusting expectations. The rules solve at least one significant problem though—they help to take the step-parent out of a role he or she will almost certainly fail to satisfy; pretending to occupy a space in the child's life equal to the space occupied by the child's biological or original parents. A step-parent can be a great part of their step-child's life without having to try to be something different than what they are and will always be.

ADOPTION, FOSTER CARE, AND IDENTITY

My interest in adoption and foster care is both profoundly personal and an important part of my professional life as a therapist working with adoptees and their adoptive families. At the age of 12, after my mother left town, and as the County condemned our house as unfit for human habitation and child protection began to investigate my father's abuses, my great aunt told me she wanted to adopt me. She thought she was going to "rescue" me from the fate of my family. I said "no," despite both of us knowing I might not survive if I didn't leave my birth home soon. A year later, I was in a very nice foster home. I had bed sheets for the first time in my life, a nice house, plenty to eat, a good school, and no parent beating me. My foster mom asked me if she could adopt me. She told me I wouldn't be able to visit my biological family if I agreed to be adopted. I'd also have to change my last name. I said "no," even though my "prior life" had been such a mess. She kicked me out. There began several years in and out of different group homes, treatment centers, a halfway house, back home, until finally finding a foster family that was able to love me, while respecting my need to find an identity that did not require me to deny where I had come from. I still have contact with that foster family, and think of them as a second family, which doesn't replace, but adds to my biological family. My personal history explains my enthusiasm for providing therapy to families with adopted and foster children.

Although this chapter has a pretty specific audience (adoptive and foster families and their adopted or foster children), if you are not part of a family that has experienced adoption or foster care, I want to suggest that this chapter might still be useful to you. You may have friends who have considered or who have adopted a child. You may have friends who were adopted or lived in foster care. You may have extended family members who have adopted or been adopted. If any of these cases apply to you, I hope you can learn something from this chapter about how to be more supportive and encouraging to adoptive parents and their adoptive children.

The primary problems that occur when families add a new child through adoption or foster care involve:

1. Transition and rule/role changes within and outside the new family;
2. Identity concerns for the child;
3. Identity concerns for the adoptive family (hopefully); and
4. Belongingness or attachment between the child and their new and old families and communities.

Transition issues are not unique to adoption or foster care—they occur when any family adds a new child. This is natural, even when the added child is born to the parents in the family. In that sense, it is an issue that can be addressed openly, logically, and effectively in most families. When the child is added through foster care or adoption, families can struggle with openly addressing these issues because these issues also require members of the family to address identity, belongingness and attachment with the new child. Depending on the circumstances involved, the importance of each of these areas of concern can be very different with adoption than they are with foster care, but not necessarily so. This chapter will take a look at each of these areas of concern and describe common ways they occur in adoption and foster care scenarios, followed by suggestions for ways families can cope with these various areas of concern in a way that recognize the needs of everyone involved.

In its simplest terms, when a family adds a child through adoption or foster care, a child moves from one family to another, facilitated by an outside agency. At a minimum, this process always involves the following "stakeholders" or interested parties:

1. The adopted or foster child(ren);
2. The child(ren)'s biological family;
3. The adopting family;
4. The facilitating agencies (county social workers and other staff); and
5. The communities of the biological family and the new family.

Although this list seems obvious, in many adoptive or foster care situations, many of these stakeholders might be completely or partially ignored. This has changed considerably in recent years, but can still be a very serious problem. This chapter focuses specifically on the needs of the adopted or foster care child or children (to which I will simply refer as the "child"). However, we must attend to the needs and perspectives of everyone on this list to encourage a system that can fully support all of the needs of the child.

In the best of all worlds, everyone involved has as their primary concern the best interests of the adoptive or foster care children. Even so, it can be easy to make assumptions about the best interests of the child that ignore the most significant needs of the child because other concerns take priority and the child may not be aware of those issues or how to express them (due to age, fear, confusion, etc.). This is perhaps the most tragic of all circumstances: when the assumptions about a child's needs trump their actual needs in a way that prevents either the child or the parents and helpers from addressing the real needs of the child.

Ironically, the more someone is emotionally invested in the process, the more they may find it difficult or impossible to understand how they are not meeting the needs of the child. Take my story of my first foster mother above. I have no doubt that her heart was in the right place—that she thought her offer of adoption was doing me a great favor, by rescuing me from the terrible place I had been before coming into her home. In that sense, her willingness to make me "her" child was in its way a beautiful and tender-hearted gesture. It may have been for this precise reason that she was then unable to see that my identity and my sense of belongingness were still very much attached to that other "horrible" place, because it had already begun to define me and I had strong attachments to my siblings and even to parents who had neglected and abused me. And for that reason, even though she offered me something that on the surface seemed so much greater, it was still foreign to me, and felt uncomfortable, and even unreal. When I did not prize her offer in the way she did, she rejected me, not thinking that, by doing so, she sent me into a foster care system that would further the abuse she was trying to help me avoid.

Every child is different. Every child has come from a different place, is going into a different place, and has different needs of their own. Nonetheless, every child who faces adoption or foster care or both, no matter what their age, gender, and other factors at the time they enter a new family, will inevitably face issues of identity, belongingness and attachment that are unique to adoption and foster care. I mean *every child, without exception.* In my practice as a therapist, I have witnessed many adoptive and foster families steadfastly refuse to acknowledge this simple fact about their adopted child, which is usually the main reason they are at my office. The issues of identity, belongingness and attachment need not lead to serious mental health or behavioral issues for the child or any other member of the family. Identity issues almost always surface later on in life, either in adolescence or adulthood, which can be adequately addressed by a supportive and understanding family that allows the child to explore these issues without fear of reprisal or accusations of disloyalty or ingratitude. In the best cases, this supportive and open environment begins when the child first comes to the adoptive home and lasts throughout their stay in the home.

Adoptive parents often come to my office with their adopted children convinced that what the child needs most is to be steered back toward the family as the only unit of importance for the child. Yet, this is simply not true. And the more the parents push this agenda, the more trouble they will have with their child, and the more difficult it will become for the child to resolve their issues of identity, belongingness, and attachment. Even in the worst case scenario, where a child's biological parents are either unattainable, or there are legal and practical reasons the child should have no contact with their biological parents, the child will still want to know where they come from (belongingness questions), what this means about who they are (identity questions), and whether they have any desire to form an attachment with their biological family of origin in addition to their adoptive or foster care family (attachment questions).

Having worked for several years in the child protection system in Hennepin County, I both understand and appreciate the legal necessities involved in terminating the parental rights of a parent who poses a danger to their children. I have witnessed on several occasions court proceedings that led to this result, and rightly so, for the sake of the child. This result can also provide much needed stability and comfort to a family wishing to adopt a child and know that the child will no longer be subjected to the negative influences of their biological parents. Yet, this does not end the matter for the child, even if it does for the Judge, the County, the biological parents, and the adoptive or foster care parents. The child will still need to satisfy himself or herself that they are where they belong and how they feel about themselves (who they are as people) in light of where they come from. Trying to convince that child that they should not bother themselves with such questions will not work.

The kinds of differences between the biological family and the new family can greatly influence a child's ability to adjust to their new surroundings and how they end up resolving differences between where they come from and where they are. For instance, it is not surprising that a white child born to a middle-class mother and father in Minneapolis who is adopted by a white middle-class family in Eagan may have less adjustment issues than a Korean baby born to a working-class, single mother in Korea, who after several years in an orphanage, is adopted by that same middle-class white family on the other side of the planet. The white child and white adoptive family will simply have less to adjust to than the Korean child, either because there is less difference in how they look and feel with their new family (and the way others view the child with their new family), or because the family is more able to support the child's search for their own identity when that child's origination is more similar to the adoptive family's own origination. A middle-class white family in Eagan does not need to reach as far beyond its own understanding of culture, race, and class to help a white adopted child find a place of comfort and satisfaction with themselves than they would have to reach for the Korean child. In many cases, though, the adoptive family may make little or no effort for the white or the Korean child to understand their identity at all, believing that the best way to encourage attachment and a sense of belongingness for the child is to either ignore or actively discourage the child from learning anything about their biological family and community. Likewise, a child of color adopted by a white family may feel prohibited from calling attention to the racism she experiences in her white suburban school and neighborhood because her white adoptive parents might take it as a sign of ingratitude or blame. So she may try to ignore or deny the racism and other identity issues, leading to feelings of powerlessness, resentment, shame, self-hatred, alienation and loneliness then and later on in her adult life.

The best thing I can do for a client who was adopted or in foster care is to give them permission and a space to begin asking the very questions they have been asking silently all along, without any expectation or agenda about how they should ask or answer such questions. "Where do I come from (place, culture, biology, other family, community, history of my people)?" "What does this mean about why I am not still there (why they abandoned me, or was it the right thing to do, to take me from them)?" "What does my leaving that place mean about how I am still connected to that place (should I go back and find out or leave it alone, am I still one of 'them' even though I was raised here)?" "What does it mean about my sense of loyalty and belongingness to my new family that I still care about these other questions, these other people?" "Does it make me ungrateful to want to explore these ideas?" "Is it my adoptive parents' fault that I was subjected to racism at school, by other kids, by their extended family?" "Should I resent my adoptive parents for discouraging these questions when it is clear now that I have been damaged by such discouragement?" "Does it mean I am not really attached to my new family if I want to know more about my biological family and their history?" "And if I do not feel attached to my adoptive family in the same way as others who are not adopted, does this mean that I am not attached to anyone?" "Can I be attached to anyone?" "Where is my home?" When adoptive parents freely give permission to the adopted or foster care child to ask these and many other similar questions, everyone can become involved in growing their attachment to each other, without letting insecurities about such issues keep them hidden and unresolved.

PART SIX:

CONFLICT

The following chapters were originally included in the Family and Relationship Issues part of the book because conflict cannot happen outside the context of relationships between at least two people. In the end, I decided to include these chapters in their own part of the book because we often experience conflict outside the context of our family and personal relationships (work, public life) and I wanted to offer these ideas as potentially helpful whether you experience conflict in your marriage, partnership, family, a friendship, at work, the grocery store, wherever. The hope is that these ideas will encourage you to address conflict, rather than avoid it, in most circumstances, by changing your outlook on the purpose and origin of conflict, and your belief in your ability to control the outcome of conflict without resorting to or accepting undue levels of hostility.

CONFLICT, PART 1:
"WHAT IS CONFLICT?"

In this series of chapters, I will discuss some of the ways conflict comes up in our lives and how therapy can be used to assist in the resolution of conflict. After reading these chapters on conflict, I hope you will discover at least two things. Conflict is much more common than you had previously thought, and therefore not especially a bad thing. And conflict is very often not nearly as difficult to resolve as we thought it might be.

I define conflict much more broadly than most people. When people tell me about conflict happening in their lives, they are referring to what I consider a subset of conflict, which I will call "hostile conflict." Not all conflict is hostile. In fact, most conflict does not involve any kind of hostility. When we think of conflict as always leading to hostility, it's no surprise that we do whatever we can to avoid conflict, even if that means being stuck in patterns and situations that are really pretty awful because we cannot resolve the continuing conflict we are avoiding. If we can re-orient the way we see conflict, as involving issues that can be addressed, often without hostility or the risk of not knowing what to do with highly emotional reactions, the thick wall that prevents us from dealing with conflict can go away.

Here's my definition of conflict:

Conflict exists when two or more people (or businesses, groups or nations) believe there aren't enough resources to meet everyone's needs in a given situation, leading to disagreement about how to divide those resources to meet their respective needs.

I know this definition is fairly general and maybe not very clear. So, I will spend some time giving details about what I mean. There isn't anything in my definition of conflict that requires the disagreement to be expressed or acknowledged by everyone involved in the conflict. Think about times when someone has been giving you the "cold shoulder" and you do not know why. You ask, and it opens up a discussion about something that has been bugging the other person about wanting something from you and you had no idea. Conflict still existed, because you and the other person did not agree about your respective needs, even though you didn't know there was a disagreement about needs until you asked.

I suppose it's also worth pointing out that my definition of needs is equally as broad as my definition of conflict. "Need" can be something as small as who gets to use the bathroom next or as large as needing to know which nations helped Osama Bin Laden commit acts of terrorism. I often find it amazing how family members can have highly aggressive and hostile conflict over needs that start out very insignificant. The reason almost always has very little to do with the immediate issue involved in the conflict and is far more related to failure to resolve past conflicts in a way that leaves both participants feeling satisfied. These highly energized conflicts erupt over trivial matters precisely because trivial matters are those that we are not prepared to deal with—they just come up when we least expect them, and then the buried conflict comes flying out, where there is no preparation for it or filtering to avoid it.

Sometimes conflict is really a matter of mistaken interpretation. The mistake might be one or both people (or groups) thinking they need something the other group needs, when in fact, either they don't really need it, or the other person or group doesn't really need it. When I was a business law attorney, this was often the case. We'd spend tens of thousands of dollars and many months or even years arguing over how to settle a dispute. Then both parties would sit down at a mediation, go through their various points, realize their disagreement was not as large or insurmountable as they both thought and could be resolved without the need for a trial and more time and money.

These mediations were most successful when both parties were in a position to hear something they hadn't previously considered (often because they were tired of spending precious time and money on the problem). Let's call this way of resolving conflict "creative reconsideration" (if you are wondering if I just made that up, I did). When we are willing to be creative in reconsidering our own needs and how we can also help someone else meet their needs, it is often the case that the conflict wasn't about "insufficient resources" to meet the needs of both, but about an overly narrow view of those resources and needs. In one legal case I remember, a business argument over who gets which clients when two people split up the business was solved without a lawsuit when both people realized they had more than enough growth potential to go around by clearly defining boundaries going forward (for instance, by geographical territory and size of clients). Both new businesses got what they wanted without losing something to the other business. This was conflict, and it was resolvable without the need for hostility.

That's easy though—to think of conflict as the result of a simple mistake. But, what about when conflict really is about not having enough resources to meet everyone's needs? In therapy, I sometimes use the example of a four-way stop intersection to illustrate that even when conflict is real and unavoidable, there are ways to face it and resolve it, if everyone respects everyone else's needs as a first step. Whenever there are two or more cars heading in different directions at a four-way stop, this is always instant conflict. You might be thinking it's not conflict because in the vast majority of cases everyone passes through the intersection without the slightest edginess, anxiety, fear, anger, yelling, screaming, etc. (insert here whatever you think when someone says "conflict"). You are right that most of the time there isn't "hostile conflict," but that doesn't mean there isn't conflict.

Every time you pull up to a four-way stop sign and someone else is either already there or coming to a stop from another direction, both of you must decide who gets to go first. You can't both go, even though you both want to go first. You'll crash if you do. That is conflict! How then does it get resolved without hostility? Well, first, it doesn't always. I've had people flip me off when I went first and they thought they had that right (and sometimes they were right, although flipping me off did seem a little petty). When we do resolve a four-way stop without hostility, we do it because we are both mindful in the moment that there are preset rules to help resolve the conflict about who goes first. Who got their first? Who was fully stopped? Were there other people in front of that person who already went? Are there other reasons the other person can't go (e.g. pedestrians in their way)? Everyone knows these rules (okay, they should know these rules), and if the rules are respected, and there is a general feeling among all involved that the next guy's right to go first is just is important as mine, then the rules will dictate how to resolve the conflict. The outcome is nearly certain most of the time, and the anxiety or hostility that often comes with conflict is not necessary or helpful in anyway for resolving the conflict. In other words, "my need" to cross the intersection will (almost always) be noted by the other person according to the rules already in place before we both pulled up to the intersection.

Where conflict really gets messy is when the rules are much less clear, so the other person's reaction to the conflict is unclear and risky, and the final outcome of the conflict is also much less clear. In other words, when it isn't at all clear that we will get what we want, that the other person cares or hears what we want, or that they will play by the same rules (our rules) about how to decide who gets what they want... most. Conflict is scary and messy when we don't know the outcome, like a fog with no clear exit. Conflict avoidance is often mostly about this fear. Conflict avoidance, how we do it, why we do it, what ways it causes problems, and how to solve it, will be the topics of the next chapter in this series of chapters on conflict.

CONFLICT, PART 2:
THE PROBLEM OF CONFLICT AVOIDANCE

Why do we avoid conflict? We fear loss of control. When we can't control a situation, we have far less ability to predict whether we will get what we need out of that situation. Also, when we have a need and recognize that our need might interfere with another person's need, expressing our need could very well result in all kinds of responses we do not want to invite. At the lowest end of troubling responses is simply "No, I am not going to meet that need." At higher ends of troubling responses we might find things like, "I can't believe you thought it was okay to ask me to do that for you," or sometimes just as bad or worse, we hear, "Your need is so unimportant to me, I am not even going to respond." Here's the really tricky part, and we all have this problem—when we hear those kinds of responses, we sometimes learn later that we were just plain wrong, and the other person didn't say anything of the kind. Why do we have such strong tendencies to misinterpret things during conflict? For the same reason we avoid conflict in general: we fear loss of control, which often translates to feelings of considerable insecurity and vulnerability. When we feel exposed and vulnerable, we often hear anything other than "Of course I will be glad to meet that need" as rejection or hostility or both. This is especially true when patterns of conflict engagement over time cause us to use defensive coping skills while we have conflict with others.

If I am right here about all the trouble that can come from conflict, it makes sense for people to avoid conflict wherever possible. Okay, I can get behind that. We should avoid conflict whenever we can meet our needs just as well without conflict. That's not usually the problem though. There are not that many people that actually want to have conflict in their lives (and I didn't say there are none). Most people do a good job avoiding conflict when it isn't necessary. The problem is that most people do avoid conflict when they should not avoid it, with all kinds of pretty bad consequences, including actually increasing the level of hostility during the later conflicts they can't somehow manage to avoid.

There are two basic fears we have when we confront conflict:

1. We will not get what we think we need, which will make us feel bad somehow; and

2. The other person will respond to our need in a way that negatively affects us and the relationship we have with that person.

In both cases, there is almost always more at stake then the actual immediate need we are trying to meet in the potentially conflictual situation. We also have the need to have our needs respected and understood and we have a separate need to have stability, reliability and connectedness in our relationships. The more important the relationship, the more desperately we want to have our needs respected and the more fear we have that conflict will disrupt the stability and connectedness we feel with the other person. This is part of why we get into arguments and sometimes say things to our partner or other family members that we cannot imagine saying to someone at work (especially our boss, even though we might have felt like it). It's not only because at home we can't get fired (because we can); it's because the relationships we have with those at home carry much more powerful underlying emotional consequences for us if they lose their stability and connectedness due to conflict.

Think about finances. If you ever deal with any kind of finances at work, it's probably fairly hard to imagine it causing the kind of conflict it might cause at home (unless you are self-employed and finances at work directly impact your family and home life). Suppose you need to spend company money on something you know will help you do your job better (e.g. a new laptop). Your boss hears your argument, maybe even pretends or actually does try to get it into a new budget, but then comes back and says no, it's not possible right now. You might feel irritated, like it's a pattern with that company, or that your boss is kind of lame. Not that big of a deal, right?

Now you are at home, same issue. You want a new laptop to get a bunch of creative stuff done, books, web stuff, home business, whatever it is, pretend it is important. You go to your spouse, partner, parent, whomever decides such things with you. They say no. They say there are other things we need to spend money on—a new garage door opener, a clothes dryer, food, etc. Not unreasonable perhaps, but at some level, no is no, and it doesn't feel very good. There is a good chance that, in addition to accepting the answer, there are other feelings that go with it like a much more deeply seated sense of betrayal, dismissiveness, or resentment. Not necessarily, but likely. Again, this is because we are not only concerned about getting what we need in the moment (the laptop) but because at home we have other longer-term needs we don't have at work which have little to do with the immediate need we are seeking (wanting to be loved, to be a priority, to be appreciated in a deeper way, more uniquely important, etc.).

When we seek to have our needs met, especially in an emotionally intimate relationship like with a family member or partner, we are always increasing our vulnerability, no matter how confident we might be in the other person's response, so we can tend to become defensive, even when it seems from the outside there isn't any reason to be defensive.

The most extreme level of defensiveness might be not asking at all. I'll use a kind of funny kinetic analogy to demonstrate. If you hold your hand out in front of you to another person, they can slap it down. Even if you don't think they will, even if slapping it down seems almost unthinkable, while your hand is out in front of you, it can be slapped down. That is a kind of vulnerability. One way to avoid that kind of vulnerability is to keep your hands to your side, or better yet, clasp them behind your back. This is where the analogy looks like serious conflict avoidance.

I've been describing conflict in overly simplistic ways to get to a basic understanding of why we avoid conflict. I've tried to explain that there are actually many layers of needs we might have going on when we enter into conflict. Those layers of needs include what we are saying we need right now, but also include what we need but are not saying we need. So far, I've only given the example of saying "I need (something)" and they say "Yes," "No," or "I don't care...." We know better though. We know that real conflict almost never ends there. Because after they say anything other than yes (which is actually pretty often it turns out), we have something else to say, like "Why not," or "Too bad," or "Okay" (but we might say "Okay" with a tone they know means this isn't over yet). And then they say something and we say something, and so on and on and on. And even worse, no matter what happens after all of that, much of the time after things settle down, there's still the conflict that there was, which means it never got resolved, is simmering, and is just waiting for the next time it comes up.

Once again, we have all kinds of reasons to avoid conflict: *so many things can go wrong, and it doesn't seem to ever end!* This is precisely what people do then, they do their level best to avoid conflict at all costs, either in all cases, or with some people, or with some issues, because they have decided either consciously or unconsciously that there is no point in engaging in the conflict—no good will come of it. Sometimes they are probably right. Mostly, though, they are wrong, and worse, their fear of engaging in necessary conflicts will only continue the conflict indefinitely and allow the conflict to cause all kinds of problems it would not have caused if it had been addressed earlier.

Let's put it this way, conflict avoidance is really a myth, especially in family or intimate relationships. It is an illusion. There is no such thing as conflict avoidance. There is only conflict postponement or conflict reduction. Unresolved conflict is like electricity—it doesn't ever go away, it just goes somewhere else (Jamie Foxx said this about his character Electro in one of the Spider Man movies and I thought it was a cool analogy). When we avoid necessary conflict, it doesn't actually go away, it just goes underground, it simmers, and it waits, only to flare up again, usually with much more energy than it had the last time. Part of this is in the nature of conflict itself and part of it is in the nature of what we do to avoid conflict.

One of the most common methods of conflict avoidance is passive aggressiveness. Passive aggressive behavior includes any and all things people do to somehow urgently communicate a need without actually expressing it directly. Think of the different things we do to each other to get a point across without saying a single word, things like rolling our eyes, glaring, crossing our arms, the silent treatment, leaving the room while you are in the middle of a sentence, rolling over in bed with a bit of "extra gusto" when our partner reaches over for us, the overly enthusiastic assurance that everything is "fine." These and many other nonverbal cues are ways we tell each other, "There's a conflict here, whether you want to see it or not, and it isn't going away until you recognize and meet my needs." Seems silly and funny when you look at it from a distance, but it stinks to have to deal with it up close regardless of which side of it you are on, and especially if it happens often. Routine passive aggressiveness can actually destroy what might otherwise be a fairly healthy relationship.

Passive aggressive behavior is an attempt to state a need likely to cause a conflict without having to take the responsibility for appearing to have the need, stating the need, or causing the conflict.

We are in essence telling someone, "You should do this thing, and you should do it without needing me to tell you to do it (you should be able to guess what I want from you), and if you don't, there will be a problem." The benefit of this approach is not just that it avoids conflict; it avoids the disappointment or pain we might feel if the answer is no. I actually think even these two reasons do not adequately explain the frequency of passive aggressive behavior or the lengths people will go to preserve their posture in it (how long people can keep up the silent treatment). Passive aggressive behavior allows us to demand some kind of need, while avoiding having to face the possibility that what we are asking for might actually not be okay. If we didn't ask, then we don't have to take responsibility for that need. See what I mean? Still conflict there, but it's just not getting worked out.

Conflict avoidance results in resentments and other destructive patterns of interaction that become even more engrained. If conflict avoidance goes on too long and in too many ways, it can destroy the fabric of a relationship by destroying trust in the ability to get our needs met while also meeting the needs of others. When we become resigned to not being able to resolve even the most basic conflicts, we either stop seeking those needs and live in disappointment or we seek those needs elsewhere. Either way, the importance of the relationship diminishes in serious ways. This is often the status when couples come to me for therapy, in a last-ditch attempt to save the relationship.

The way to avoid these patterns is to stop trying to avoid conflict when conflict is necessary to resolve issues that won't be resolved any other way. A client once asked me if their marriage therapy should be measured by whether there is less fighting. I said I didn't think so. A couple that never fights, but is also never able to resolve conflicts, is just as troublesome as a couple that fights all the time, and doesn't resolve conflict. The measurement should be whether their arguments were actually helping them solve problems. Conflicts need to be able to be resolved before couples in any situation can believe the relationship can be saved. Then they can actually stop fearing conflicts in the ways they have in the past.

With so much at stake when conflict goes bad, it makes sense that we avoid conflict whenever we can. It doesn't make sense to avoid conflict when avoidance actually makes things worse, or when our needs are really important and avoiding conflict keeps us stuck in a place that is unacceptable. If a person needs to have space in their lives to try something new and important (go back to school, switch jobs, have a free night each week to hang out with friends), but they don't ask their partner for this, they may avoid conflict in the short term, but they may also be inviting damage to their own sense of self-worth and inviting resentment against their partner for their inability to have the space they need to grow (even though their partner doesn't know what's wrong because they didn't ask).

With so much at stake in figuring how to have conflict which is both necessary and can achieve resolution satisfactory for everyone involved, it is important to think about what it would take to feel good about having conflict when it is necessary. That leaves us with the next chapter, where we will pick apart how to have conflict without the need for hostility. And no matter what kind of hostility might be involved in a conflict (short of physical or verbal abuse), I want to explain how to have conflict that actually achieves the result of resolving underlying issues that leaves everyone feeling heard, important, and safe.

CONFLICT, PART 3:
RESOLVING CONFLICT

Conflict by itself has no purpose. It is merely a disagreement about how to meet differing needs. These differences can be asserted once, and still exist a week, a year or decades later, with no resolution. Conflict can be given a purpose, every time: resolution of those differences in a way that allows everyone involved to feel they have had their needs considered fairly, with some level of understanding, so the conflict is no longer necessary.

I have been careful in this discussion of conflict not to suggest that the resolution of conflict requires agreement. It does not. When I was practicing law, I remember courts making decisions all the time that leave one or more parties (sometimes every party) feeling like they got the short end of the stick. The result of a conflict can be less important than the process for resolving it. If a party to a lawsuit doesn't get what they want, they might still feel pretty good about the process if they feel they were given a fair chance to make their case, and the reasoning of the court is not completely unbalanced or biased. This is part of the reason we have courts, to give to others the authority to make difficult conflictual decisions, but do so in a way that everyone can agree gave them a fair shot at getting the result they expected. It reduces the importance, and therefore the fear, of the outcome to some extent by making the process more predictable (certainly more than the alternative, which is either anarchy, the Old West, the guy with the biggest stick wins, or vigilante justice).

Imagine if you could have a disagreement with a family member and know in advance that no matter what caused the disagreement, you could count on a process for resolving the conflict that felt safe—it was fair to everyone, made sure everyone felt understood, appreciated, and respected. If this were the case, there would be far fewer cases in which people felt the necessity to resort to shouting, name-calling, crying, walking out, negative assumptions, and all the other examples of how conflicts can become really difficult to endure and resolve. If conflict could be resolved in a way that felt safe and respectful to everyone involved, the outcome of the conflict (whose needs get met and how) would also be far less important. In other words, removing the unpredictability of the process of conflict would remove a significant part of the reason we are afraid of it, and often deal with it so poorly when it comes up. It's not that the outcome is not important. It is. It's just that the process leads to so many other problems that get in the way of getting to an outcome. Now we will get to the point of figuring out how to have conflict in a way that feels safe and which will make it easier and more likely to lead to a resolution of the immediate and underlying issues.

In order to "have the conflict" that you think may be coming (what outcome you want by having the conflict), it's a really good idea to think about what you do not want to have in the conflict process. Think about the underlying issues and needs of this particular conflict and how those may have played themselves out in conflicts with this person or others in the past when you've tried to deal with it. What came up for you? What were your expectations? What kinds of feelings did you have while processing it? In other words, what are your likely responses in dealing with these kinds of issues (e.g. money, time, connection, intimacy, family history, roles, etc.). Are there ways you can prepare yourself to avoid becoming overly angry, irritated, hurt, annoyed, and bothered by whatever the other person's response might be?

Then, think about the other person. How are they likely to respond? Are there things you can do to minimize likely negative responses, knowing they might come up? Are there ways of saying what you need that are less likely to make the other person defensive, hostile, or just closed to what you might want to tell them you need? Just keep in mind that there are three things you and everyone else mostly fears in conflict: the other person's reaction to your expression of a need, losing control over the outcome, and your own emotional reaction to whatever they might say or do in response to your needs. If you can at least try to account for all of these before going into a potentially conflictual situation, you will be like the driver approaching a four-way stop, having thought about the rules before you enter the intersection with others.

In the first part of this discussion on conflict, I stated conflict happens *"when two or more people (or businesses, groups, or nations) believe there aren't enough resources to meet everyone's needs in a given situation leading to disagreement about how to divide those resources to meet their respective needs."* So, the components of conflict are:

1. Your needs;
2. The other person's needs (real or perceived);
3. A belief by one or both of you that both needs cannot be fully met; and
4. Disagreement about how to fully meet both needs (or whose needs should be met and to what extent).

In order to resolve conflict, then, it seems necessary first to identify these components, starting with your own needs. How important are those needs? Why are they important? What would it take from the other person to get those needs met?

The next step is to try to identify the other person's need. The best way to do this, of course, is to ask them to tell you. You'd be surprised at how often clients don't think of this as a good strategy because entrenched patterns of conflict that go badly have made them reluctant to ask. If the other person is able to identify their needs, you are both in a good position to determine whether there is room to move on either of your needs. You can then also decide why there is disagreement about meeting your respective needs. Does one of you feel like you cannot get your needs if the other person's needs get met? Is there a question about whose needs are more important or which should be met first? Is there some underlying issue that isn't specific to this particular conflict that one or both of you are hanging onto that is the real basis for the disagreement? This really amounts to trying to figure out why one or both of you believe that there are not sufficient resources to meet both of your needs (resources can include, time, money, attention, emotional availability, or anything else that is necessary to make a decision about how to meet either or both of your needs).

Couples I work with in therapy often find it helpful to ask themselves first whether they have stated their needs in a helpful way right at the beginning of a conflict, and if they are not sure, ask the other person, "Have I explained myself to you in a way that makes sense" (use whatever kind of language works for you, as long as it is about you, not them). This provides the other person an opportunity to check with you before they might say why they have some kind of a problem meeting or supporting your need. If they give you an answer that indicates that there is disagreement about meeting your need, and therefore there is a conflict about it, you can be more sure that it is not about how you stated your need. Or if the way a need is stated is the real basis for the conflict, and they've identified it, you can re-state your need to see if that resolves the conflict all by itself.

Here's an example from my own life. Recently, my wife asked if we could buy a magazine rack. She didn't specify an amount she wanted to spend. I didn't see the need for a magazine rack, but also didn't much care either way. I wanted to know what she thought it would cost because we were a little tight on money at the time and we had just agreed not to spend money on anything unnecessary for a while. I asked how much she was planning to spend. She told me. The amount was reasonable to me. It seemed important enough to her. So, I said "sure." This is a simple example, but shows how something that began to look like conflict was resolved because her desire to have a magazine rack (her need), didn't interfere much with my desire to avoid spending money (the resource) on something I didn't care about (my need). I didn't know this at first. So I asked. My simple question gave her the opportunity to restate her need with the clarity I needed to determine whether I was willing to agree with meeting her need. We had conflict. For a moment. And it was resolved easily because both of us were open to thinking about the other person's "need" during the conflict.

If you account for your own reactions in the past and likely reactions in the future during conflict, and you consider these reactions along with what you think is a likely response from the other person, you can prepare yourself for almost any conflict with expectations that will allow you to adjust your reactions during the conflict in a way that will avoid escalating into hostility, defensiveness, and behaviors that you will later regret. This can be true, no matter what the other person's response might be. In an extreme example, I often provide therapy to people wishing to leave actual or potentially violent relationships by helping them create a safety plan for how to communicate to their partner their intent to leave, including hiring a lawyer, going to a family member's house, or a safety shelter with the kids, if kids are involved. This way, the impact of the other person's reaction can be anticipated and reduced or eliminated. This can also prevent my own client from doing something that would escalate the conflict toward violence. Less extreme examples of anticipating escalated conflict by accounting for your own as well as the other person's reaction occur every day in our lives.

Looking back over this discussion on conflict, the key ingredients to successful conflict resolution boil down to becoming aware of your own and the other person's immediate needs, any underlying issues that might be triggered by those needs, and likely reactions by you and the other person in the conflict based on past conflict history. If you know these things before you attempt to solve the conflict, you can be ready to change your expectations of the process and the outcome, regardless of how the other person responds. Of course, conflict by definition includes at least you and someone else, over whom you may have little or no control. If you and the other person want to be able to resolve conflict more successfully, and you are both willing to use the kinds of tools and ideas offered in this discussion on conflict, you will both become better at keeping the process safe and the outcome less unpredictable. The more you do this, the less likely conflict will escalate. Each time you can resolve conflict without feeling like it is out of control or pointless or just plain scary, you will each no longer need to engage in destructive conflict avoidance because you will be able to affirm your own capacity to handle conflict safely and resolve it effectively.

WHAT IS "VERBAL ABUSE?"

Couples often come into therapy with me to save their relationships. I also have a number of clients whose relationship is not in danger of dissolving. They have decided their relationship could be better and want me to help them find ways to make it better. So, that's what we do, often with great results. But, this chapter is about relationships in real trouble. A relationship in danger of ending is usually in some kind of downward spiral, either due to underlying issues they cannot identify or resolve, or due to particularly troublesome behavior of one or both people in the relationship—like addiction (alcohol, drugs, gambling) or boundary issues (infidelity). It takes two people to make a relationship work, but it only takes one person to destroy it. Whatever the reason for this downward spiral, there is usually also a pattern of interaction between the couple that is damaging and self-destructive, in which both people are suffering, and the relationship itself is regularly and repeatedly harmed by this pattern of interaction.

In order for therapy to have any chance of helping to save a relationship in trouble, this damaging pattern of interaction must first be identified and stopped. There are a few patterns of interaction so damaging to one or both people or the relationship, I must insist they stop in order to be willing to continue working with the couple at all, which includes physical violence in the family. This seems pretty obvious. Less obvious is when communication— words and actions —are damaging without amounting to violence or the threat of violence. In these cases, I do not make it a condition of continuing therapy that the behavior stops. In fact, identification of this kind of behavior is an essential part of therapy in these cases. Identification of what kinds of behavior constitute verbal abuse can be tricky and must be handled with some measure of care. I don't like to see verbal abuse happening to anyone, but I also don't like to throw around the term verbal abuse lightly either. This is the topic of this chapter: when someone tells me they are being "verbally abused," what does this mean? When do words become "verbal abuse?" How can it be identified, so it can be stopped?

I take abuse seriously. I also take seriously when someone is being accused of any kind of abuse, including verbal abuse. Let's start out by eliminating from the discussion of abuse a commonly-held belief which is not helpful, or might even be considered a myth. Just because someone is hurt by something someone else said doesn't make the person who said it abusive. Here's an example. If one partner says to the other partner, "This checkbook is so damned confusing, I can't tell how much money we have and what bills to pay." The other person might rightly think they are being accused of having done a bad job keeping up with the checking account balance, might feel degraded, even put down. They might feel very hurt, offended, they might feel abused. That doesn't mean the statement is verbal abuse. The statement might be true, and the person saying it is simply communicating their frustration about it.

Now, though, suppose a person lifts up their hands, shakes the checkbook, throws it at the wall, screams at the other person, "This checkbook is so damned confusing, I can't tell how much money we have and what bills to pay." Same exact words, but this is different. This looks a lot more like abuse. Why? This person is using behavior (the raised hands, the shaking, the throwing, the screaming) that is likely intended to intimidate the other person, make the other person afraid, feel bad, feel small, feel stupid. In both examples, the person who filled out the checkbook might feel bad. The difference is the intent of the person making the statement. By "intent," I mean, what is the purpose, the reason, what do they expect by making the statement? Why did they say it? In the first example, the reason they said it was that they were frustrated and letting the other person know this. They probably also wanted the other person to realize that their behavior (not doing a good job of keeping track of the checkbook) was causing a problem. Fair enough. They did not intend their statement to make the other person feel bad, or hurt or scare the other person. They just want to resolve the issue of a confusing checkbook. In the second example, they were pretty clearly intending to scare and hurt the other person's feelings, to make them feel bad about themselves. And that's not okay. It is destructive to both people, and it is destructive to the relationship and the therapy process.

So, here is my general definition of "abuse:" abuse happens whenever someone does something because they want the other person to feel hurt. Think about what makes something physical abuse. If someone trips on a toy on the floor, falls down, grabs their partner to avoid the fall, they both fall, and they are both bruised by the fall. This is not abuse. If someone grabs their partner in anger, and pulls them to floor in a fit of rage, this is violence. This is physical abuse—same action, same injury, but very different intent. One is an accident. The other is abuse.

"Verbal abuse" is saying something to someone with the intent that what they say will hurt the other person. If you are mad, and you are mad because someone you know has done something to make you mad, and you say this so they know you are mad, and saying this makes the other person feel bad for what they did, this by itself is not abuse. If you are mad, and you say something because you want the other person to feel bad and hurt by what you said, then it is abuse.

It's not always easy to know when something said is about venting feelings and when it becomes abusive, but there are simple things you can do to make it less likely that what you say is abusive. Examples of verbal abuse include name calling, like saying "You are such a loser, you suck at (fill in the blank), the fact that you do (something they don't like), makes you a (bad name)." Stick to what the person is doing that bothers you (statements about actions are okay). Stay away from saying what the person is or who they are (statements about the other person's character are often a form of verbal abuse). It's not abusive to say, "I don't like it when you mess up the checkbook balance so I can't understand how much money we have." It is abusive to say, "You are so stupid, why can't you keep the checkbook balance straight, what is wrong with you!" These are obvious examples, but the point is clear: look at the intent of the person making the statement to see how verbal abuse comes into your relationship. Don't engage in name-calling, or disparage the other person. Stick to what they do that bothers you, and not "who" they are because of what they do.

Verbal abuse by either person is never justified or necessary, no matter what the circumstances or what the other person said first. It is never necessary or okay to use verbally abusive language and behavior to vent anger or any other feeling. This means it is no excuse to say, later, "Hey, sorry I said that about you, I didn't really mean it, I was just angry and venting my anger." Besides, once you've said something that is verbally abusive, apologizing later doesn't undo the very real damage done. I believe in speaking your piece, saying what you need to say. I am not afraid of nor do I want others to be afraid to vent real feelings, including all appropriate levels of anger, from minor irritation, to outrage. No matter how angry a person is, though, or how much right they might have to be angry, this never makes it acceptable to say anything in which the primary intent of saying it is to cause the other person to hurt.

I am judgmental about very few things. Violence is one of them, including sexual violence. I am circumspect, though, when it comes to "verbal abuse." Whether something is actually "verbal abuse" can be a lot harder to know than, say physical abuse. Also, knowing that I myself have said things that are verbal abuse makes me a hypocrite if I pass self-righteous judgment on others for doing it. I have said things wanting the person hearing what I have said to feel bad. That doesn't make it okay, just because I have done it. I am just trying to acknowledge that I am far from perfect. The best I can do is to try to learn from it, avoid it, recognize it, and not repeat it. This is what I suggest to my clients too. I don't judge them for it, or threaten to discontinue therapy when they have used language and actions that are verbal abuse. I just suggest that to continue saying things meant to be hurtful is not okay, is damaging, and can destroy what could otherwise be a good relationship. Stopping a destructive pattern of interaction that includes verbal abuse is also the only way I can help a couple get to the underlying issues damaging the relationship. We have to "stop the bleeding" before we can get to the source of the injury.

WHEN IS AN APOLOGY REALLY AN APOLOGY?

A mainstay of my work as both a therapist and previously as an instructor of a "Healthy Relationships" class has been to create a brief but detailed list of the essential ingredients of a genuine apology. Why is this important? Well, how many times have you thought someone owed you an apology, and then they did apologize, but you somehow felt dissatisfied, even "robbed" of your right to expect the apology without really getting what you want? Too many, I suspect. Also, if an apology is not genuine, then the behavior that created the need for the apology is more likely to be repeated. A real apology is often the only way to truly resolve conflict for both people over behavior that is wrong and has caused harm.

Think about this: when someone says "I am sorry..." what do they really mean? Really? Isn't the word "sorry" really a short hand way of saying "sorrow?" Well, that's the way I think of it—like when a friend suffers some kind of major loss, like a death in the family. Then we say "I am so sorry for your loss." See what I mean. But, when someone says "I am sorry [for something I did]" it's kind of weird, and vague, and can even be kind of lame depending on what comes next. Think of the times we say we are sorry, which might actually be true, but we are mostly sorry because now we are having to deal with the consequences of what we have done (like having to discuss it, which we wish we didn't have to do). Anyway, "I am sorry..." can mean "I am sorry your feelings are hurt" or "I am sorry you took it that way" or "I am sorry we are fighting now" or even "I am sorry you have decided to make such a huge deal out of this." See what I mean. "Sorry" is really a poor word to use as part of an apology. So, what's better? That's the point of this chapter.

278

In other parts of this book, I told you I used to teach a "Healthy Relationship" class in the State prisons. While teaching that class, I used to ask class participants to give me the crucial ingredients of an apology that they could believe was real, and worthy of their acceptance. The answers are mostly the same when I ask my private practice clients the same question now. Here is the summary of the essential ingredients of a genuine apology (further discussion of these items follows this list):

1. A statement of regret;
2. An explanation of how and why the "offending" behavior or act was wrong;
3. An acknowledgment of the effect of the behavior on the person receiving the apology;
4. A commitment to do things differently in the future;
5. Allow the person receiving the apology a chance to express their reaction; and
6. Demonstrate real change over time.

A statement of regret. Using the word "sorry" can convey regret, but can also be vague. Why not just use the word "regret" or "wrong" as in "I regret doing..." or "I was wrong when I...." Even something as simple as "I feel bad because I (insert behavior)" is more clear than "I am sorry." Without something saying they feel bad about what they did, we can't tell if it matters to them personally. It is also important that the statement of regret be given without the expectation that the apology will be accepted. A genuine apology is given because we regret what we did. We may hope our apologies are accepted, but that is not the primary motivation of a genuine apology. In fact, it is this difference in motivation for the apology that distinguishes when an apology is genuine and when it is not.

An explanation of why the offending behavior was wrong. This can be a re-examination of why they did what they did, how they might have thought is was okay at the time, but now seeing it was not okay. It is important, though, that this not be an opportunity to excuse the behavior or simply state its effect on another person like "I am sorry you are hurt" because that can end up sounding like it is the other person's feelings that are the real problem. It has to have some element of why the person apologizing is wrong, to ensure they are taking responsibility for their actions.

An acknowledgment of the affect of the behavior on the other person. By this, I just mean something like "Hey, I can see now that making plans without checking with you first left you out of the loop, and made you feel unimportant to me. I would have felt the same way." No big deal to say it, but this can be really important for the other person to hear. Without this, we can't know if the apology really means anything to the person apologizing (are they apologizing because they feel bad or just to get out of having to talk about the behavior). Likewise, a person who realizes the nature of the harm they have caused to us might make them less likely to do the same thing again.

A commitment to do things differently in the future. This seems obvious, but it's still worth saying—if the person apologizing is just going to repeat the behavior, do we really even want to hear that they are sorry? Also, when appropriate (as in the apology is not just for something minor like being a few minutes late), this commitment should actually specify how they are going to do things differently in the future. This might actually be the most important part of an apology. It is at least a close second to wanting to know the person regrets what they've done. This part can also help validate the feelings and perceptions of the person hearing the apology because it requires the person making the apology to recognize the other person's needs, not just now, but if the circumstances come up again in the future. Finally, how can trust be regained if a person making an apology does not show their desire and willingness to do things differently.

Without this part, the person to whom the apology is made is left justifiably wondering if they are going to be hurt again.

Allow the person hearing the apology to state their feelings and other reactions. To the person making the apology, this can be very difficult because they are already feeling vulnerable, and this may end up feeling like kicking the dog when it is already down. This is another way the person hearing the apology get's a chance to validate their feelings, reactions, mistrust, etc. Unless the person making the apology allows the other person to grieve their differences, the apology can seem like it is more an attempt to overcome conflict than to really understand and accept responsibility. When I practiced litigation as an attorney, I often noted that parties that had been fighting tooth and nail would soften up to settlement during a mediation after they'd had a chance, maybe for the first time, to lay out their complaints to the other side face to face. Multimillion dollar cases that had lasted months or even years would sometimes settle within a day.

Demonstrate real change over time. This is not something the person apologizing says to the other person, but whenever a person makes an apology, they need to be prepared to demonstrate the genuineness of their regret and their desire to do things differently by actually changing their behavior over time. The more serious the behavior leading to the apology, the more time the person making the apology will need to give to the other person to regain their trust and accept the apology as legitimate and heartfelt. My father once actually got on his hands and knees crying and grabbing my hands begging for my forgiveness for what he had done to me as a child (beat me, and otherwise treated me very badly). I was overjoyed, wanting so badly to believe he regretted what he had done. I think he probably did really feel bad in the moment. Within a few months he had bloodied the face and neck of a younger sibling in a rage over milk (yes, milk), so I knew he would never change. Time is a telling thing. Don't underestimate its value.

Thankfully, not every apology needs to be this formal, detailed or long. If that were the case, we might end up spending half our lives apologizing to others or listening to them apologize to us. If we are a few minutes late for a coffee date, a simple "Hey, sorry I am late" might suffice. If someone is perpetually late though, this apology will likely and should fall flat as meaningless because the latecomer doesn't realize or seem to care that their behavior over time proves their apology isn't genuine. No matter what kind of behavior gave rise to the need for an apology, if an apology is accepted too quickly, just to move on from the conflict, residual resentment can fester, making conflict about that topic, but also other topics, more likely in the future. This is why we need to make sure the apologies we both give and receive are genuine. In therapy sessions in which there has been a more egregious or harmful act, an apology which does not contain all six of the "ingredients" listed above often leads to failure to resolve the issue, which can lead to even more mistrust and defensiveness.

Once all of these ingredients are on the table, discussed, understood, and acknowledged, sometimes even very harmful behavior can be reconciled and forgiven. Following something like this simple process of apologizing doesn't need to be complicated. We role model this process in sessions all the time, and when it comes naturally, which it can eventually, its not a big deal at all, and it really saves a lot of wasted energy on conflicts that can be fairly simply resolved. In my next chapter on this issue, I will spend some time talking more about the person harmed—their options for reacting to harmful behavior, with or without these six ingredients of a genuine apology. Those options include holding onto the feelings left over from whatever was done to forgiveness or even just letting go with or without forgiveness.

FORGIVENESS AND LETTING GO, PART 1

I had originally planned to write this chapter on forgiveness as a fairly direct follow up to my recent chapter entitled "When is an apology really an apology," but then needed some time to sort through my thoughts about the issue. Forgiveness seems to follow naturally from accepting an apology. If an apology is genuine, then forgiveness seems to be a good way to resolve the issue. I've been struggling with how to approach the issue of forgiveness. First, is forgiveness "earned" or is it "given," or both? Second, what do you do when you can't justify forgiving someone, but you also do not want to hang onto the negative feelings you have about something someone has done? Can you just "choose" to forgive them, even when they don't "deserve" your forgiveness?

Is forgiveness something that one must earn from another? If someone does something to you that you believe is wrong, that injures you somehow, either emotionally, financially, or in some other way, should you just forgive him or her? Should you offer forgiveness whether they apologize or not, whether they are sorry or not, whether or not they are willing to take responsibility for what they have done, even if they might do it again?

I had been pretty clearly in the camp of "no forgiveness without earning it" until a client recently gave me another point of view, which they considered a fundamental part of their deeply held religious faith: we should be willing to forgive others even if they do nothing to earn it, even if they do not ask our forgiveness, even if they might do it again. I had been thinking of forgiveness as a kind of transaction (that might be the lawyer in me rising up). In other words, "I will forgive you, but you must do the following things first... (insert condition)." This client pointed out that forgiveness was a gift we should be willing to offer freely, for ourselves, for others, to make the world a better place.

At first, I'll be honest, I thought this was a bit naïve, and might lead to exposure to continued injury. Take a battered woman. Her husband gets drunk, beats her. Next day, he is sober, sorry, remorseful, asks her for forgiveness. I'd say, even with the remorse, she ought not forgive him. Why should she believe he is really sorry right after he did this to her. Besides, even if he is sorry, what difference does that make to her, while she has bruises on her face and a swollen cheek and the emotional trauma of what he's done still swirling around her mind? Is he going to change? The jury is still out on that isn't it? Shouldn't she wait until she knows if he is going to really change, to prove just how sorry he is and how safe she will be, if she forgives him? Better yet, get out, take the kids with you, get a restraining order, be safe, and then think about forgiveness (maybe)!

Why do we even bother with forgiveness at all? Why does it matter? Should we do it because we think it makes the world a better place to "forgive those who trespass against us?" I don't know if it makes the world a better place. Maybe it does, sometimes. Doesn't everyone deserve a second chance? Maybe. Again, I don't know if everyone in every circumstance deserves a second chance. Anyway, that's not really for me to decide.

Here's why I care about forgiveness. As a therapist, forgiveness is often the only way to repair a damaged relationship. Some damaged relationships are worth repairing. So, forgiveness is an important part of the healing process. Maybe even more importantly, forgiveness is sometimes the best way someone, as an individual, can really resolve their issues from a past event. With forgiveness, the person can begin to move past their resentment, trauma, or other emotional limitations and embrace the possibility of real change. Think of the work done by the Truth and Reconciliation Commission in South Africa after apartheid and minority white rule gave way to true democracy. Many abused people in that nation were willing to forgive so they and their nation could heal.

There's a problem, though. It can feel really good to forgive someone for something, so you can get on with your life, but what if that person didn't really "deserve" your forgiveness. What do you do with your forgiveness, already offered, if they didn't really change anything, and they continue to do the same thing? Do you ignore it or look the other way? Do you take your forgiveness back? Is that even possible? Even if they don't repeat the offending behavior, what if you weren't really ready to forgive, and you offered forgiveness only so you would feel better? This can lead to deep resentment, or a lingering sense of unfairness, or unresolved pain, which becomes difficult to get at, because it is now lying underneath a layer of what felt like forgiveness, and now might feel more like denial or repressed anger.

Let me approach this issue with an alternative. Is there any way to move past feelings of hurt and anger toward someone who has done something that feels really wrong without forgiving them? The answer is actually yes. Forgiveness says something like (use your own words here if you like), "I am okay with you despite what you did, and now we can be fine again." If repairing the relationship is important, and the person seeking forgiveness is truly remorseful (see the chapter, When is an apology really an apology), this is the ideal approach. When preserving the relationship is less important than finding a way for you to heal, there is an alternative short of this "clean slate." It is, simply, letting go. Letting go of a feeling like resentment, or an attitude or judgment toward someone is a choice. It is a way of saying, "I am not okay with you because of what you've done, but I also don't like the way this feeling I have about what you did affects me now, so I want to get rid of it." In other words, you don't have to be okay with the person in order to let go of the difficult feelings associated with whatever they did.

I am not advocating withholding forgiveness when it is the right thing to do for you to repair an important relationship. I am simply saying there is an alternative, called letting go, which can be a better option when forgiveness is not earned, deserved or even wise. Choosing to let go of difficult feelings can bring us the relief that we need from those feelings without creating the need for denial of anything through premature or a false sense of forgiveness, including the possibility that we are not okay with that person, even though we want to overcome our feelings about what they did.

This still leaves us the question of when should we choose to forgive, which includes letting go, and when should we choose to let go, but without forgiveness. That's what I will discuss in Forgiveness and Letting Go, Part 2.

FORGIVENESS AND LETTING GO, PART 2

Have you ever had a moment when you were willing to let go completely of all of the things that had ever been done to you? When you didn't care who did this or that, why they did it, whether they might try to do it again? When you are seemingly filled to the brim with compassion for everything? Some call this serenity. Some call this nirvana. I will call it the possibility of a generous spirit.

In my first chapter on this topic, "Forgiveness and Letting Go, Part 1," I focused on how to decide when you can allow yourself to forgive others for their transgressions against you and when you might decide to let go of feelings even if you can't completely forgive. Basically, I suggested that forgiveness seemed to require that the other person be willing to change their behavior, and maybe even that they have had an opportunity to demonstrate their desire for change was genuine (that they could both "talk the talk, and walk the walk"). I also said letting go is possible when you believe the person is not going to change, but you decide you are not interested in carrying around resentments and other negative feelings based on their behavior, but are not willing to give them the gift of forgiveness or the benefit of the doubt because you don't want to open yourself to the vulnerability of being hurt again or pretend that things are resolved between you when they are not.

I still think this is all true, but it has limitations and there is a third possibility: forgiveness even when you know the other person is not likely to change.

The distinction between forgiveness and letting go based on whether someone has shown real change applies only in a circumstance when you want to continue to have a relationship with that person that depends on their ability and willingness to engage in that kind of change. Take for example a relationship you might have had with a friend that seems one-sided. You are always the one calling (or texting, emailing) them. You tell them this. They tell you they can see what you mean, and will make a real effort to put energy into the friendship. They call you a few times, you get together. You feel better. Over time, though, they fade, again. Until you realize you are back where you started. They didn't "walk the walk" (make the change you wanted). So, you let the friendship fade. You feel hurt. Maybe sad, but also a little resentful that they didn't care more about keeping the friendship going. You decide to let go of your feelings. You have other friends, and can't be bothered by the feelings of remorse, resentment, missing this one friend who isn't a very good friend anyway. You hang onto forgiveness though because you don't want to fall into the trap of believing they want a friendship with you again, when it is clear to you now that it is just an act they put on occasionally to keep you in their life. So, you let go of your feelings, but remain guarded, unwilling to completely forgive them for their seemingly irresponsible behavior to you which feels very inconsiderate to you. On the rare occasion when they do call (or text or email), you go through the motions of a friendship to avoid offending them or getting into a conflict, but are uninterested, not invested. If this were a client I was referring to (and yes, it applies to many clients over the years), I would readily suggest they have done a good job of navigating a delicate and difficult situation.

A more serious example, which I have used in other chapters, is a marital or other long term partnership in which one person has been injured numerous times in a way they both acknowledge. Perhaps it involves physical or verbal abuse or infidelity. Maybe it also involves addiction, and multiple failed attempts at recovery. The addict begs for forgiveness, she pleads with utterly sincere earnestness of her intent to mend her ways, to repair damage, to change. Her partner wants to forgive, to give her another chance, but without risking further injury. He decides he can do both. He can give her another chance, but withhold forgiveness until he sees real change in her. So, he begins to let go of the pain from past transgressions while watching her make necessary change for recovery, while holding back on complete forgiveness. Like the ignored friend above, this too seems like a good way for my client to navigate a difficult and potentially devastating situation. If she stays in recovery, he can begin the process of going beyond letting go of his feelings and begin to forgive her, changing his way of perceiving her, not based on pain, but based on hope, losing the fear of the past repeating itself. If the partnership ends, though, will my client ever be able to forgive his ex?

There is another alternative, which can involve a third way to forgiveness. If you are the ignored friend, you could be honest with your feelings, tell them you are no longer interested in a friendship with them on terms you find hurtful. If they really do not change, and you no longer hear from them, can you forgive them? Yes. If you choose to. In this case, you could forgive without being vulnerable to repeated hurtful actions.

We all have within us the capacity for enormous almost limitless compassion (okay there are rare exceptions, people who are not capable of compassion, but not anyone reading this book). This means we have equally vast capacities for forgiveness. If we use compassion as a way of seeing others, we can nearly always forgive them for whatever they might have done to us or to others. Compassion is a state of being in which we recognize that the experience of others is unique to them, that we cannot ever know completely what that experience is like for them, and that we can accept that their experience explains everything that they do, no matter how bad it might be. Compassion involves an acceptance that we can never really leave our own subjective experience, but can readily, almost completely, accept the experience of others as something completely different than our own. Only with compassion, can we say, "I cannot agree with what they have done, or even understand why they did it, but I can accept they had their reasons." With compassion, we don't even have to go through any logical analysis of a person's motivation. We can say, "I will never understand or agree with you, but I trust that you either thought what you were doing was justified, or there is some other reason I cannot begin to understand that compelled you to do what you did, and I can accept that and leave it at that."

Forgiveness, like compassion, is a gift. They are gifts we can find within ourselves and offer to others, even if we also know they might not "deserve" it. We do not have to offer forgiveness to anyone, but we can, if we choose to do so willingly. Forgiveness, though, is a gift we must choose to use only when it is genuine. Simply wanting to be compassionate and forgiving in the wrong circumstances can actually be harmful to ourselves and others. If the husband above uses compassion to avoid the difficult decision to leave his partner if she relapses again, he will make himself vulnerable to the damage of her addiction and might also in the process enable her to continue to be self-destructive. On the other hand, if he uses compassion wisely, says to himself that he doesn't understand her addiction, but can accept that for her it is real, difficult, and terrible for her too, he can give her a chance and give himself a chance to forgive her.

The point of this chapter is that he can forgive her whether she relapses or not. If she does not relapse, he can begin the process of forgiveness as they rebuild their relationship. If she continues to relapse, and he makes the decision that he must leave to protect himself (or his children too) from her addiction, he can still say, with deep compassion, 'I wish you had been able to recover from your addiction, but I am not you, I cannot ever completely understand what it is about being you that prevents you from recovery, and I am sad for you, and love you, and wish you could find it within yourself to recover, and I forgive you for all that your addiction has done to me."

He can give this forgiveness as a gift of compassion. Notice, though, that this generosity of spirit need not come with continuing to make himself vulnerable to her addiction.

The same can be said for the ignored friend. She can tell her friend (or just herself), "hey, I will never understand why our friendship didn't seem as important to you as it did to me, but I am not you, and I can accept that your needs are not the same as mine, and leave it that, let you be you, and forgive you for actions which caused me pain."

Forgiveness, with compassion, but without continued vulnerability, can be given in any circumstance. We have seen on the news mothers forgive those who killed their children. I have known children who have forgiven parents, other family members, and even strangers for unspeakable things done to them as children. Our generous spirit gives us the capacity to say, "I am not you, you are not me, you have your needs, your motives, your history, your struggles, your limitations, your humanness, just like I do, and I can accept that whatever you have done, you have done because you are you, and I choose to accept this, and let it be." This is the ultimate gift of forgiveness. As you can see, it requires no vulnerability to future harm. It only requires the generous spirit of compassion. In the process of offering forgiveness, you will feel better by releasing from yourself the burden of negative feelings and perceptions about that person and you will at least give the other the gift of freeing them from the burden of your feelings to change or not change, whichever they decide, whichever they are able to do. When we forgive, we give ourselves the gift of knowing deep generosity and we give others the gift of freedom to be whoever they are or might become.

PARTING THOUGHTS

On my laptop, there are over a dozen unfinished "bits of writing" (I am not sure what else to call them) that might find their way onto my website, or be used as a handout at a future workshop or be given to a client if the issue they address is relevant to a client's struggles. I might finish all of them, as the start of a new book, or add them as a new version of this book. I might not finish any of them. Whatever I do, there is already a good indication that I will continue to write my observations of what I have learned from working with clients in therapy and share them as I complete them. If you have found these chapters interesting, useful, a good read, the best way to find out if I have added to this collection is to visit my website: jupitercenter.com. Check the blog page, or if I have written another book or revised this one, I will make a note of it on the home page.

The caveat (again) for mental health issues: seek help when needed!

I put this at the beginning of this book, and am repeating it, because it deserves repeating. I hope you have enjoyed and found useful some of the ideas and tools offered in my book. If you think anything in this book might be valuable to someone else, of course it is your book and you are free to give it to whomever you like. Please keep in mind, though, that many of the topics in this book cover mental health issues that are serious, deep, protracted, and even life-threatening (e.g. depression). Even if you think the examples given in this book sound very much like the situation you or a friend or family member are currently experiencing, everyone is different, everyone experiences things differently, everyone's reaction to circumstance or the guidance of a loved one could be unanticipated. If either you or someone you know is suffering from a mental health issue, I strongly encourage you to seek the help of mental health professionals, educated and qualified to provide the help you or they may need. I say this with all the sincerity I can muster, because I myself have found the need to do this, for myself and others in my life, on many occasions.

Thank you (again) for reading my book!

Made in the USA
San Bernardino, CA
08 June 2014